D0850848

*When the Marching
Stopped*

SUNY SERIES IN AFRO-AMERICAN STUDIES
JOHN HOWARD AND ROBERT C. SMITH, EDITORS

Other Books by Hanes Walton, Jr.

Invisible Politics: Black Political Behavior

Black Republicans: The Politics of the Black and Tans

The Study and Analysis of Black Politics: A Bibliography

The Poetry of Black Politics

Black Politics: A Theoretical and Structural Analysis

Black Political Parties: An Historical and Political Analysis

The Political Philosophy of Martin Luther King, Jr.

The Negro in Third Party Politics

WHEN THE MARCHING STOPPED

The Politics of Civil Rights Regulatory Agencies

HANES WALTON, JR.

STATE UNIVERSITY OF NEW YORK PRESS

PUBLISHED BY
STATE UNIVERSITY OF NEW YORK PRESS, ALBANY

©1988 STATE UNIVERSITY OF NEW YORK

FOR INFORMATION, ADDRESS STATE UNIVERSITY OF NEW YORK
PRESS, STATE UNIVERSITY PLAZA, ALBANY, N.Y., 12246

LIBRARY OF CONGRESS CATALOGING-IN-PUBLICATION DATA

Walton, Hanes, 1941-
    When the marching stopped.

    (SUNY series in Afro-American studies)
    Bibliography: p.
    Includes index.
    1. Afro-Americans—Civil rights.   2. Civil rights—
United States.   3. Administrative agencies—United
States.   4. United States—Executive departments.
I. Title.   II. Series.
E185.615.W325   1987   353.0081'1   87-7081
ISBN   0-88706-687-9
ISBN   0-88706-688-7 (pbk.)

To Doctor Elmer J. Dean
whose leadership, administrative skills, and devotion
to scholarship made possible from his position
as chairman of the division of social sciences
a new black civil elite and through them
a more viable black community in the years ahead.

Come, Let Us Celebrate His Growth

He used to blindly and emotionally
get things done,
What CBS news was calling militant.
He's more scientific now,
what CBS news,
When they mention him at all these days,
is calling practical.
In the cut he is, thinking,
what he calls a theorist.
This means he don't do diddley
but lay chilly
And see the good and bad in everything.

—Lee R. Haven
Copyright *Catalyst* ©

CONTENTS

TABLES

ix

FIGURES

FOREWORD

The most striking aspect of Walton's book is his understanding of the effect on civil rights progress of the institutionalization of enforcement agencies in the federal government. As he explains, once a movement gains legislation and a bureaucracy to enforce it, a perceptible decline in commitment results. Political and budgetary resource considerations come into play, and managers in agencies naturally move with more care and less risk-taking than movement people. Also those who participated in a movement may have a tendency to turn their attention to other things, placing little pressure on the bureaucracy to act. Therefore, another non-violent, direct action movement using different strategies and tactics may be necessary in order to stimulate greater attention to providing an equal opportunity for health, education, employment, and other concomitants of a satisfactory livelihood in our society.

I am also impressed with Walton's understanding of the role destined for the U.S. Commission on Civil Rights in our national government. During my first years on the Commission, we took seriously our "watchdog" and conscience within the government role. We urged and prodded Presidents and the Congress to adopt strong, broad interpretations of their powers to act to enforce voting rights, the right of access for women and people of color to quality education, non-discrimination and affirmative action in employment, and quality integrated housing. For our troubles, President Reagan tried to fire not just "liberal" or Democratic Commissioners, but all of them. In the Bob Jones University case, when we tried to prevent giving a tax credit to segregated schools, we offended the Administration. It was a classic example of the Commission at work. We wrote letters to the President and Congress drawing upon analyses and reports we had done over the years, pleaded to the public on the grounds of law and policy, and having no enforcement authority, used to the maximum the powers of persuasion. Our view prevailed on the Supreme Court ultimately, but the Commission suffered. Chairman Arthur Flemming and Commissioner Stephen Horn, both Republicans, were fired, and substitutes were nominated for the rest of us. Clarence Pendleton, Jr. was appointed Chairman, and for the first time in the Commission's history, a presidentially imposed Staff Director, Linda Chavez Gersten, was appointed to manage the agency day to day according to President Reagan's policies.

This change did not occur without controversy. Blandina Cardenas Ramirez and I sued the President in Federal district court and won reinstatement. But when the Commission's authority expired, in the reauthorization legislation, President Reagan gained the majority which he had been seeking. The House of Representatives wanted to take authority to appoint Commissioners completely away from the President because he had abused it. The Republican-controlled Senate insisted on a compromise. For the first time in the Commission's history, one-half of the members were appointed by the Congress with no required Presidential involvement and one-half by the President with no advice and consent by the Seante. The President used his appointees, as well as those of the Congressional Republicans, to gain a majority. Ramirez and I, appointed by the Senate and House Democrats, respectively, were left in a minority. The statute made no changes in the functions, authority, or powers of the Commission, but soon Chairman Pendleton announced that the Commission was part of the Reagan Administration. Contrary to a proud tradition, the Commission became just another agency acting in conformity with Administration policy.

The clearest public example of the reauthorized Commission at work occurred when Pendleton thought it was acceptable to oppose minority business set-asides, consistent with the Administration's opposition to affirmative action for women of all races, and minorities. However, traditional black Republicans made clear that their support of the party was in part based on the espousal of business set-asides dating from Nixon's presidency. White House officials announced their opposition to a report condemning set-asides just as the Commission's Reaganite majority was about to approve it. The Reaganite Commission retreated, voting to send the report back for further study from which it has not emerged.

There is no way to know what contribution the Commission would have made after 1984 to prevent further erosion of civil rights enforcement. In Reagan's first term, one measure of its effectiveness in redirecting civil rights policy can be seen in the firings. It is not often that a President accords so much attention and capital to such a small agency.

The analysis and description Professor Walton provides can help us to understand how fragile and problematic civil rights enforcement becomes when it is institutionalized. It can also help us to understand what must be done by concerned people in order to press any administration to emphasize enforcement, rather than letting it languish.

MARY FRANCES BERRY

Professor of History and Law, Howard University
Member, U.S. Commission on Civil Rights

PREFACE

This is the first comprehensive and systematic study of the sundry civil rights regulatory agencies in the various cabinet departments created under Titles VI and VII of the 1964 Civil Rights Act. Any review of the literature on these regulatory agencies that deal essentially with human rights and their violations in this democratic society will reveal several books on the Fair Employment Practice Commission (FEPC), the first experiment in this area, one on state civil rights agencies, one on the Commission on Civil Rights and several studies on the Equal Employment Opportunity Commission (EEOC).[1] But as for Title VI Compliance, with the exception of some reports by the Civil Rights Commission, there are but two books in this area.[2] In brief, there is a significant void in the literature.

My interest in this subject grew out of a year as a visiting scholar in the office of Civil Rights Compliance in the Law Enforcement Assistance Administration (LEAA). In January 1975, the staff director of the National Association of Schools of Public Affairs and Administration (NASPAA), Dr. Don M. Blandin, informed me that I had been selected as an NASPAA Fellow and could spend a year interning in Washington, D.C., with a federal agency that had interest in my credentials and training. In February, Nan Shute of LEAA called and indicated her interest in having me work with the agency as special assistant to the director of the Office of Civil Rights Compliance, attorney Herbert Rice. The internship was to last for a full year—August 1, 1975, to July 31, 1976.

Director Rice, unlike some agency heads, involved me in every aspect of the functions of the office. I traveled with different divisions, did complaint investigations and resolutions, was project monitor for two of the office's large grants, and was given full use of the office files, correspondence, records, appointment calendar, the director's travel log and weekly activity reports to the head of LEAA, newspaper clippings, governmental reports, and interoffice memos.

During my internship year the director asked me to assemble a history of the office. That work was the start of this project. However, because the office underwent a reorganization and the director resigned under fire, the project was left unfinished, and lay dormant for several years.

I returned to the project with funds granted by the Rockefeller Foundation under its Research Fellowship Program for Minority Group Scholars to survey all civil rights compliance offices, in the cabinet-level departments and in selected federal agencies. Therefore, I spent another year gathering federal reports and documents, interviewing directors of civil rights offices of compliance, and analyzing vast amounts of data generated by these new regulatory bodies in the attempt to structure and organize the material so that a comprehensive study and report could emerge. This report, I hope, will not only fill a void in the literature but will provide some practical and scholarly insight into yet another experiment by this political system—its attempt to deal with conflicting human relationships in our society and with the questions of inequality. Shortly after I finished the Rockefeller-sponsored research year, a new administration came to power, with much talk about deregulating federal functions and revising government's approach to civil rights. I needed to consider what impact this new Reagan administration would have on the fledgling civil rights regulatory agencies. A chance came in 1983–1984, when the American Political Science Association selected me as one of its congressional fellows. During that year, while working in Congressman Mervyn Dymally's (D-Cal.) office, I had the opportunity to gather more data and gain insight into the influence of the Reagan administration. When the fellowship year ended, Congressman Dymally generously permitted me to work out of his office to continue the project. I finished the project in March 1985, just as Reagan was ginning his second term. I now had a full picture of his impact after four years in office, immensely enhancing the project and the contribution it will offer the reader.

The project out of which the book emerged stretched over approximately 12 years and three fellowship opportunities: NASPAA, Rockefeller and APSA. These fellowships helped me to assemble the data and coordinate and write it so that it provides basically a longitudinal study by a participant observer. I hope from these different levels of vision there will emerge a new understanding of the new civil rights regulatory agencies.

I would like to acknowledge several people for their assistance and help. At LEAA, I would like to thank the division heads: Andrew Strongly, Henry Tribble, Roberta Dorn, Al Wilson, and Curtis Neal. On the staff side, I would like to express my appreciation to Gloria Carey, Julia Dicoco, Donna Donato, Winifred Duntin, Eurnie Fuentes, Norma Harrison, Laverne Henderson, Gladys Hooper, Rose Kelley, Bill Cummings, June Langely, Linda Medina, Ida Miller, Phyllis Moore, David Trevelin, Doris Ware, Calvin Watkins, and troubleshooter Ronald Branch.

Attorney Branch, through our many—in fact almost daily—discussion sessions during that year and since, made me aware of the innumerable bureaucratic games, the in-house tensions between those who saw LEAA as a program agency and those who saw that it needed to include a regulatory mission in its function, the unresolved problems, the clashing personalities, the staff problems between black and white workers in the same office[3] and how the administration used those problems to further its own goals and personal ambitions and the real questions involved in civil rights regulatory activity. Attorney Branch has spent his entire career working with these agencies and is still employed in one. His advice, insights, and help proved to be the clarity that a professor needed from a keen and skillful practiner. In many ways, this is his book.

I would like to express thanks to Dr. Bruce E. Williams, assistant director of the Research Fellowship Programs for Minority-Group Scholars, at the Rockefeller Foundation for his unending aid and assistance at crucial times in the project.

I would like to thank Dr. David Johnson, Ms. Theta Shipp, Ms. Brenda Young, and Mary Twitty in Congressman Dymally's office for their help in obtaining elusive federal data and statistics. Finally I am deeply indebted to Congressman Dymally, who did all he could to assist the project. Without him and his office staff, the full impact of the first Reagan administration on the civil rights regulatory agencies would not have been seen by the author.

Although I have acknowledged most of the people involved in helping me on the current project, I cannot fail to mention those who laid the educational foundation and background for this work. In public administration, there was Professor Tobe Johnson at Morehouse College who in his year-long course, made his students aware of his unique and pioneering research on the New York Port Authority. It was exciting, stimulating, and revealed to us how one could conduct a study on a public bureaucracy that had regulatory functions.[4]

At Howard University, Professor Joseph David Cooper was endlessly enlightening in his public policy and public administration courses. His insight into organizational bureaucratic behavior led his students to see public organizations in a much different light and perspective.[5] And then there was the ever-erudite Samuel DuBois Cook at Atlanta University. Being a political thinker and analyst of the first order, he made his students see the struggle for civil rights within the question of justice in a democratic society. In his carefully reasoned analyses, this effort was not simply group interest but a fundamental matter at the heart of the democratic enterprise.[6]

In addition to Cook, there were Professors Robert Brisbane, Harold Gosnell, Emmett Dorsey, Morris Levitt and Brian Weinstein, to say nothing of the prolific Bernard Fall. I hope they can see their ideas and wisdom, especially in Chapters Five and Six. Truly all of these men were ahead of their time and the discipline.

Another group of individuals I would like to acknowledge are those who contributed directly to this manuscript. First, there is the profound poem of Professor Lee R. Haven. From the beginning of the civil rights movement, Professor Haven has captured its human essence in moving and telling verse. This work on the transformation of a black activist to someone inert is a continuation of his commitment, talents and skill. I thank him and continue to watch with admiration his rise in the literary and poetic world.

Then, there is the contribution by my friend and former graduate school classmate, Civil Rights Commissioner, college professor and activist Dr. Mary Frances Berry. I have over the years marveled not only at her staggering and well-deserved achievement and honors, but at her commitment and keen sense of outrage. She has truly been the lone warrior and voice crying out at the currently embattled Civil Rights Commission. I am very pleased that she took the time from her very busy schedule to read the manuscript in its entirety and to write her profound insights about problems at the commission. She has stayed the course and given the reader a first hand account. I appreciate it.

Among the people at Savannah State College that I would like to acknowledge are Professors Annette Brock, Otis Johnson, Delacy Sanford, Ronald Clark, Willie T. Yancey, and E. J. Dean. Andrew McLemore and his staff provided constant assistance in helping me track down lost and hard-to-find items. He personally permitted me to work in the library long after the regular hours had passed. The help of his staff permitted the work to go very smoothly and systematically.

In the Secretarial Center at Savannah State College, the director, Mrs. Doris Jackson, and her assistants, Mrs. Carol Haywood and Ms. Regina Hopkins, worked untiringly with the manuscript through all its changes with great kindness and understanding. I owe them many thanks. And to the secretary who finished the last two drafts of the book, Ms. Margaret Mitchell-Ilugbo, I express my sincere and deep appreciation.

During my numerous research sojourns in Washington, a home-away-from-home was furnished by Mrs. Margaret Lowman. Her lovely home and fine facilities and congenial environment made the long hours of writing and analyzing much much easier. I will always appreciate her hospitality and generosity. Many thanks to her.

Thanks also to Professor Joseph McCormick who went through his files and shared with me a document which he prepared for a transportation research project. This document *(Develop a Methodology for the Evaluation of Civil Rights Programmatic Input on the Transit Industry)* included a good literature review of materials dealing with Titles VI and VII. However, Professor McCormick went beyond just providing me with this document. He gave the manuscript a profound and intensely close reading; nothing missed his critical eye. His knowledge of the public policy literature and all of its sundry nuances is simply unexcelled, and he shared this knowledge with me in some lengthy discussion sessions. With his help in these sessions, I was able to reorganize and reformulate several of the chapters to improve their precision, focus and clarity. Professor McCormick not only made these probing insights, but went to his files and placed numerous key documents, essays, rare articles and books in the author's hands that were subsequently used to improve the overall thrust of the work. My debt to this professor and fraternity brother is indeed great. To him, I offer my greatest thanks.

Finally there are the series editors. Professors Robert Smith and John Howard are first of all to be congratulated for their efforts to launch the series. If Black Politics as a field and area is going to grow, an outlet for innovative as well as critical perspectives has to be found. This series is filling a massive void in the literature. While no such series existed after the Reconstruction Period, the appearance of one during this period of renewed black political activity and governmental intervention lays the intellectual and scholarly foundations for a new generation of political insights. Thus, an entire segment of the black political experience will not be lost or left up to a single discipline to recapture and re-interpret. One knows full well how some of these recapturing and re-interpretation efforts came out in a biased, prejudiced and negative manner.[7] Hence, an entire generation of black scholars had to devote its time and effort and energies to correcting these realities, i.e., errors of fact, judgement, interpretation, ommissions and harmful theories.[8] By launching their series when they did, Professors Smith and Howard have already made a great and significant contribution.

I would like to personally thank Professor Smith for working with me very closely on my two projects for the series and seeing them to completion. Further he has shown vision and insight in choosing readers for these manuscripts who have complete mastery of their subject matter and have brought this mastery to bear upon the manuscripts. Such scholars have populated the discipline for years, yet their talents have gone unused, particularly in the area of black politics. If their talents had been utilized, some of the distortions and illusions that dominate the literature about the area would have never surfaced in the first place. But being outside the "ole" boy network, they were simply not used. Professors Smith and Howard are bringing these well-read scholars into the intellectual forefront of an exciting new field of study. It will be all the more illuminating because of their presence.

Lastly, let me thank Professor Smith for suggesting the two main titles for my works in the series. As with any good series editors, Professors Smith and Howard have carried their creativity far beyond the mere conceptualization of the series. I wish the very best to them as the series expands and evolves in the years ahead. My work and the emerging area of Black Politics will be much much better for their brilliant efforts.

Finally, I must say thanks to my family—Alice, Brandon and Brent, parents, Estelle, Arie, and James, Dennie and Flossie—for all of their encouragement and complete support. They saw me through all phases of the project. The product of this effort reflects my shortcomings and not theirs, for cooperation and assistance was the first order.

H. WALTON, JR.

Fuller E. Callaway Professor of Political Science
Savannah State College

1. The Institutionalization of the Civil Rights Revolution

Of the grand civil rights coalition and movement of the sixties, there are many questions still to be asked. Some people want to know what happened to it; others want to know whether it can be revived; still others are curious about its death and decline. A few are concerned about its impact. And some would raise the question, looking at the current plight of black people, if the movement occurred at all.

There are numerous answers. For instance, a lieutenant of the Reverend Martin Luther King, Jr., the Reverend Wyatt T. Walker, saw the apex of the movement in 1963. Social activist Bayard Rustin saw the transformation of the movement from protest to politics in 1964.[1] Some analysts date the demise of the movement, and therefore of the coalition that gave impetus to the movement, with the rise of the "Black Power" slogan in 1966, while others view it as the response to white backlash and consider the riots and burnings of 1968 as its death knell. Still others blame the Vietnam War, the death of black leaders (especially King and Malcolm X), and the election of Richard Nixon to the presidency in 1968 for the disruption of the movement and collapse of the coalition. A few would credit the political appeal and rhetoric of George Wallace

1

and his American Independent party as the lethal weapon. And so the argument about the coalition and the movement continues. Despite the wide array of opinions, the fact remains: the coalition and its movement did exist, and they did shape public policy in American society.[2]

Whither the Civil Rights Movement: The Coming of the Civil Rights Regulatory Agencies

The civil rights movement has, to some extent, been institutionalized in America. It has become, along with some of its goals, *legitimate* and *acceptable*. As civil rights became a policy concern of the government, the government itself sanctioned the need to struggle for this cause. It agreed to place part of its power and authority and financial resources behind the quest for and the establishment of these rights and concerns. In short, the government came to support civil rights, at least in part. But as recent events and shifts in governmental policies have shown, the achievements of the movement can also become de-institutionalized. We are presently in an era where a sitting President has systematically attempted to de-institutionalize the gains made by this movement in the early 1960s. The government can drop its concern for, lessen its authority to and reduce its financial support of, civil rights regulatory efforts. But let's look first at how and why the civil rights movement became institutionalized in America.

There are two important reasons for this. First, the movement took both a political and moral approach to the resolution of fundamental problems to policy not just a moral one. About this tendency in sociopolitical movements, Pendleton Herring has observed that "when these movements enter national contests they are forced to fight for power rather than for principles . . . If they refrain they are thrown back upon criticism and theorizing rather than seeking to create through legislation appropriate administrative devices for achieving their ends."[3] The civil rights movement never succumbed to the temptation to fight only for principles. Several factions in the movement compromised its moralism by forcing it to enter the political melee and fight not only for a change in the hearts of people but for a change in their behavior, as it is regulated through social legislation.[4] Even King, the principal spokesman for the movement, would respond to his critics, who argued that the government could not legislate morality, by stating that he was not trying to legislate morality but that human behavior could be regulated.[5] Stateways could impact folkways.

One should clearly separate the coalition from the movement, if only for analytical purposes. The coalition was composed of a broad array of groups, and its unity was from the outset precarious and very fragile. Segments of the coalition were political. Some of these were groups or factions within the parties; many were elected officials. Not all who were thus involved were black; for example, the late Senators Hubert Humphrey and Everett Dirksen took the moralism of the movement and fashioned it into a legislative reality. The civil rights movement in the streets also became a movement in Congress.[6] There was also support from the White House. President Lyndon B. Johnson made some of the concerns of the movement concerns of his presidency. Eventually, the judicial branch of government was also led into the struggle behind the legislative and executive branches. This combination of political tactics and moral appeal assured the movement a significant policy impact. However, it should be noted that those forces opposing the civil rights coalition also had a political element—for example, Senators Richard Russell and John Stennis—that fought valiantly to see to it that the legislative desires of the pro-civil rights forces never came to fruition or were only minimally realized.[7] And as the first coalition had some impact, the second coalition, a counter group, as we shall later see in this work, had some impact on policy as well.

The civil rights movement's dual focus on morality and practicality was only one of the reasons that the civil rights movement became institutionalized. The second reason lies in the range of alternatives open to citizens of a democratic society (though some would argue that it is a nondemocratic society).[8] The first option can be called a do-nothing alternative. The government could simply ignore the movement, its demands and its leadership. Various sociopolitical movements, including earlier civil rights efforts, have been ignored by the government. Usually this means that the movement is not considered to be *legitimate*, it can be openly attacked by various segments of society, with implicit and indirect governmental assistance. Under pressure from this type of opposition a movement usually runs out of steam, as its grand coalition of support slowly trickles away. American history is filled with the stories of such sociopolitical groups that failed to influence governmental policy. Earlier civil rights attempts are clear-cut examples.[9]

A second option is for the government to fully support the movement. In this instance, the government *legitimates* the movement, supports its concerns, its leaders and its aims and objectives, even to the point of making the movement a functional part of the government. When the government takes this approach, it can pass laws of the land, put its leadership in governmental roles, or assign specific governmental departments and agencies a function that expresses the group's demands. Or finally, it can create departments and agencies. In the case of the civil rights movement, there are the government–created offices of civil rights compliance within various federal agencies.

A third option is a mixture of the first two, where the government alternates between supporting and opposing a socio-political movement. Many earlier civil rights efforts have suffered such an off-and-on relationship with government, one whereby the government sometimes frustrates the aims of the movement and sometimes supports its aims. The government compels the movement to undergo a cyclical process, alternating between high points of success and low points of defeat. Such instability puts the movement in limbo, for it never knows quite where it is or what kind of support it might get next.

Government has a fourth option, to actively oppose the movement. An apt example is the government's response to radical economic movements that have tried to gain a foothold in American society. These groups have found themselves harassed, intimidated and undone by various federal agencies. Under this type of pressure, a movement usually fades from the social and political scene.

These four options are not static or fixed. The government may shift among them in dealing with any one movement. In short, the four options are malleable, useful according to the realities of the environment and the variables of the moment. The survival of a socio–political movement can depend on how well it responds to shifts among the options.

Robert Tucker has developed a theoretical framework to show why governments eventually institutionalize revolutionary movements. These movements, he indicates, cause instability, internal conflict, stagnation, deadlock and a good deal of distraction and disruption. He writes, "when a radical movement grows large and strong, acquires a big organizational structure, a mass social constituency and a recognized place in society, this very wordly success fosters deradicalization."[10] He continues, "moreover, when society begins to accord a measure of acceptance to a radical movement, this may tend to weaken, if not eventually dissipate the sharp sense of alienation from this world and the commitment to a future order which characterized the movement in its earlier phases."[11]

Arthur Schlesinger reveals that American democratic society has absorbed many socio–political movements. "Every great period of social change in American history," he notes, "has been set off by the demand of some excluded but aggressive group for larger participation in the national democracy; in the age of Jackson by the frontier farmer, the city worker, the small entrepreneur; in the Progressive era by the by-passed old upper classes of the cities; in the New Deal by labor in mass production industries, the unemployed and the intellectuals."[12] In the last two decades such groups have included women, consumers, pacifists, environmentalists and young people in addition to blacks and their supporters in the civil rights revolution. Some have had an impact on public policy, some have become institutionalized and some have simply been co-opted.

The civil rights movement was institutionalized with Titles VI and VII of the 1964 Civil Rights Act.[13] Title VI of the act set up provisions for the enforcement of nondiscrimination in federal financial assistance programs, and Title VII provided for the enforcement and prohibition of discrimination in employment. Title VI and the civil rights compliance agencies that have emerged as a result of that act are the foci of this work. Title VI of the 1964 Civil Rights Act created the basis for a new group of federal regulatory agencies. This work will explore the nature and scope of these agencies in light of historical realities and political conditions which have changed over time. Put differently, one of the achievements of black protest and electoral politics have been not only civil rights (or anti-discrimination) laws but administrative agencies which could regulate behavior that violated these laws. It is *now* crucial that a comprehensive assessment and evaluation of these regulatory agencies be made.

The Civil Rights Regulatory Agencies: A Brief History

There are precedents for these sort of governmental regulatory agencies. First came the well-known federal regulatory agencies, especially the essentially economic ones.[14] A second group grew out of the brief and limited attempts by the federal government to create civil rights employment regulatory agencies.

The economic regulatory agencies grew out of the Populist movement, the Progressive movement and the New Deal. Such agencies as the Securities and Exchange Commission (SEC), the Federal Power Commission (FPC), the Federal Trade Commission (FTC), the Interstate Commerce Commission (ICC), and the Federal Communications Commission (FCC) were regulatory agencies created to oversee and control economic monopolies and natural resources and to manage access to and use of limited national holdings. Regulations were aimed at corporations, conglomerates, and private partnerships to protect the public from exploitation and manipulation. A furor attended the coming of these regulatory agencies; they were rarely accepted by those forces they were intended to regulate. Legislative and political fights are still waged over the scope of authority held by these agencies, even though they are many decades old.

An example of such furor is that which attended the creation recently of a new agency, the Environmental Protection Agency (EPA). The establishment of this agency was fought by business, labor, farmers, politicians, newspapers, and many others. The EPA came into being despite their opposition and continues to struggle in the face of opposition. The EPA survived, but a proposed consumer protection agency never quite made it. Congress never passed a bill to set one up; the opposition to it proving to be too much.

The point is that regulatory agencies never have smooth histories. They face, at times, stiff and formidable opposition. They suffer setbacks, defeat, and sometimes even death at the hands of their opponents.

Whether one is examining the old or new regulatory agencies, all of these agencies eventually emerged out of congressional legislative mandates. This is certainly not true with the *initial* attempts to create civil rights regulatory agencies. The control of *key* congressional chairs by Southern congressmen made it all but impossible at least until the sixties, to try to establish civil rights regulatory agencies via congressional legislative mandates. A former congressman writes: "In 1963-64, 24 southern committee chairmen could be arranged against" a civil rights bill.[15] In addition to this institutional power, congressional opponents of civil rights laws had such legislative weapons as the Senate filibuster, the right to offer amendments that could severely weaken the bills, and the well-known tactic of compromise that could remove or dilute sections of a bill that proved to be too strong or unacceptable. Finally, southerner's had the legacy of a weak legislative history of civil rights bills. No strong civil rights bill had ever made it through Congress and particularly the Senate. Here the famous southern filibuster prevailed. Not even Cloture or Rule 22, a device to limit debate, had ever succeeded or prevailed against the great southern weapons used to halt legislation that would mandate a civil rights regulatory agency. "Tried 11 times on civil rights bills, it had failed 11 times."[16] Therefore the road to establish civil rights regulatory agencies had to take other, and often circuitous, routes. Let's look briefly at such efforts.

The Civil Rights Section in the Justice Department: 1939

The first efforts to create a civil rights regulatory agency came from the federal bureaucracy, the Justice Department, while the second one came from the efforts of the president, Franklin D. Roosevelt. Thus, the federal bureaucracy and the chief executive moved before Congress on this matter. Of the Justice Department's effort, Robert Carr, who first recorded that effort, writes: "In 1939 the federal government was jolted out of its cautious tradition when Attorney General Frank Murphy issued his order erecting a civil liberties unit in the Department of Justice." The "Order of the Attorney General, No. 3204; February 3, 1939" reads as follows:[17]

> Effective this date (February 3, 1939) there is established within the Criminal Division of the Department of Justice a unit to be known as the Civil Liberties Unit.
> The function and purpose of this unit will be to make a study of the provisions of the Constitution of the United States and Acts of Congress relating to civil rights with reference to present conditions, to make appropriate recommendations in respect thereto, and to direct,

supervise and conduct prosecutions of violations of the provisions of the Constitution or Act of Congress guaranteeing civil rights to individuals.[18]

However, "in June, 1941 when Victor Rotnem became chief of the unit, he asked that the name be changed to 'Civil Rights Section'."[19] This title was used until the section was upgraded to a division by the 1957 Civil Rights Bill.

The creation of this bureaucratic unit was done singlehandedly by Attorney General Frank Murphy, because of his special concern for this matter, his public record, and his commitment to civil liberties. Carr, who interviewed Murphy, writes: "He created the Civil Liberties Unit as a warning that the might of the United States government was on the side of oppressed people in protecting their civil liberties."[20] Moreover, he was well aware of what happened to Americans' civil liberties before, during, and after World War I.[21]

In this instance then, "Establishment of the unit was solely an act of administrative discretion. . . ." Funds for its operation were made available from the amounts already appropriated for use by the criminal division of the Justice Department and "if the creation of the unit didn't result in the setting up of new or elaborate machinery, it did provide an important impetus to the federal government's civil rights program."[22]

Although the creation and establishment of this bureaucratic regulatory device was relatively easy, giving it a firm legal basis and techniques for carrying out its program was not. Understanding that it couldn't get enabling legislation and greater powers from Congress, "the Civil Rights Section had to start almost from scratch in devising administrative techniques and procedures," as well as the legal justification and constitutional foundations on which to regulate racially discriminatory behavior.[23]

Murphy, as described by Carr, felt that government had both a duty and a role to protect civil liberties in a democratic society. And that this protection had to be both a shield and a sword.

> The shield, then, is a negative safeguard. It enables a person whose freedom is endangered to invoke the Constitution by requesting a federal court to invalidate the state action that is endangering his rights. The sword is a positive weapon wielded by the federal government, which takes the initiative in protecting helpless individuals by bringing criminal charges against persons who are encroaching upon their rights.[24]

Therefore, to provide this new bureaucratic regulatory unit with a legal basis for action, two departmental attorneys prepared a detailed circular setting forth the constitutional foundations upon which a federal sword could be wielded. Since the Bill of Rights at this time could not "serve as a basis for a program of positive governmental action directed toward the protection of civil liberties," such a federal program of safeguarding civil rights had to rest on the Civil War amendments (13th, 14th, and 15th) and those provisions of the Civil Rights Acts passed by Congress during Reconstruction which had not been invalidated by subsequent Supreme Court decisions.

These three amendments, which grant freedom, citizenship, and the right to vote were later buttressed by seven different pieces of congressional legislation. Robert Carr goes on to say:

> These acts admittedly were motivated by a general concern on the part of Congress for the newly freed Negro, and by a specific desire to safeguard his rights. But, without exception, no mention is made of the Negro as such. Instead the wording is sufficiently broad to cover the rights of all citizens, if not all inhabitants or persons.[25]

Therefore, after clarifying its constitutional foundations, the authors of the circular went on to clarify the statutory legal bases for the new unit. Here, the attorneys went to the *United States Codes*, "Section 44 of the same title," and used these criminal sanctions to develop a federal civil rights regulatory protection device. With these legal bases—one resting in the constitution and the other in statutory criminal law—the new unit moved to regulate discriminatory behavior.

Overall, "the task which confronted the CRS—(Civil Rights Section) was a unique one. It was expected to build a program to safeguard civil liberty throughout America, by using certain fugitive and largely moribund statutory provisions, all nearly seventy-five years old."[26] Thus, with such a shaky legal foundation, this regulatory unit of the Justice Department began a cautious and experimental program. It remained "a small agency with limited powers and resources of its own." For instance, "CRS had no field officers of its own to report civil rights violations to the Washington office" and it had to rely on FBI agents in their local field offices to pass complaints on to it.[27] Needless to say, many southern offices were reluctant to do so. But even with this cumbersome complaint procedure the unit had 8,612 complaints in 1942, 13,490 in 1943, and 30,000 by 1944. But the resolution of these complaints was not only slow and cumbersome, but the successful prosecution of cases was at best only minimal. Not only did it not find much support in the Federal Courts, but Congress ignored this unit. Thus, this first bureauratic initiative to sidestep Congress and devise a civil rights regulatory unit that would have sword-like powers saw at best only marginal success. Yet it did set the stage for the executive branch of government to act in this policy area.

The Executive-Created Civil Rights Regulatory Agencies

Civil rights regulatory agencies created by presidential order are rooted in the efforts of President Franklin D. Roosevelt. Much of this initiative can be directly linked to President Roosevelt's Executive Order 8802, issued on June 25, 1941, when blacks under the leadership of A. Philip Randolph, president of the Brotherhood of Sleeping Car Porters, threatened to march on Washington, D.C. Roosevelt's order banned "social and religious discrimination in defense industries and government training programs."[28] On July 19, 1941, less than a month after the order was issued, the President selected the five unsalaried members of the Committee on Fair Employment Practice, or the FEPC as it was popularly known, and put it under the Office of Production Management. It was later transferred to the War Manpower Commission. However, on May 27, 1943, by Executive Order 9346, the FEPC was reconstituted, enlarged from five to seven members, and established as an independent regulatory agency in the Executive Office of the President.[29]

In its new form, the "FEPC was given power to receive and investigate complaints of discrimination prohibited by the executive order, to conduct hearings, make findings of fact, "and to take appropriate steps" to eliminate discrimination."[30] But this forerunner of the current civil rights regulatory agencies had very limited success, to say the least.[31] Robert Brisbane writes: "The greatest weakness of the FEPC was its total lack of power to enforce its orders. The powers to subpoena witnesses and records, to compel testimony and to enforce directive through the courts or the Attorney General" did not exist. He continues: "But, like all other bodies which originated from the war powers of the Chief Executive, the FEPC had to refer noncompliance cases to the President for his disposition. He could order governmental seizure and operation of the plant involved."[32] President Roosevelt chose not to do this, and when Congress refused to make the FEPC a permanent agency of the government in 1947, it ceased to exist.

During the Truman administration this agency was revived with a new name, the Committee on Government Contract Compliance, but it had no significant power. When President Eisenhower came into office in 1953, he issued a new executive order that created the Committee on Government Contracts and made the Vice-President its chairman. The Committee was authorized to receive complaints against government contractors and was required to "send such complaints to the federal agency holding the contract with directions to investigate the charges and take appropriate action to eliminate any discrimination found to exist."

By 1955 Eisenhower set up the Committee on Government Employment

Policy "to supervise the nondiscrimination program within the federal establishment."[33] This committee was created to review the employment practices of the departments and agencies of the federal government and to determine if such practices had been nondiscriminatory.[34] This new committee, created in 1948 by another executive order, replaced the Fair Employment Board created by President Truman in the Civil Service Commission.[35] But this new board, like its predecessors, had very little power to impact the entire system. What Eisenhower had done was to create a second toothless administrative structure.

On March 5, 1961, shortly after he took office, President Kennedy issued Executive Order 10925, which combined these two committees and their functions into a single new one called the Committee on Equal Employment Opportunity.[36] His executive order not only designated the vice-president as chairman and the secretary of labor as vice-chairman but it went on to spell out in great detail the expanded duties and enlarged powers of the new body.

Three years later Title VII of the Civil Rights Act of 1964, would create a legislative agency, the Equal Employment Opportunity Commission (EEOC), with five members, each having five years' tenure with one member selected as chairperson by the president and another member as vice chairman. This title empowered the Commission to eliminate, through certain devices, discrimination in employment because of race, color, religion, sex, or national origin. Yet this new commission, created by legislative initiative like its counterpart created by the executive branch, met with only limited success. Therefore, Congress subsequently amended Title VII of "the 1964 Civil Rights Act with the addition of the Equal Employment Opportunity Act of 1972, banning all employment discrimination within the Federal employment sector. The Civil Service Commission (CSC) was given the authority to enforce the promises of this act." In 1976 a new president considered a new approach to the matter.[37]

In February, 1977, "within three weeks of taking office, President Carter noted that there were a number of agencies responsible for implementing equal employment opportunity requirements and stated that it was his goal to move toward consolidation of these functions." He subsequently created a "Civil Rights Reorganization Task Force within the Office of Management and Budget."[38] And, although he did not establish one civil rights office, his task group did help him shift all contract compliance functions from all the other agencies into one location, the Office of Federal Contract Compliance Programs in the Department of Labor. Additionally, the EEOC got a new, vigorous chairman who promised swift action.

In sum, there have been numerous attempts by the executive branch and one by the legislative branch of the federal government to create civil rights regulatory agencies. All of them, however, have had only limited success. However, their emergence did have some impact, for they fostered the formation of counterparts on the local and state levels.

Efforts by the States

After World War II several northern and western states created civil rights agencies based on the FEPC model. "Prior to 1945, thirteen states had statutes prohibiting discrimination in various fields of employment, although no state had a fair employment practice law."[39] Then, on March 12, 1945, "Governor Thomas E. Dewey signed into law the first state fair employment practice statute enacted in the United States. It became effective on July 1, 1945."[40] The law created a state commission of five salaried members. This body was empowered to "eliminate and prevent discrimination in employment because of race, creed, color, or national origin by the employers, labor unions, and employment agencies" through persuasion or a cease and desist order which could be enforced by a court decree. Violation, willful resistance, and refusal were treated as a contempt of court matter and the fines were five hundred dollars and/or a year in jail.

By 1960 the number of states with FEPC laws stood at seventeen, while the number of municipal or local governments with such ordinances stood at forty. Local governments in California, Michigan, Minnesota, Ohio, and Pennsylvania had passed local fair employment ordinances before the legislatures acted to outlaw discrimination in employment on a statewide basis."[41] In July 1966, the number of states with such laws stood at thirty-three; of that number, twenty-eight, or more than half, had commissions. Only one state, Nevada, has a statute that gives enforcement powers but establishes no commission. Despite their numbers, these state and local commissions have proven to be of extremely limited power and effectiveness, much like their national counterpart.

One observer, Herbert Hill, labor secretary for the National Association for the Advancement of Colored People (NAACP), has been even more critical. "Given the significant developments in the American economy during the last twenty years together with the current status of the Negro wage-earners in the states with FEPC laws, we must conclude on the basis of the evidence that State FEPC laws have failed. They have failed because their potential was in fact never realized."[42]

Two academics looking at the same laws made a slightly different evaluation. They wrote, "in states and cities having established and enforceable laws, racial discrimination in employment is considerably less prevalent today than it was prior to the enactment of the laws."[43] Yet, the most recent analysis of these laws and commissions, that by Duane Lockard, agreed with Herbert Hill's; Lockard noted that "there are reasons beyond discrimination in hiring that account for job inequality. But, even by a less exacting standard of achievement it seems fair to say that the experience with FEPC has been a failure to meet its potential."[44] It is Lockard's opinion that these failures stem from a "predominant concern with individual cases, the failure to pursue contract compliance procedure, the bureaucratic slowness of many agencies, the failure to establish real contact with the Negro slum dweller and other shortcomings."[45]

Despite the problems with the state and local civil rights agencies and the failure of the first one established by the executive branch of the national government, the executive branch which was quite conscious of these weaknesses and the budding civil rights movement, attempted to move in that direction again in 1957.

On September 1, 1957, Congress created the Commission on Civil Rights. President Dwight D. Eisenhower had requested such in his State of the Union Message on January 10, 1957. Martin Luther King, Jr., had led his first march on Washington (called the Prayer Pilgrimage) on May 17, 1957. Needless to say, southern congressmen in both houses vigorously fought the bill and succeeded in severely restricting the power of the commission. Bernard Schwartz writes, "As finally passed, the 1957 statute scarcely deserved the title of Civil Rights Act." Opponents, he said, were right to be "jubilant," for they "well knew" that they had "a mild measure" with "little substance."[46] Senator Richard Russell, the leader of the southern bloc that reduced the power of the commission, called his effort "the sweetest victory of my 25 years as a Senator."[47] This new attempt to fashion a civil rights regulatory agency ended up creating a fact-finding agency composed of six commissioners and a staff that would submit its report to Congress and the president "not later than the last day of the fiscal year 1958" and within sixty days after that would cease to exist.[48]

Eventually, the life of this commission was extended. President Eisenhower, in a special message to Congress on January 5, 1959, made the request: "I recommended legislation to extend the life of the Civil Rights Commission for an additional 2 years . . . because of the delay in getting the Commission appointed and staffed, and additional 2 years that should be provided for the completion of its task and the making of its final report."[49] Because the Senate Judiciary Committee was under the control of southern opponents of civil rights legislation, nothing was done in the Senate to pass this new bill and extend the life of the commission. Therefore, a rider that would extend the life of the Commission two more years was added to the foreign aid bill that was passed in September 1959.[50]

Although the commission was saved for a while longer, the attempt to enlarge its power and scope failed. "Proponents of civil rights legislation" in both houses of Congress "failed in their efforts to add strengthening amendments, notably one providing for a voting registrar" plan through federal enrollment officers and one adding the third part of the original 1957 Civil Rights Act.[51] The southern filibuster which made the addition of these elements impossible did relent in its opposition once the bill was severely weakened. The president signed the legislation into law on May 6, 1960. The Civil Rights Commission at this time was limited to fact-finding about voting rights or discrimination, although it could explore other areas.

The new Civil Rights Act signed into law on July 2, 1964, contained eleven titles. Title V extended the life of the commission for four years, broadened its scope, and increased its powers. The first historian of the commission, Foster Rhea Dulles, notes: "The section dealing with the Civil Rights Commission did not break very much new ground. It established certain new requirements in respect to the conduct of hearings . . . broadened existing functions with authority to serve as a national clearing house for Civil Rights and to investigate voting practices as well as denial of the right to vote."[52]

This new law gave the members of the commission a boost in morale, as they gained confidence and a sense of a new direction. But there were problems. Although the new law gave the agency certain additional functions, its scope was far from clear.[53] The commission had to seek a new focus. In Father Hesburgh's view (Theodore Hesburgh, both at this writing and then, was president of the University of Notre Dame), its old fact-finding function had been enlarged. The commission held a lengthy session to explore and define its new role and future orientation.[54]

However, even under the new law, this quasi-regulatory agency continued to have difficulty carrying out its functions. Donald Strong has shown that the commission had great difficulty in simply getting cooperation to get the facts. At a January 1959, public hearing in Montgomery, Alabama, held by the commission, "Attorney General Patterson (then governor-elect) made every effort to frustrate the Commission's activities. On his own advice, the Macon County registrars took refuge in the Fifth Amendment and refused to testify or produce any records."[55] Even when the commissioner, a former governor of Virginia, pleaded with them to be more cooperative, they refused to give even rudimentary facts.

The Commission on Civil Rights never had the power to become a true regulatory agency. At best, all it could do was gather facts and report behavior that violated the constitutional principles of the nation with regard to human equality and equal rights. Such action can have impact, but exactly how much it can reshape and refocus behavior is not determinable. The best that a fact-finding body can hope to achieve is to plant the seed for stronger action and policy initiatives in the future. In fact, the commission is a future-oriented enterprise.

Prior to 1964, the history of civil rights regulatory agencies in America was short, nebulous, and evolutionary. Two experiments had been tried on the national level; they set into motion carbon copies of themselves at the state and local levels. Efforts at all these levels were weak.

The first experiment, the FEPC, was created by the executive branch of government during the early years of World War II. It was reorganized by each succeeding president. The second experiment, the Commission on Civil Rights, had been created by the legislative branch. All attempts to give it powers beyond fact-finding ended in failure, but the commission itself continued to exist. Despite these failures, a modest beginning was made between 1939 and 1964 to create civil rights regulatory bodies. These early efforts would see new life with the passage of the 1964 Civil Rights Act.

The Administrative Impact of Titles VI and VII of the 1964 Civil Rights Act

Titles VI and VII of the 1964 Civil Rights Act set into motion two new attempts at regulating racially discriminatory behavior. Specifically, Title VII created the Equal Employment Opportunity Commission (EEOC) and in so doing brought to culmination the FEPC and related attempts by several presidents to bring about equality of job opportunity for all Americans through the use of executive orders. Much has been written about the EEOC and its role in trying to get compliance in the employment field.[56]

Title VI, on the other hand, did not specifically mandate a compliance agency, but it made provision for quite a few. Little has been written about the numerous civil rights regulatory agencies that have come into existence as a result of Title VI. Few analyses have been made of their activities, and no effort has been made to put them into perspective, judging their performance in the light of work by past and current agencies or to assess what their role might be in the future.

Title VI is based on one of the powers vested in Congress by Article I, Section 8, i.e., the power to tax in order to provide for the general welfare. The power to tax, it has long been settled, includes not only the power to spend but also, just as significantly, the power to lay down the conditions upon which federal funds are to be dispensed. In this title, Congress used these powers to mandate that "no person in the United States shall, on the ground of race, color, or national origin . . . be denied the benefits of, or be subjected to discrimination under any program or activity receiving federal financial assistance" (Section 601). Section 602 of the title asserts that "Each federal department and Agency which is empowered to extend federal financial assistance to any program or activity by way of grant, loan or contract . . . is authorized and directed to effectuate the provision of Section 601 with respect to such programs or activity by issuing rules, regulations, or orders of general applicability.[57]

If Section 602 makes possible the creation of compliance components in all the federal departments and agencies, then that same section provides them with the authority to deal with discrimination when they find it. Discrimination or noncompliance can be dealt with by: (1) "the termination of or refusal to grant or to continue assistance under such program or activity to any recipient as to whom there has been an express trial on record . . . " and by (2) "any other means authorized by Law."[58] Over the years, the phrase "any other means authorized by law" has meant the use of judicial enforcement procedures.

Title VI is not without its limitations, however. The Commission on Civil Rights itself declares straightforwardly: "Title VI does not cover all forms of federal financial assistance." In most cases it does not cover direct assistance extended by the federal government or contracts of insurance guaranty. Moreover, its application to employment discrimination is limited and it does not prohibit sex discrimination.[59] The areas that Title VI does cover are immense and pervasive. As the Civil Rights Commission points out, "Federal financial assistance extends into every area of . . . national life." Such assistance has "helped to build hospitals and private health care, to construct airports and highways, to revitalize urban areas and aid in . . . orderly growth, to provide housing, to improve education and recreation facilities and to assist economically disadvantaged individuals and communities."[60] Occasionally this same federal financial assistance has, in addition, provided for the surviving spouses of war veterans and foster care for children.

In short, "federal financial assistance covered by Title VI is extended through more than 400 programs totaling an estimated $50 billion annually. These programs are administered by approximately 25 agencies," which are themselves responsible for enforcing Title VI. Thus, this title, simply because of the vast number of programs that it covers, has the power to cut off or withhold vast funds. It certainly has a major potential to create and set into motion a different type of regulatory agency in the area of American civil rights policy.

The Civil Rights Regulatory Agencies: A New Approach

The initial effort to create a civil rights regulatory agency, as the previous discussion indicates, came from *one* agency in the federal bureaucracy. The second effort came from various chief executives, beginning with Franklin D. Roosevelt in 1941. Congress was finally prodded into action in 1957 and 1960, but both efforts were negated and compromised by the formidable opposition of Southern congressmen.

Therefore, in 1964, Congress tried a third time and on this occasion overcame the solid and stiff opposition of the Southern congressmen and passed legislation that would allow for the creation of the most unique and comprehensive civil rights regulatory agencies to evolve to date in this society. And to accomplish this reality it had taken the federal government a quarter of a century—1939-1964.

Commenting on this problem of elapsed time, Duane Lockard writes: "Where there is a dominate majority race, the white majority gives in, if it does at all, at its own pace and in its own manner . . . Furthermore, where the domi-nate majority race is being pushed to act, there is a tendency for the resistors to convert actual liberating policies into symbolic gestures, appearing to act stav-ing off change by only pretending to change or inserting into programs reserva-tions that undercut operational measures."[61] Lockard's remarks about the time lag situation are quite clear, whether his remarks about efforts to "undercut op-erational measures"—have any validity will be examined in detail in the forth-coming chapters.

At this point in the discussion, it is necessary to describe the nature and scope of these new civil rights regulatory agencies. In this work, such an agency is defined as an organization on the federal, state, or local level that uses the law and provisions or techniques provided by the law *to regulate or to promote human relations in such a way that the conflicts and tensions between different social groups will be ameliorated, their causes removed, and positive action taken to relieve unjust conditions and to eliminate unjust actions affecting mem-bers of one or more groups.*[62] These organizations were made possible by Title VI of the 1964 Civil Rights Acts and have come to be known federally as offices of civil rights compliance. They are new structures in the federal bureaucracy. Unlike the old regulatory agencies that tried to oversee and control economic monoplies and national resources, they are aimed at the protection of the public by regulating human behavior. In his recent book on regulatory agencies, James Q. Wilson labeled these offices as those concerned with "processes," agencies "that regulate nonbusiness organizations."[63] Jeremy Rabkin, who wrote an ar-ticle on the Office of Civil Rights in the Department of Health, Education and Welfare (HEW) for the Wilson book, describes that agency's regulatory focus as being concerned "with vast social engineering schemes" and setting forth "complex schemes of social regulation."[64] Although both men understand that these agencies are new, and quite different from the more traditional agencies, they are rather vague and overly optimistic in their descriptions of them. The very essence of these new agencies is that they have been created to deal with much different realities and forces in the socio-political environment than was the case with regulatory bodies of the past.

The Commission on Civil Rights notes that there were six reasons why Congress created these new regulatory bodies as it did. First, there were numer-ous ambiguous federal statutes on the books that provided federal financial as-sistance on a nondiscriminatory bases but that at the same time permitted, through certain provisions, "separate but equal facilities for minorities and non-minorities." "These separate-but-equal provisions were enacted before the Sup-reme Court's decision, in *Brown v. Board of Education*, that separate but equal is inherently unequal, but that decision did not directly invalidate those provi-sions."[65]

The second reason was that private individuals had to follow a slow, costly, and tortuous road in bringing private lawsuits to resolve discrimination that they encountered in their daily lives.

The need for a clarification of duties and functions was the third reason that Congress established these new agencies. Long before 1964 several federal departments and agencies like the post office, labor, and commerce had acted on the assumption that they could cut off funds where segregation or discrimination was found. Other federal agencies did not operate on such an assumption. The new law gave each federal agency and department the same basis for action.[66]

The famous so-called Powell amendment, a nondiscrimination amendment attached by the black congressman from Harlem, Adam Clayton Powell, to nearly every bill that came to the House of Representatives, was the basis for the fourth reason.[67] Such amendments were time consuming; they led to extensive debates every time there was an attempt to reject the rider. The new law, ironically, resembled the old "gag rule" that forbade the reading of antislavery petitions in the House early in the nineteenth century.

Morality in the commission's view was the fifth reason for the creation of these agencies. Commissioners used President Kennedy's message to Congress on civil rights to illustrate their point. He stated, "Simple justice requires that public funds, to which all tax payers of all races contribute, not be spent in any fashion which encourages, entrenches, subsidise or results in racial discrimination."[68] Such a position was carefully considered and used in the passage of the law that created the new agencies.[69]

The sixth "and possibly the most important reason" for the new law, argued the commission, was that in the "early 1960s discrimination was pervasive in federally assisted programs," such as those in higher education, medical care, and agricultural assistance. In the South many governmental agencies operating with federal funds retaliated against the black protest movement by refusing them federal assistance, funds, and products.

Overall, then, the commission saw legal, practical, and moral reasons for Congress creating a different type of regulatory agency. Essentially, liberal congressmen supported the passage of the legislation for the same reasons. On the other hand, the southern congressmen who opposed the creation of the new regulatory agencies felt that such action would lead to (1) bureaucratic tyranny by bigoted bureaucrats who would impose foreign social customs in the South; (2) a more powerful federal government—one that could involve itself in nearly every facet of the individual's life; and (3) a more massive and expensive federal bureaucracy. They attempted to defeat the bill, and failing that, to eliminate the sections of the legislation that gave the new agencies significant powers. These were the same strategies they had followed in opposing the FEPC and the Commission on Civil Rights. The bill passed over their vociferous opposition and became the Civil Rights Act of 1964. In failing to amend the bill so as to affect the structure and operation of the new agencies, the southern members of Congress only helped to bring about their worst fears. The structure and regulatory approaches in the new agencies were left up to the bureaucrats themselves.

A key point to be made here is that the legislative struggle over the new regulatory agencies did not concern a definition of their structure and regulatory approaches but, rather, whether these agencies were to exist and whether they were to have any real enforcement powers. This was, to say the least, a very narrow though crucial basis for debate concerning the creation of such pioneering bureaucracies. But the southern congressmen had by and large set the lines of battle. Ironically, southerners in the House of Representatives showed little interest in Titles VI or VII. For instance, when Title VI was called for discussion and debated in the House on Friday, Feburary 7, 1964, only one southerner Oren Harris (D-Ark.) offered an amendment that would (have) drastically weakened the section and removed all provisions for judicial review. It was voted down 80-205.[70]

When Title VII was called by the clerk for debate and discussion, Howard W. Smith (D-VA.) rose and offered an amendment—which would insert the word "sex." He had hoped that "by adding the word sex to the list of discriminations (race, creed, color, and national origin) prohibited in employment," the men in the House would vote the title down. It was, however, accepted by a vote of 168-133.[71]

In the Senate, the southerners concentrated not on these titles per se, but on either defeating the entire legislation, or on getting a compromise which would give them the right to remove several of the titles they considered most objectionable. If these two tactics failed, a third one was to offer a series of amendments calling for a Trial by Jury for Title XI.[72] All of these tactics failed. But if there were problems of a lack of unity around tactics among the southerners—there were also some among the civil rights movement.

The civil rights movement had not itself defined exactly what it wanted. Even Martin Luther King, Jr., considered by many to be the chief spokesman for the movement, never specifically called upon Congress to pass legislation creating civil rights regulatory agencies. Scattered throughout his writings are calls for legislation that "would eventually alter peoples' social habits," and in his last policy-oriented book he called for a "bill of rights for the disadvantaged." But he made no specific request for agencies like those which were developed to administer and enforce provisions of Title VI.[73] In fact, David Garrow has shown that although King and his associates drafted and sent to President John F. Kennedy a 115-page policy proposal brief called the "Second Emancipation Proclamation,"[74] the Kennedy administration did not even inform King of its plans to send to Congress a comprehensive Civil Rights Bill.

Garrow writes: "Martin King knew little about the government's decision to propose comprehensive civil rights legislation until Tuesday, June 11, 1963," when President Kennedy went on national television.[75]

When the Johnson administration took over and decided to back the Kennedy sponsored legislation, King had little or no input. Although the administration did summon black civil rights leaders to the White House to keep them informed, the actual drafting and shaping of the legislation took place in the Justice Department with the assistance of several key congressional leaders.[76] In effect those most responsible for making civil rights a national concern were literally forced to stand on the side lines in the *policy formulation* stage and could do little more than criticize in the *policy adopting* stage. At this stage of the policy process, when southern Senators threatened to weaken the legislation, King declared: "I would rather see no bill at all than a bill devoid of these sections" (i.e. public accomodations and fair employment title).[77] To stop the Senate from eliminating these titles, King promised a "Massive Freedom Army" operating during the summer of 1964 in Alabama, and in face to face meetings with President Johnson, he asked the president to fight to keep them in the bill. However, even after the 1964 Civil Rights Act was passed, King gave no indication of the directions the Title VI agencies might follow, and there is little on record of attempts by King to get any Title VI agency to deal with racial discrimination. In sum, King appears to have overlooked the *role* of the federal bureaucracy by not giving any attention to the issue of policy implementation. As Lockard has indicated, in this instance the majority race took complete control of both the policy formulation and policy adoption process and shut the minority reformers completely out.

Seemingly then, the idea that federal departments and agencies might withhold federal funds to enforce desegregation began with President Kennedy's request to Congress for discretionary withholding authority. By the spring of 1963 the Commission on Civil Rights would urge President Kennedy to issue an executive order "forbidding federal funds to segregated facilities."[78] He rejected the request, but by the summer of 1963 "the House Judiciary Committee had transformed President Kennedy's request for *discretionary authority to a mandatory enforcement provision.*"[79] Thus, only a small number of congressmen were behind the Title VI fund-termination proposals, and these congressmen, like people in the civil rights movement, were more concerned with the passage of the legislation than with the structure and regulatory processes of the new agencies. In fact, throughout the legislative debates there is little about how the Title VI agencies might resemble the traditional regulatory agencies, nor is there any comment about earlier attempts to fashion such civil rights regulatory agencies along the lines of the FEPC, the state and local human relation agencies, and/or the Commission on Civil Rights.[80]

The Policy-Oriented Literature on Civil Rights Regulatory Agencies: Two Trends

When these new regulatory agencies began to operate, they attracted quite a bit of journalistic and scholarly attention. Shortly after their emergence, the scholarly literature began to reveal a series of impact or compliance studies. These studies analyzed the attitudes of those being regulated and usually contrasted the attitudes of those who complied with the new law *with those* who did not comply. Scholars working in this area have typically sought to identify the demographic correlates of those communities where compliance took place. The empirical findings of the impact studies generally reveal how well "compliance law" is doing its job at the local level throughout the country. Thus, these impact studies show "how environmental and psychological variables interact to shape" the individual's and the decision maker's "compliance behavior."[81]

In part, these studies grew out of the behavioral movement in political science, a primary concern of which was individual motivation. Compliance impact studies do just that, reveal which attitudes are correlated with observed behavior. The second field of scholarship influencing these studies came out of the area of judicial behavior which focuses on U.S. Supreme Court decisions and their impact on society.[82] Many of these studies date from the late 1950s and the 1960s, following the 1954 *Brown* decision and the various landmark decisions in religion, criminal justice, social welfare, and school desegregation.[83] Findings made in the subfield of judicial behavior found their way into the study of the impact of civil rights laws.

For instance, a pioneering study by Frederick Wirt looked at the impact of civil rights laws on one Mississippi county—Panola—to determine the five conditions that made the implementation of the law successful.[84] Wirt's book established a standard for rigor and scholarship, setting into motion a host of subsequent studies. Another such study was done by Charles S. Bullock and Harrell R. Rodgers, Jr., which dealt extensively with Title VI and the Office of Civil Rights Compliance in HEW.[85]

Using the work of Wirt as a guide, Rodgers and Bullock conducted an impact study of the behavior of thirty-one Georgia school districts from 1965-66 to 1973-74 to identify "the variables that determine whether the school officials involved would comply with the law" as well as whether individuals would do so.[86] This study, which included 189 whites and 61 blacks, reviewed its findings in the light of then current compliance impact literature.[87] Although the authors found that certain attitudes and demographic factors were strongly correlated with compliance, they concluded that "federal enforcement activities" were particularly critical in the desegregation of schools. "The coercion necessary to eliminate dual schools in a community was associated with factors assumed to measure local decision makers' perception of the costs of compliance. In communities in which compliance costs were perceived to be high and rewards low, the most severe coercion was required."[88] Wirt had found earlier that "in civil rights matters, southerners move very little toward the goal of equality unless under direct federal pressures which threaten specific, injurious sanctions."[89]

The merit of the impact studies lies in what they reveal in specific instances and cases. They show the strong relationship between federal enforcement and compliance behavior. But their weakness stems from the fact that they are case studies and do not provide much insight into other, dissimilar cases. Second, they emphasize a "micro" perspective; i.e. they look at the behavior at the point of impact and do not give much emphasis to the larger enforcement system and process. These studies tend to emphasize the coercive aspect of the federal enforcement system without conveying some understanding as to how the larger system is organized, structured, and operates. Third, by not giving much emphasis to the larger system, these studies foster the notion that the entire enforcement apparatus is working in a proper fashion and thus incorrectly evaluate the enforcement process based only on what they have observed. For instance, at the same time that the Bullock and Rodgers study looked at the impact of HEW's Office of Civil Rights Compliance in Georgia in the area of education and found it to be successful, the General Accounting Office (GAO), civil rights groups, and Congress found that this same office failed to enforce Title VI in regard to health facilities in several parts of Georgia, and other places.[90] One therefore has to be very careful about accepting generalizations based on the single-case impact studies.

Finally, these impact studies suffered from the same limitation that beset most behavioral studies.[91] By focusing *solely* on individual psychological attitudes, they ignore the enormous role that the government itself can play.

The earlier impact studies have been supplemented by more recent implementation studies, which analyze *how* federal agencies carry out the law at the local and state level. They rely essentially upon government statistics about complaints and government accounts of the ways those complaints are resolved.

Like the earlier impact studies, this new implementation literature takes a single case approach to the data. Yet it differed in that it looked at basically only three areas: voting rights, job discrimination and school desegregation and busing. Although the job discrimination books were not always case site specific, it was essentially true for the other two areas—school desegregation and voting rights. In fact scores of books appeared on school desegregation particularly in the large metropolitan cities, while the works on voting rights looked at the south in general or specific parts of the south where black voter participation was facing grave obstacles. In fact, at one point, these implementation studies were so skewed towards voting rights, education and school desegregation that it was hard to determine federal government regulating effort in other areas.

To put it bluntly, something of an intellectual and academic logjam had taken place in terms of the focus and emphasis of these implementation studies. Although new studies proliferated and some questionable generalizations emerged in the area of school desegregation, there was little outward movement in the area. Then, Bullock and Charles Lamb started to look at civil rights regulatory agencies from the standpoint of a comprehensive implementation approach. They attempted to generate a *standard* list of crucial variables that would " . . . explain why a policy meets with a greater success at one time or another . . ." And besides the construction of a standard list of variables they broaden the scope by looking at other regulatory agencies. They explored the traditional voting rights, school desegregation and the job discrimination matters but added fair housing and the matter of equal educational opportunities.

The Bullock and Lamb effort was not only new in its approach and conceptualization, it argued that it was possible to compare different areas of civil rights policy and thus to explain variation in patterns of implementation over time. They write: "Such an exercise would go beyond the case study approach which although valuable in identifying potential explanatory variables, is not suited to determining whether the causes of implementation success are broadly applicable or are limited to a unique fact situation."[92] Thus, with this work a break began to appear in the intellectual logjam.

Therefore, into this morass of single case studies and a narrow focus on thr e regulatory areas, i.e. voting rights, job and school desegregation, Bullock and Lamb's volume had tried to forge a new path. But, basically speaking, this direction and path was in the area of implementation. Bullock and Lamb write: "Books, lectures and courses in policy implementation" have now become "a recent phenomenon in political science." Civil rights regulatory matters got submerged under the concerns with implementation problems and realities. But regulatory activity, civil rights or otherwise, is only partially concerned as we shall see with the realities of policy implementation.

There were other problems with this new volume besides its implementation emphasis. Several scholars looking at implementation in the civil rights regulatory areas had developed their own *standard* list of crucial variables.[93] Hence, students of this literature found themselves facing competing lists of explanatory variables about implementation success and without any basic criteria for choice among them. The other problem which is typical of much of the civil rights implementation literature is that it does not sufficiently link implementation performance with the multifaceted capacity or lack thereof, of the bureaucracy to execute the law. Several factors, as the forthcoming chapters will reveal, impact the bureaucracy's capacity to make the law effective. Thus, while bold and daring, the Bullock and Lamb volume had some severe limitations.

But when they are taken collectively, i.e. the single case implementation studies and the broad gauge studies of Bullock and Lamb and Augustus Jones, a key theme emerges for which most of these studies offer significant empirical proof. And this theme is that as one of the many variables shaping the successful outcome of implementation, management is related to implementation performance. And this finding in the civil rights implementation studies is quite similar to the findings in most implementation studies. And perhaps, it was this key finding that has drawn the ire of several critics, most notably among them is Lester Salamon.

Salamon writes: "The new field of implementation research has already become stuck in a rut. Like Antimochus' hedgehog, which knew only one big thing, both students and practitioners of implementation have taken to discovering repeatedly a single, simple truth: that programs cannot work if they are poorly managed."[94] He continues; "without doubting the critical importance of good management, it seems clear that 'public management' is fast becoming for students of policy implementation what 'political culture' became for students of political development: a kind of universal solvent expected to unravel all mysteries and explain all problems."[95]

These insights then lead Professor Salamon to conclude: "most important . . . while demonstrating that, poor management is associated with poor performance, no one seems to be able to show that the converse is true, giving rise in some quarters to the conclusion that it is not the absence of management, but the presence of government, that is the real explanation of public-program failure." At this point one must hasten to add that this is not the intention of the civil rights implementation literature. Yet many of the current conservatives and neo-conservatives who have read and analyzed these studies and some of the conservatives who are writing these civil rights implementation studies have come to the conclusion that it is the *presence* of government and/or poor management that is responsible for the problem. But it is Duane Lockard's insights that the white majority adds reservations that undercut operational measures which enables one to see these *presence* of government arguments as little more than a smoke screen. Not everything as Salamon reminds us, can be attributed to poor management and the presence of government.

The reason for this narrow vision, argues Salamon, is that " . . . the major shortcomings of current implementation research is that it focuses on the wrong unit of analysis, i.e. the individual programs."...Or even a collection of programs grouped according to major 'purpose'..."The focus, as Salamon sees it, should be on the "techniques of social interventions."

Perhaps the most important part of all, before one looks at how a law is implemented, one needs to see how the designated departments and agencies are themselves prepared internally and organizationally to carry out congressional mandates. *Thus, anterior to the question of implementation is the question of whether the responsible parties themselves are prepared to undertake the task of implementation. In sum, there is a stage before implementation that is crucial in shaping the outcomes of implementation.*

Given these severe and unresolved conceptual, methodological, analytical and interpretative problems in the impact and implementation literature, any new study and/or reexamination of these new civil rights regulatory agencies must began with a new and different approach—recognizing that these new civil rights regulation agencies are unique and different in their own right.

When Congress included Titles VI, VII and to some extent Title XI (it establishes a Community Relation Service agency within the Department of Commerce to help states and communities resolve discrimination disputes) in the Civil Rights Act of 1964, it had in effect, created the basis for an entirely new type of regulatory structure. In short, the law created a two-dimensional regulatory structure.

Title VI created, or at least made possible, a civil rights administrative unit "within *each* federal agency and department, whose congressional mandate is not solely limited to the enforcement of civil rights laws."[97] As Professor Michael Preston states: ". . . policymakers tend to take an existing instrument (a government agency) and use it regardless of the similarities between its present function and the new uses to which it is to be put."[98] He goes on to write: ". . . where new programs are grafted onto old structures without a proper assessment of the relationship between the existing instrument and the new purpose, the results are likely to lead to faulty implementation of new programs . . ."[99] The Cabinet-level department and agencies in which created Title VI regulatory units were developed saw themselves and their mission as one of dispensing benefits and desired programs and not as bureaucracies with civil rights regulatory authority. Thus if Preston insights are correct, we will be able to see problems inherent in the very creation of the new regulatory agency immediately.

Title VII on the other hand created the classic regulatory body, the Equal Employment Opportunity Commission (EEOC). It is an independent and separate agency not unlike the earlier economic regulatory agencies, e.g. SEC, FCC, ICC, and the FPC. Much like the economic regulatory agencies, the EEOC's chairman and members are selected by the President and approved by Congress and attempt to operate independently of Congress and the chief executive. President Reagan however, has clearly sought to alter this previous pattern in a host of regulatory agencies and particularly in the civil rights area.

Looking at regulatory bodies that are structured organizationally the way that Title VI and Title VII civil rights regulatory agencies have been structured, one academic observer has categorized those regulatory bodies that are within cabinet departments (like Title VI units) as "Dependent Regulatory Agencies," (hereafter DRAS) and those outside such departments (like the Title VII unit)[100] as "Independent Regulatory Commissions" (hereafter IRCS). While this is an intriguing typology and has been little explored, this study will reveal if this dual approach has one unit being more successful than the other.[101]

Besides these two different types of civil rights regulatory agencies—a traditional and a new one, the 1964 Civil Rights Act also with Title X gave the Department of Commerce—the Community Relations Service agency and continued the Civil Rights Division within the Justice Department. Thus, from the outset, this new law created an entirely different and unique set of regulatory bodies for civil rights. Why this mixed approach? Lester Salamon writes: "The problems the Federal government has recently been called upon to resolve— poverty, urban distress, environmental degradation, (civil rights), etc.—can rarely be solved through individual programs."[102] To address them meaningfully requires the successful orchestration of a number of different activities."[103]

Moreover, "Federal *regulatory activities*, once primarily economic in focus, have now become major vehicles for the promotion of a wide array of health, safety, environmental and social goals." Beginning in the 70's there was a significant expansion of social regulatory agencies and these agencies had new and different types of techniques and procedures for managing their spheres of activity.[104]

One scholar sums it up as follows: "The proliferation, expansion, and extension of these and other tools of Federal policy have substantially reshaped the landscape of Federal operations. Instead of a single form of action, virtually every major sphere of Federal policy is now made up of a complex collage of widely assorted tools involving a diverse collection of different types of actors performing a host of different roles in frequently confusing combinations."[105]

Not only had the 1964 Civil Rights Act created a new and broad type of regulatory structure, with a new and different type of regulatory powers, i.e. cutting off of federal dollars, but it had also created a new type of internal environment within the federal bureaucracy, which had employees of different races working to carry out these laws. Frank Thompson called these efforts, the making of representative bureaucracies.

Burton Levy writes: "Most civil rights agencies have developed a degree of internal interpersonal conflict with some aggressiveness and hostility directed by employees against the agency itself."[106] Black public servants and their white allies might find "racism" inside the bureaucracy that hindered them in their efforts to do something significant for people who had been discriminated against. Such internal tensions added a new dimension to these already unique and different agencies.

Moreover, rather than look at one agency or a collection of these agencies, this study will analyze and evaluate *each* and *every* one of the federal cabinet departments for both its Title VI and Title VII functions. And although it will cover specifically and in detail these regulatory bodies, it will also include some analyses of the EEOC and other independent federal agencies that have Title VI units, particularly in terms of the budget and personnel practices.

The analysis starts in *1964* and covers each agency through *1984*—for a full two-decade look. And furthermore, where possible it will include some budgetary and personnel and organizational data through 1986. The point here was to avoid some narrow and limited time frame and actually do a time series analysis so that the reader can see changes, continuities, and tendencies in these new regulatory agencies. This would avoid the old snapshot and episodic studies now in the literature.

Being a time series analysis, this study has gathered, where possible and available, governmental statistics on organizational structures and flow charts, budgets, personnel numbers, number of complaints and compliant resolutions as well as pre- and post-award analyses.

Needless to say, federal data, particularly on these new social regulatory agencies has not been competently kept and data is non-continuous and spotty and sketchy as well as very unreliable. But where such conditions exist in the data, the reader is constantly made aware of it and in every case the most reliable data available is used. Thus, the portrait drawn about personnel, budgets, and enforcement efforts is drawn from a careful empirical assessment of the data.

Once the data is analyzed, the interpretation of it is rooted in a historical context. Historians of the Reconstruction period have collected some data for the 1870-1877 period and this data permits some degree of historical continuity to be shown in a reliable fashion by comparing the regulatory efforts of that period with the new regulatory efforts of today. Thus, a sense of success and failure in the federal government's civil rights regulatory effort past and present can be made.

But for some, success and failure rest not on the nature, scope, and realities of the regulatory machinery but in the very nature of the regulatory policy itself. For instance, one student of the civil rights regulatory effort has asserted that: "In the final analysis, what has blocked bargaining over official compliance standards for OCR is the notion that Civil Rights cannot be compromised, that 'civil rights' like constitutional guarantees, must stand as an outer boundary on the free play of political preferences."[107] But it is precisely this historical continuity and overview which will permit the reader to see beyond the supposedly inherent nature of civil rights policies that lead to certain regulatory consequences and observe how the question of management, and the political process itself have developed sundry techniques and devices which resulted in compromises that lead to debilitating regulatory consequences. Hence, a historical perspective is central and germane.

Finally, this study seeks to avoid the problems of values that many students of implementation studies carry with them when they see civil rights regulatory efforts as redistributive programs and policies instead of as protective regulatory programs. Randall Ripley and Grace Franklin write: "Redistributive policies and programs are intended to readjust the allocation of wealth, property, rights or some other value among social classes or racial groups in society." Then they define protective regulatory programs as policies that "can both prevent certain types of private activity and require private activities in explicit terms."[108] Yet, they write that "equal rights programs are often thought of as protective regulatory efforts. However, we think they should be treated along with other redistributive programs because their aim is to enlarge the political, economic or social rights of persons whose rights are limited on the basis of some sort of racial, ethnic, or sex discrimination."[109]

They conclude that policymakers who support such programs and policies do not feel this way, i.e. seeing them as redistributive programs. But what counts is "that a number of whites view equal rights and affirmative actions programs as taking their rights from them in some sense in order to give them to minorities."[110] And since the dominant white majority objects, these authors feel that such programs and policies ought to be labelled redistributive. This clever and sleight of hand device makes justice in this society rest on the will of the dominant white majority. Might in this instance becomes right.

Thus, such a picture raises all sorts of philosophical and ethical and moral questions which Ripley and Franklin quickly brush aside. Rights can be affirmed or denied. Whether they can be redistributed is another question all together. And such reasoning and typology permit and justify the existence of groups, individuals, and academic studies and support for the very people that the regulatory programs are designed to restrain. For instance, one recent academic study justifies an end to busing because, using this topology, busing is considered a redistributive policy and under this policy whites lose too many of their rights—conversely it could be argued that the rights that they have, are ones that they are not willing to share with blacks so that blacks can have equal education under the law.[111] Therefore, to avoid this value problem and ideological stance, this study sees the new regulatory programs as essentially protective regulatory bodies and nothing else.

When the marching of the grand civil rights movement stopped—in fact just before it stopped —there were already in place in America a substantial new set of civil rights regulatory units within the federal bureaucracy. The grand civil rights movement had given rise to these administrative units and the federal government had literally gone into the civil rights business. The civil rights movement had become institutionalized in the structure of American government. And just what did this new institutionalization via civil rights regulatory units mean? How did the federal bureaucracy perform after Congress enacted a law designed to meet the challenges of the civil rights movement? To what extent did the behavior of the federal bureaucracy in its implementation of civil rights policies change over time? These are the questions that this study will answer.

2. The Politics of Creation: Structure and Personnel

The enabling congressional legislation for these new civil rights regulatory agencies was designed in part to stop the marching of the grand civil rights movement. David Garrow writes: "The president used the signing ceremony (of the 1964 Civil Rights Act) not only to congratulate those who had contributed to the passage of one of the legislative milestones in modern American history, but also to caution the black leaders about how they should greet this new achievement. After the public ceremony, the President spoke in private with King, Roy Wilkins, Whitney Young, and other black representatives. He told them that there had to be 'an understanding of the fact that the rights Negroes possessed could now be secured by law, making demonstrations unnecessary and possibly even self-defeating'."[1] Marching and/or demonstrations, both the president and Congress felt, could now subside.

However, with the passage of this new law and the Supreme Court's decision that the law was constitutional, the matter of actually creating these new regulatory bodies, particularly the Title VI agencies, was left up to the various cabinet secretaries and chairmen of the sundry independent commissions and federal agencies. Put differently, in the absence of guidelines from the president or from Congress, the sole initiative to structure an Office of Civil Rights Compliance within each cabinet level department and elsewhere was left with

28

the cabinet secretaries and commission and agency heads.

But the question of *responsibility* in the creation of these new civil rights regulatory agencies is only *one* of the key concerns in this chapter. The enabling legislation, the 1964 Civil Rights Act, also required each department and agency to fulfill its Title VII responsibilities. Title VII required that the Equal Employment Opportunity Commission (EEOC) be established, but at the same time it required all departments and agencies to ban in-house discrimination in employment, hiring, firing, promotion, and raises. Each federal department, commission, and agency was congressionally mandated to monitor itself to see that its in-house functions were free of employment discrimination. The EEOC was also authorized to monitor such activities both in the federal government and in the private sector. If an agency or department could not resolve a matter itself, the EEOC would become directly involved.

Therefore besides the question of *responsibility*, another key concern in this chapter is that of *structure*. Organizationally, how did the various cabinet-level departments approach compliance with Title VI and Title VII of the 1964 Civil Rights Act? Some agencies established separate Title VI compliance offices while in other agencies these functions were combined with Title VII compliances. But once a structure has been created, it is possible in human organizations for that structure to be changed, abolished, or reorganized. This is, then, one of the realities that this chapter wants to explore in great detail and a longitudinal approach permits such an analysis.

Once the task of creation and structure has been handled, the next concern is that of staffing—first at the top administrative levels, i.e. cabinet secretaries and then Title VI and/or Title VII heads. Here, the study will probe for stability and continuity in these positions at both the secretarial and sub-secretarial levels.

When administrative staffing of these new civil rights regulatory agencies has been analyzed, this chapter will then review departmental staffing, by both size and programs function, to determine where the staff have been placed and what functions actually have been given to these individuals as they perform their regulatory duties.

Finally, the findings about when and how these agencies were created, the nature and types of structure, and the size and functions of their staffs will be analyzed and evaluated in light of their regulatory operations of *policy-making* and *enforcement*. But with this effort there are some problems. As one scholar has indicated, "Does regulatory structure make any real difference in the operation of regulating agencies? Surprisingly, existing opinion on that question consists mainly of impressions and conventional wisdom rather than being based on careful research; there is very little of the latter."[2] If this is the case of structure, the literature on creation and staffing and how they impact regulatory efforts is even less available. But given our data bases, some tentative and inferential linkages will be made.

In sum, this chapter will explore, analyze, and evaluate who had the responsibility for creating these new regulatory agencies, when and how they were created, and, once they were created, whether they were changed, abolished or reorganized, how they were structured to carry out their mandates, how they were staffed at both the top administrative and departmental levels, including the stability in this staffing as well as the functions and duties of this staff. And finally, we will try to explore how there regularities impact upon regulatory policymaking and enforcement given the vagaries of federal regulatory data.[3]

The Politics of Creation

No one—not the president, the Congress, the Commission on Civil Rights or any black civil rights organization—had a comprehensive list of the names and/ or location of the various civil rights compliance agencies. On March 3, 1980, a letter was sent to Louis Martin, the black special assistant to President Jimmy Carter for Minority Affairs, at the White House. A reply was mailed from the White House on July 28, 1980. Robert A. Malson, assistant director of the Domestic Policy Staff, answered for Louis Martin: "I have discovered as you did before me, that no such comprehensive list exists and therefore, I am attempting to prepare one. I will send you a copy when I have completed the list."[4] Such a list was never received from Malson.

With no response from the White House, letters were sent to members of Congress in the Georgia delegation. Senator Sam Nunn (D - Ga.) and Congressman Ronald "Bo" Ginn (D - Ga.) responded by sending a Xerox copy of the *Civil Rights Directory* and suggesting that the author should check with the Commission on Civil Rights. Their responses clearly indicated that Congress— or at least their offices—could not provide a comprehensive list.

Finally, a letter was sent to the Commission on Civil Rights, not only because Congressman Ginn had suggested it but because the commission had prepared an evaluation of the Office of Civil Rights Compliance in six cabinet-level departments and one independent agency—the EPA—in its 1975 report.[5] However, the Commission did not have a comprehensive list of Title VI regulatory agencies. Cynthia Norris Graae, associate director of the Office of Federal Civil Rights Evaluation, who responded on behalf of the Commission to my inquiry, stated that her agency had never made a comprehensive list.

In short, none of the *policy formulators* (the civil rights organizations, Congress, the presidency) nor the *policy leadership* (the executive office of the president, congressional oversight committees), nor the *policy evaluators* (Commission on Civil Rights) knew how many federal agencies had complied with Title VI and Title VII requirements, or if they had not complied. Nor did they know how these agencies had responded to putting Title VI regulatory bodies into effect. Thus, sixteen years after the Civil Rights Act of 1964 was passed, officials of the federal government had little knowledge of how the federal government had responded to an important congressional mandate. It appears that the creation of civil rights compliance offices within cabinet-level departments was not a legal question, but a question of administrative will.

The point to be made here is that no one had taken the responsibility to ensure compliance with the enabling legislation. With no centralizing force or body engendering conformity, then from the outset the responsibility would be at best a decentralized one. Each and every cabinet department, commission, and independent agency would respond on its own at its own pace. Put differently, exactly how that federal department or commision was to meet its Title VI and Title VII requirement was left up to the department. For instance, in the U.S. Department of Labor, Title VI responsibilities were carried out in the department's Employment and Training Administration and were not assigned to a separate office until October 28, 1980 via the labor secretary's order number 8-80; its organizational location was prescribed by secretary's order number 2-81.[6]

In other words, creation of an office in each department to handle Title VI and VII requirements originated exclusively with the department's secretary since there were no uniform guidelines from Congress or the president.

With a clear understanding that cabinet secretaries, commission chairpersons, and agency heads had wide discretionary powers in responding to the enabling legislations, we can now explore when each cabinet-level department complied with the legislative mandate.

The number of cabinet-level departments fluctuated somewhat between 1964 and 1982, and, until 1972, only a portion of them created an office to carry out Title VI responsibilities (Table 2.1).[7] In 1964 only the Justice Department had a Civil Rights Division, which it had been required to create by the 1957 Civil Rights Act. From the outset, then, it had the administrative means to handle Title VI responsibilities mandated by the 1964 Civil Rights Act. It took nearly two years before any other cabinet-level department reflected in its organizational chart an internal division that was created to deal with and carry out Title VI responsibilities. It was eight years before all cabinet-level departments had created such offices and divisions. The last two to do so were Agriculture and Treasury; the first to come on line beside Justice were Commerce, HEW, Housing and Urban Development (HUD), and Labor. Transportation created such an office within a year of its establishment by Congress, and the Energy Department created its compliance office the same year that it was established.

Each department instituted regulatory units at the discretion of the secretary in office. Two-thirds of the departments initiated regulatory units during the Johnson administration, while the remaining third did so under the Nixon administration.

Table 2.1   Cabinet Departments Having Title VI Offices 1964–1982

Years	Number of Departments	Number with Title VI Offices
1964	10	1*
1965	10	1
1966	11	5
1967	12	7
1968	12	8
1969	12	8
1970	12	9
1971	11	9
1972	11	11
1973	11	11
1974	11	11
1975	11	11
1976	11	11
1977**	11	11
1978***	12	12
1979	12	12
1980	13	13
1981	13	13
1982	13	13

*Justice Department
**Department of Energy authorized.
***Health, Education and Welfare reorganized to create a Department of Health and Human Services and a Department of Education
Source: U.S. Government Organization Manual (1964–1982).

Having now seen when each department created a unit and how long it took the federal government to comply with its own enabling legislation, we can now probe the data to see if these Title VI offices were single and separate offices or whether they were combination offices designed to handle the Title VII regulatory concerns also.

The data in Table 2.2 reveals that the majority of the cabinet departments created combined offices. Although an office that had responsibility for both Title VI and Title VII might have separated their administrations internally, the office was nonetheless headed by one person. Only in 1969 did the two types of structures reach a similar level with each other, when the Department of Transportation, which had combined the two regulatory functions, reorganized and created a separate office called the Office of Civil Rights

Compliance to deal solely with Title VI responsibilities.

Table 2.2 The Structure of Civil Rights Compliance Offices in Federal Departments: 1964–1972

Years	Separate Title VI Offices	%	Combined Title VI/EEOC Offices	%
1964			1	100.0
1965			1	100.0
1966	2	41.0	3	60.0
1967	3	43.0	4	57.0
1968	3	37.5	5	62.5
1969	4	50.0	4	50.0
1970	4	44.4	5	55.6
1971	4	44.4	5	55.6
1972	3	27.3	8	72.7

Source: The United States Government Manual (1964–1972).

That year, 1969, was the peak year for separate Title VI compliance offices. By 1972, only slightly more than one-fourth of the civil rights compliance offices were separate. In 1972, the Department of Defense—which had maintained a separate office called Civil Rights and Industrial Relations—reorganized, changing its title and combining its functions with the EEOC office. In fact, all of the combined offices had the "Equal Opportunities" label, suggesting that the emphasis and concern may have been more with Title VII than with Title VI.

In the ten years between 1972 and 1982 eight of the thirteen departments reorganized their compliance offices with a change in departmental secretaries (Table 2.3). The greatest number of reorganizations took place in 1978 and 1979, following President Carter's cabinet shuffling, and in 1975, the second year of the Ford presidency.

The Commerce Department saw four significant changes over six years. In 1974 the department changed the title and division. In this department, Title VI functions had been combined with employment opportunity functions, and the director, Luther C. Steward, Jr., was called the special assistant for employment opportunity. By 1974 he was called the special assistant for civil rights. In the following year his office was completely abolished, disappearing from the organizational chart when the new secretary, Rogers C. B. Morton, took over. However, the very next year, when another new secretary, Elliott L. Richardson, took over, the section was reestablished with Steward as special assistant. By 1978, departmental secretary Juanita M. Kreps shifted civil rights responsibilities from her office to that of the assistant secretary for administration. The office was then given a new title, Office of Civil Rights Compliance, but no director was named until 1979.

Table 2.3   Reorganizations of Title VI Offices: 1973–1986

Departments	'73	'74	'75	'76	'77	'78	'79	'80	'81	'82	'83	'84	'85	'86	Total
Commerce		R	R		R	R									4
Defense			R							R					2
HEW						R	R								2
HUD	R						R						V		2(1)*
Labor						R	R								2
State							R								1
Transportation			R	V	R		R								3(1)*
Treasury			R												1

Source: The United States Government Manual (1964–1986) and data collected from various agencies.
R = Reorganized
V = Vacant
* = Vacancies

The Department of Transportation Title VI office has undergone almost as many changes. Under its first black secretary, William T. Coleman, Jr., the office was shifted to the secretary's office, and the director of the Office of Civil Rights Compliance was made, a special assistant to the secretary himself. When the Carter administration took office, a new secretary was brought in, and the office was reorganized so that the director was no longer special assistant to the secretary. In 1980 the position would once again go vacant. In short, four major changes ocurred in a five-year span.

Under Joseph A. Califano, Jr., HEW underwent a reorganization in 1978 and the second change in 1979, a separate Department of Education was created and a new secretary, Patricia Roberts Harris, who had been secretary at HUD, was brought in. HUD had seen major reorganization in 1973, when an Office of Civil Rights Compliance and Enforcement was created in the equal opportunity division. In 1975 the directorship of this office was vacant, but a year later when a new director was appointed, it underwent a minor revision. The number of sections in the equal opportunity division went from five to nine. However, in 1979, under Secretary Harris, the number of sections would fall from nine to six and then rise to seven. By 1985, the office would be vacant.

In the Department of Labor a change in both title and organization took place. The Title VI office was separated from the Office of Federal Contract Compliance and given a new name, Federal Compliance and State Programs. By 1980 it had been placed under the direction of the Office of Equal Opportunity and its director was the assistant secreatry for administration and management.

In 1975 two departments, Defense and Treasury, made their single reorganizational efforts. Defense reorganized its administrative structure so that the newly-combined office stayed under the direction of the deputy assistant secretary for equal opportunity but it was moved further down the organizational chart—a long way from the secretary's office. In Treasury, the Office of Civil Rights was a section of the Office of Equal Opportunity Program that was housed in the general counsel's office. In 1975 the Civil Rights office was taken out of the general counsel's office, also located in the secretary's office—and placed in one of the under-secretary positions, two levels of administration lower. Secretary William Simon was responsible for the move.

Finally, the Department of State, under Cyrus R. Vance's leadership in 1979, moved the combined office out from under one of the deputy under-secretaries (the third administrative level) and moved it up to the direction of one of the under-secretaries (the second administrative level). This sort of movement in departmental office and civil rights office was not typical, for it involved a move up in the organizational hierachy rather than down.

To summarize: it took eight years before all of the federal departments at cabinet level had created units to carry out the Title VI congressional mandate. The structure of the units created to carry out the mandate have varied greatly. Some departments created separate offices of civil right compliance; others combined them with equal opportunities divisions; some tried both. Currently, the trend is toward combined offices, which increases the number of functions, forces an office to work at cross-purposes, thereby reducing overall effectiveness.

Finally, after the structures were put into place, nearly every department underwent some reorganization and left the directorship of the compliance office vacant for a time. It would seem, then, that organizing an administrative structure and developing a comprehensive system to carry out Title VI and VII mandates has been difficult. The status quo leaves much to be desired. Leaving the *creation* and the *structure* of these new regulatory agencies up to the "will" of the cabinet secretaries demonstrates that there was from the outset, a lack of uniformity in *when* these regulatory agencies got started and a lack of uniformity in the structure of these agencies, i.e. some had single and others had dual functions. Thus, these new civil rights regulatory agencies lacked any type of systematization as they sought to deal with discriminatory behavior. Basically, the federal government's spending of federal funds moved piecemeal along the front line of battle with racist behavior. Different federal agencies came into the regulatory battle at different times over the eight-year period. Such an approach made the federal regulatory stance in civil rights not only uneven but it quite possibly encouraged resistance because some recipients of funds saw others, at least for the time being, escaping regulation.

Now, having seen how the creation of these agencies took place, let's turn our attention to how they were staffed, beginning with the top administration; a new regulatory agency must have staff if it is to operate. Regulatory activity cannot take place unless a vehicle has been created to handle the responsibilities, and that entity cannot operate without people.

The Politics of Personnel: Top Administrators

In this section, we will look first at the cabinet secretaries and then at the Title VI or VII department heads and at what relationships occurred between the two, and particularly the degree of stability. Stability at this level suggests the *potential* for greater continuity and possibly more uniformity in carrying out the regulatory mandate. Instability at these levels, on the other hand, suggests the great potential for discontinuity and disruption in carrying out the regulatory mandate.

Each cabinet secretary usually comes into a federal bureaucracy with his/her own goals, strategies, and perspectives.[9] Sub-cabinet level departments tend to have similar outlooks. And these individual outlooks tend to differ from person to person—despite the fact that the bureaucracy is perpetual. These individual mangerial predispositions have regulatory consequences.[10] First, let's look at the stability and instability in these organizations.

During the period under analysis there were five different presidents, yet, as the data in Table 2.4 indicates, there have been a far greater number of secretaries and Title VI department heads. In some instances the number of secretaries has been more than double the number of presidents; the number of Title VI heads has also been high. Clearly, little stability has been maintained. Each department has had its own ebb and flow, independent of changes of administration and of changes of other cabinet-level departments. Commerce, Justice, HEW, Treasury, Transportation, State, and Defense have suffered the largest amount of turnover. Energy and Education are at the bottom of the list because of their recent creation.

One department, HUD, has had more frequent changes of its Title VI director than secretarial changes: eight Title VI directors and seven secretaries between 1964 and 1982. All of the other cabinet-level departments except Defense, Labor, and Education have seen more secretaries come and go than directors of Title VI units. Treasury has had three times as many secretaries as civil rights directors. Energy, Interior, and Transportation have seen twice as many secretaries as civil rights directors. The personnel running these units has been in constant flux over these eighteen years. This leadership instability has caused uneven implementation, as the outlook and emphasis of each individual director and secretary make themselves felt.

Table 2.4   Cabinet-Level Secretaries and Title VI Heads under Five Presidents: 1964–1982

Departments	Number of Secretaries	Number of Title VI Heads
Agriculture	5	4
Commerce	12	6
Defense	7	7
Energy	4	2
HEW	11	8
HUD	7	8
Interior	6	3
Justice	11	8
Labor	8	8
State	7	4
Transportation	8	4
Treasury	9	3
Education	2	2
Mean	7.5	5.2

Note: These numbers do not indicate the number of times either office has been vacant.
Source: The United States Government Manual (1964–1982).

A few of the directors of civil rights units did run these offices for comparatively long periods of time. For instance, in the Interior Department, Edward D. Shelton ran the Title VI office for thirteen years, from 1969 to 1982.[11] Next to Shelton in longevity are: Luther C. Steward, Jr., in Commerce, who held the position for eight years, from 1968 to 1974 (in 1975 the secretary of the department disbanded the office), and David Sawyer in the Treasury Department, who also held the job for eight years from 1970 to 1977.

One person held the same position in two different agencies for a total of seven years. J. Stanley Pottinger was head of the civil rights office in HEW under Secretary Elliott Richardson for three years (1970–1972); when Richardson moved to head the Department of Justice, he took Pottinger along with him. Although Richardson left in 1973, Pottinger stayed on to run the office for four years (1973–1976). Another person, James Frazier, headed the civil rights unit in two different agencies for a total of nine years. From 1972 to 1976, he ran the Title VI office in the Department of Transportation, and from 1977 to 1980, he headed the same office in the Department of Agriculture.

A much larger group, twenty-two individuals examined in thirteen cabinet-level departments between 1964 and 1982, stayed in office for only one year. Out of the sixty-nine civil rights offices, nearly thirty-two percent—a whopping one-third of all the people running these offices—held their positions for less than a year. The mean length of stay for heads of Title VI agencies is 2.5 years (Table 2.5). Two-thirds of all the Title VI heads were gone by the end of the sec-

Table 2.5   The Longevity in Office of Title VI Officers: 1964–1982

Length of Stay in Office (mean = 2.5)	Number of Officers	Percentage of All Officers
14	1	1
9*	1	3
8	2	3
7*	1	3
4	5	7
3	11	16
2	24	35
1	22	32

*Denotes one individual holding two offices.

ond year, a staggering turnover rate. The quality of enforcement and its consistency obviously were negatively impacted, as personalities shifted and programs changed rapidly over the years. Although some agencies were not as hard hit as others, the mean time in office for all Title VI officers was below the four years that mark regular changes of administration. As people came and went, so did commitment, enforcement, standards, policies, and practices.

   The analysis based on Tables 2.4 and 2.5 has focused on departmental level Title VI units, i.e., units that were directly connected to the departmental secretary's office by having department-wide jurisdiction. However, within various cabinet-level departments, Title VI (or civil rights) units were also to be found below the level of the departmental secretary. Figure 2.1 provides an organizational chart for the U.S. Department of Transportation. In the third tier the department is divided into seven modal units, covering a specific type of transportation—the U.S. Coast Guard (USCG), the Federal Aviation Administration (FAA), the Federal Highway Administration (FHA), the Federal Railroad Administration (FRA), the National Highway Traffic Safety Administration (NHTSA), the Urban Mass Transportation Administration (UMTA), and the Saint Lawrence Seaway Development Corporation (SLSDC). Within each of these units is an office of civil rights to deal with Title VI problems in its respective area. Each of these offices reports directly to the Office of

Figure 2.1
The Offices of Civil Rights in the Department of Transportation

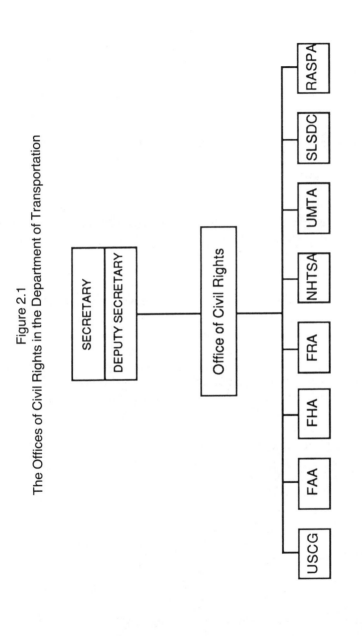

Civil Rights in the secretary's office. The question here is, what about turnover and vacancies at the subsecretarial level? The data in Table 2.6 answers this question. Of the seven units, only one had a civil rights director who lasted thirteen years, William T. Hudson of the Coast Guard. (He is the current departmental director of civil rights in the secretary's office.) His longevity is followed by that of Leon C. Watkins in the FAA, who stayed in office for eleven years; Harold B. Williams of UMTA remained in office for ten years; and Barbara E. Walsh held office at FRA for eight years. (Her office underwent two title changes—one in 1973 when it was called the Equal Employment Opportunity Office, and a second one in 1975 when it was changed back to the Office of Civil Rights.) R. Edward Quick held his position of FHA for eight years. The mean number of years for these five individuals is 10.5.

But the picture of change is more significant. An office of civil rights was not created in each of these seven units until 1969, two years after the department was created and one year after a Title VI unit was created in the secretary's office. For this first year, 1969, five of the seven civil rights directorships were vacant. In fact, the Saint Lawrence Seaway unit let its position stay vacant for the first seven years. In all, there have been fifteen years of vacancies in the modal units.

Turnover at this level is also high. The FHA has seen four directors, the FRA three, and all the other units except the Coast Guard have had at least two directors since the creation of the Title VI units. All total in the Department of Transportation there have been nineteen different civil rights directors in the seven modal units over a period of sixteen years.

This is the picture on the federal level in Washington, D.C. Organizationally, each cabinet-level department has an office within each of the ten federal regions of the United States.[12] Therefore, a wholly different situation and picture prevail at the regional level. For instance, in the regional offices for each cabinet-level department, there is a Title VI office which is directly under the control of the director of the regional offices.[13] If cabinet secretaries run their offices and whatever units come under them, then the regional directors control their Title VI offices. Although Title VI directors are usually civil servants, they serve in this position at the pleasure of the regional director. Thus, the regional director's position toward the monitoring and enforcement of Title VI rules and regulations can be expressed through his or her control over the person appointed to direct the regional compliance office. Through the use of rewards and incentives (or the promise to use them), the regional director can manage the pace and flow of Title VI administrative activity. The key here is the influence of structural authority on policy, not merely the influence of shifts in personnel. Structurally-rooted authority can have as much impact on the implementation of policy as do personnel changes.

The preceeding pages have offered a discussion of top level staff and per-

Table 2.6 Change and Continuity of Title VI Heads in Department of Transportation: 1969–1984*

	Coast Guard	FAA	FHA	FRA	NHTSA	UMTA	SLSDC
1969	Vacant	Quentin Taylor	Alexander Gaither	Vacant	Vacant	Vacant	Vacant
1970	William T. Hudson			Joseph Walker			
1971				B. E. Walsh	R. L. Harper		
1972		Leon C. Watkins				Harold B. Williams	
1973			Lester A. Herr				
1974			Alexander Gaither		Hanley J. Norment		
1975							
1976			Vacant				Richard C. McCarthy
1977			R. Edward Quick				
1978							
1979							
1980							
1981				Jenne E. Randall			
1982						Barbara A. Ibarra	Evan Baumberger
1983						Robert C. Owens	Nonexistent
1984	Walter R. Sommerville			Niles S. Washington			

*A check of the 1986–1987 Manual reveals that Sommerville, Watkins, Quick, Washington, Norment, and Owens are still running their offices.
Source: The United States Government Manual (1969–1984).

sonnel and the degree of stability and instability in the top administrative offices. The next step then is the analysis of the staff of civil rights regulatory agencies in each and every cabinet-level department. With such an analysis, a much more comprehensive portrait of personnel stability and instability can be had across each department and not just at the top.

The Politics of Departmental Personnel

After the creation of civil rights regulatory agencies, the next matter was that of staffing them. Data on the full-time permanent Title VI staff members in each federal cabinet department was not always systematically reported by the federal government and consequently such data is not comprehensive, but we began our analysis with the most reliable data available.

Before 1983, the Justice Department reported in its *Title VI Forum*, personnel data for Title VI offices for 1976, 1977, and 1978. In these three years there was an overall growth of seventy-one persons in the Title VI staffs, yet only four of the sixteen departments grew larger; seven departments suffered a decline (Table 2.7). Most of the growth occured in HEW, which by 1978 had added 265 persons to its staff. The next largest increase took place in the Department of Agriculture, but its growth was minor in comparison. During the 1970s civil rights violations in education were getting the most attention, which accounts for the hugh increase in HEW. In the 1980's another picture emerges.

The Office of Management and Budget (OMB) did not start reporting budgetary data on the civil rights regulatory agencies until 1971, and it was not until 1983 that data on the supporting cast of employees in the civil rights agencies surfaced in OMB's special analysis of the federal budget (Table 2.8A). The five departments with the largest staffs were (in order of size): (1) EEOC, (2) Defense, (3) Labor, (4) Education, and (5) Justice. The five smallest were (1) State, (2) Energy, (3) Commerce, (4) the Small Business Administration (SBA), and (5) the Office of Personnel Management (OPM).

The data shows also which agencies deal with civil rights matters in states and localities all over the nation, leaving only a very small percentage of staff to handle in-house matters. EEOC was found to assign ninety-seven percent of its people to external programs; Labor, ninety-five percent; Education and Justice, ninety-nine percent each; and Health and Human Services, sixty-five percent. In contrast, the small agencies—State, OPM, and Commerce—have the majority, if not all, of their staff members working on in-house civil rights matters. Overall, most federal civil rights personnel, at least by 1983, were concerned with monitoring Title VI compliance outside of the federal government. (Outside or external civil rights programs dealt with Title VI, while internal or inside civil rights programs dealt with Title VII or Equal Employment Opportunity (hereafter EEO) concerns within the cabinet departments.)

Table 2.7   Full-Time Permanent Title VI Staff Members in Federal Departments: 1976–1978

Agency	1976	1977	1978	Change
Agriculture	22	23	29	+ 7
Commerce	28	20	24	− 4
CSA	12	0	5	− 7
Defense	156	0	4	− 152
EPA	0	−	−	
HEW	565	720	830	+ 265
HUD*	0	0	0	
Interior	10	10	9	− 1
Labor	71	73	68	− 3
LEAA	0	0	0	0
SBA	41	41	41	0
Transportation	48	41	16	− 32
VA	6	0	0	− 6
Others	NA	4	0	− 4
Energy	−	−	2	+ 2
TVA	−	−	2	+ 2
Total	959	936	1,030	+ 71

SBA (Small Business Administration), VA (Veterans Administration), TVA (Tennessee Valley Authority), CSA (Community Services Administration).
*Not Reported
Source: Title VI Forum—1977, p. 6; Title VI Forum—1978, Title VI Forum—1979, p. 5.

In 1984 the five top departments were (1) EEOC, (2) Defense, (3) Labor, (4) Education, and (5) Justice. The five departments having the smallest staffs were (1) GAO, GPO, (2) OPM (3) SBA and Energy, (4) Veterans Administration (VA), and (5) Commerce (see Table 2.8B). Thus, in a single year several shifts took place in terms of which departments had larger staff. But, with the exception of the Department of Defense, the top agencies continued to have the majority of their civil rights staff employed in dealing with matters external to their departments. Title VI matters still drew the attention of the majority of department personnel.

Once again we would like to remind the reader that several departments had combined Title VI and Title VII units and the references to staff members with external functions refer to Title VI concerns, while references to those with internal (EEO) functions deal with Title VII matters.

Table 2.9 looks at the civil rights staff in 1983 and 1984 from the standpoint of programmatic categories. In 1983, the largest number of civil rights personnel were involved in monitoring activity in the private sector; the next largest number were concerned with the federal and military sectors, while those monitoring discrimination in federally assisted programs, civil and constitutional rights, fair housing, research, and voting rights followed in that order.

Table 2.8A Total Full-Time Permanent Civil Rights Staff by Executive Department and Agency, Fiscal Year 1983 (Estimate)

	Internal EEO Programs	External Programs	Total
Agriculture	94	71	165
Commerce	52	3	55
Defense	NA	NA	NA
Education**	** 14	**1,070	1,084
Energy**	** 9	12	21
Health and Human Services	282	524	806
HUD	25	451	476
Interior	195	30	230
Justice	8	859	867
Labor	50	1,041	1,091
State	17	17	0
Transportation	144	55	199
Treasury	213	41	254
EEOC	18	3,215	3,316
Commission on Civil Rights	2	213	215
OPM	60	0	60
SBA	16	38	57
VA	57	14	71
All Other Executive Agencies			
Total	3,566	7,633	11,369

*Agency totals for FTP. Internal EEO and FTP External program staff in some cases are less than figures for total civil rights FTP because some personnel have duties in both areas.
**Was scheduled for termination in 1983.
Source: Office of Management and Budget, *Special Analysis J: Civil Rights Activity*, 1983, p. 27.

Data in Table 2.9 reveals that in 1984, the largest number of civil rights staff were involved in monitoring compliance in the *public* sector, with federal and military service having the largest number of personnel. The next largest number were concerned with the *private* sector. This is followed by nondiscrimination in federally assisted programs, civil and constitutional rights, fair housing, equal credit opportunity, and voting rights respectively.

This comparison shows that within one year, the federal bureaucracy shifted in emphasis from the *private* to *public* sector and it also *reduced* its manpower commitment to monitoring civil rights compliance in other private areas like fair housing, and other civil and constitutional rights. Increases in manpower have come only in the voting rights area, equal credit opportunity, and nondiscriminatory federal programs. Now that we have compared civil rights staffs by programmatic categories in order to observe shifts and differences between 1983 and 1984, let's do a similar comparison by cabinet-level departments to gain additional insights.

Table 2.8B Full-Time Permanent Civil Rights Staff by Department and Agency, Fiscal Year 1984 (Estimate)

	Internal EEO Programs	External Programs	Total
Agriculture	109	64	173
Commerce	79	7	86
Defense	2,407	33	2,486
Education	15	950	965
Energy	41	9	50
Health and Human Services	179	509	688
HUD	47	535	582*
Interior	220	4	224
Justice	156	749	905
Labor	66	1,150	1,215
State	—	—	—
Transportation	88	31	119
Treasury	214	254	40
EEOC	18	2,962	2,980
Commission on Civil Rights	3	233	236
OPM	45	—	45
SBA	14	32	50
VA	70	3	73
Postal Service	416	NA	416
GAO, GPO	26	26	52*
All Other Executive Agencies	500	345	16
Total	4,558	7,327	12,074

Agency totals for FTP Internal EEO and FTP External program staff in some cases are less than figures for total civil rights FTP because some personnel have duties in both areas.
*Not included in totals.
Source: Office of Management and Budget, *Special Analysis J. Civil Rights Activity*, 1984, p. J-34.

A comparison of the personnel changes in a single year shown in Table 2.10 indicates that although the grand total appears to have increased over the year, when missing data is compensated for the number of full-time federal employees on civil rights staff actually dropped by thirty-two, or roughly four percent in a single year.

Table 2.9   Personnel Changes by Program Category: 1983–1984

	1983	(%)	1984	(%)	Differences
Private Sector & Nonfederal Public					
Sector Equal Opportunity	4,409	(39.3)	3,202	(22.1)	− 1,389
Federal Service Equal Opportunity	3,566	(31.2)	5,365	(39.2)	+ 4,365
Military Service Equal Opportunity	NA		2,566	(18.8)	
Nondiscrimination, Federally					
Assisted Programs	1,907	(17.0)	1,939	(14.2)	+ 32
Other Civil and Constitutional Rights	673	(6.0)	370	(2.7)	− 303
Fair Housing	402	(3.6)	168	(1.2)	− 234
Research	213	(1.9)	*		
Voting Rights	52	(1.0)	96	(1.0)	+ 44
Equal Credit Opportunity	8	(0.0)	151	(1.1)	143
Total	11,230		13,675		+ 2,658

*Excluded from calculations because data exist for only one year.
Source: Office of Management and Budget, *Special Analysis J: Civil Rights Activities, 1983 and 1984.*

The largest drops came in EEOC, Education, and Health and Human Services, and there was a small though sizable drop in the Department of Transportation. The largest increases occurred in Labor, HUD, Commerce, and Energy. The Commission on Civil Rights had more than a modest growth rate in personnel. But overall some 681 people were dropped while only 359 were hired, giving the civil rights staffs in over eighteen federal agencies a net loss of 322 individuals in a single year. Reagan's reduction in force, or "RIF" as it was called, affected the size of the civil rights staff in federal service between 1983 and 1984. Moreover, the personnel gains were in internal programs, where staff was involved in checking the federal government for its equal employment opportunity record (Table 2.11). This was a clear-cut avoidance of civil rights enforcement in the private sector, clearly in line with Reagan's conservatism and the Republican party's contention that regulation of the private sector (including that in civil rights) should be significantly reduced.

If such a functional comparison reveals loss, reflecting Republican ideology, what then does a comparison of program categories reveal? The data in Table 2.9 reveals a corroborative pattern.

The major losses of full-time civil rights personnel were in programs focused on the private sector, including fair housing and other civil and constitutional rights. All programs having an external thrust, which attempted to ensure civil rights compliance in the larger community, were severely cut back in a single year's time, from 1983 to 1984. The federal government turned its attention instead to monitoring its own civil rights compliance record. As previously mentioned, important exceptions were in the areas of equal credit opportunity and voting rights. The first is in keeping with the Republican philosophy that black economic advancement is the best way to help blacks to achieve their rightful place in American society. And perhaps voting rights are such fundamental constitutional rights, fully backed by the courts, that they have come to be an accepted reality.

Table 2.10   Civil Rights Staffs by Department, 1983 and 1984

	1983	1984	Differences
Agriculture	165	173	+ 8
Commerce	55	86	+ 36
Defense		2,486	*
Education	1,084	965	− 119
Energy	21	50	+ 59
Health & Human Services	806	688	− 118
Housing & Urban Development	476	582	+ 106
Interior	230	224	− 6
Justice	867	905	+ 38
Labor	1,091	1,215	+ 124
State	17		*
Transportation	199	119	− 80
Treasury	254	254	0
EEOC	3,316	2,980	− 336
Commission on Civil Rights	215	236	+ 21
OPM	60	45	− 15
SBA	57	50	− 7
VA	71	73	+ 2
Postal Service		416	*
GPO		26	*
All Other Agencies		500	*
Total	8,967	8,645	− 322

*Data excluded from totals.
Source: Office of Management and Budget, *Special Analysis J: Civil Rights Activities, 1983 and 1984.*

Thus, the apparent wide growth in federal government civil rights personnel between 1983 and 1984, belies the fact that the focus of civil rights enforcement was carefully shifted so that it was in keeping with the philosophy of the Republican party and its conservative constituency. Title VI oriented pro-

grams, designated in Table 2.9 as "nondiscrimination,—federally assisted programs," have seen only a modest increase in staffing.

Table 2.11 Personnel Shifts in Federal Civil Rights Compliance Offices, 1983–1984*

Years	Internal Programs	External Programs
1983	1,239	7,637
1984	1,364	7,278
Difference	+ 125	− 359

*Calculations were derived from number of staff members assigned to each function.
Source: Office of Management and Budget, *Special Analysis J: Civil Rights Activities, 1983 and 1984.*

One other small item in the OMB special budget analysis dealing with staff
and personnel is useful here. In 1984 OMB, for the first and only time to date,
listed the total number of full-time federal employees involved in compliance
review, both those preceding the award of funds and those following award[14]
(Table 2.12). The majority of full-time personnel is conducting compliance re-

Table 2.12 Civil Rights Staff Members Involved in Pre- and Post-Award Compliance Reviews:
1981–1984

Years	Pre-Award	Post-Award
1981	76	386
1982	74	422
1983[1]	64	435
1984[2]	65	434
Mean	69.75	419.25

[1]Estimated.
[2]Projected.
Source: Office of Management and Budget, *Special Analysis J: Civil Rights Activities, 1983 and 1984.*

views after the fact. In 1981, some eighty-four percent were so involved, and
for the entire four-year period (1981 to 1984) a mean of eighty-six percent of the
employees in this area worked on post-award reviews. However, OMB felt that
too many personnel were assigned to post-award reviews and that for the fairly
small amount of discrimination they had uncovered, their work was not cost effective. On this point, OMB wrote: "Even when the problematic SBA desk audits are subtracted, the rate at which even routine reviews resulted in correction
of illegal discrimination was a disappointing two percent." They continue: "In

addition to the enforcement anomaly discussed above, current arrangements for enforcing these statutes raise serious questions of cost effectiveness: The cost of interagency expenditures of coordination of these statutes . . . exceeds the enforcement expenditures of all but four of the agencies coordinated. In addition to these expenses there are the considerable outlays for administration overhead and legal support necessary to maintain separate programs in each agency."[15]

OMB recommended that the Civil Rights Division of the Justice Department work with the current President's Task Force on Regulatory Relief to develop, revise, and coordinate regulation so as to address these problems. OMB backed its reform efforts knowing full well that "substantial improvement in this area may require basic reforms in the organization and structure of the administration's enforcement of these provisions." The point is that perhaps personnel for compliance review will not exist at all in the future. At least that is what OMB hopes.

The overview from the budget documents of full-time civil rights staff can be enhanced if departmental records are examined. James P. Hood, the freedom of information officer of the Civil Rights Division of the Department of Agriculture, wrote: "The line and staff sizes from 1972 to present grew from 6 to 101 positions and then began a decline in the late 70's to its present size of 50 positions."[16] The number of black staff members in the equal opportunity office in the Agriculture Department for 1977 and 1980 are compared in Table 2.13.

Table 2.13   Blacks in the EEO Office of the Department of Agriculture: 1977 and 1980

Year	Number of Blacks	% of Blacks
1977	44	62.9
1980	33	61.1
Differences	11	1.8

Source: USDA, *Equal Opportunity Report: USDA Programs 1979* (Washington, D.C.: Government Printing Office, 1980), p. 22. See also, USDA, *Equal Opportunity Report: USDA Programs 1980* (Washington, D.C.: Government Printing Office, 1981), p. 5.

The total number of employees dropped by nearly one-third over a three-year period. The facts corroborate the letter from the division reporting that the number of employees in this section had been steadily declining. However, the latest report shows that the number has risen from thirty-three to thirty-eight, though the total is still below the peak of 101 in the early years of the agency.

The story from the Department of Defense is quite different (Table 2.14). Its Title VI report, of July 10, 1980, submitted to John P. White, deputy director of OMB, indicates that Title VI employees had become essentially only part-time employees. Richard Denzig, deputy assistant secretary of defense, who prepared the report, writes that between 1977 and 1978 "full-time staff appears to have dropped from 1,287 persons to only 6," but "the problem," he says, was more shadow than reality. The dollars and people did not exist, as previously reported; several components of the department had "phantom" budgets and staff." He found that the 1973 staff was in reality only a part-time staff—the only component of Defense with any semblance of a full-time staff in Title VI enforcement was the National Guard Bureau. Of the six full-time employees in 1978, the Guard had four and the Office of the Secretary of Defense had two. Other components like the Army, Navy, Air Force, and the Civil Defense Preparedness Agency had no staff whatsoever.

Table 2.14 Full-Time and Part-Time Title VI Enforcement Staff in the Defense Department, 1977–1979

Year	Full–Time	Part–Time
1977	1,287	45
1978	6	84
1979	7	52

Source: Department of Defense, *The Department of Defense Title VI Enforcement Effort and Related Matters*, June, 1980, p. 12.

The upshot of this analysis is that the personnel changes on the departmental level, given the state of available and reliable data, reveals a modest amount of instability in the mid-seventies but rather rapid, and to a degree more, instability in the eighties.

But besides the shift and losses in full-time permanent civil rights staff, the other most disturbing and perhaps unique finding is the rapid change in focus and functions assigned to the staff. First of all, OMB data shown in Table 2.8A and 2.8B reveals where the various cabinet-level departments had assigned their personnel, i.e., Title VI (external programs) or Title VII (internal EEO programs). In 1983, we find that the majority of full-time permanent civil rights staff was involved in Title VI regulatory work. One year later, 1984, a majority of the staff was still involved in Title VI programs, but as Table 2.11 reveals, a significant shift in personnel to internal (Title VII) regulatory matters had taken place. The percentage increase in focus was six percent.

Moreover, data in Table 2.9 not only corroborates this shift but it shows that if personnel changes are analyzed by programmatic categories, the shift to the *public* (governmental-internal) sector as opposed to the *private* (Title VI-external) sector is quite clearly revealed. And we discover that this shift in functions is in keeping with the philosophies of President Reagan and the Republican party.

Available data for the Agriculture Department reveals that when staff changes are analyzed by race, this department has lost full-time permanent staff members. Data for the Department of Defense reveals the massive drop in full-time employees—because Defense simply inflated its own figures.

Finally the analysis reveals that most full-time permanent staff members have been engaged in post-award, instead of pre-award, compliance reviews. Post-award reviews mean that after Title VI departments disperse their funds, agency personnel check to see if the money had been spent in a non-discriminatory fashion. However, OMB has felt that no compliance reviews, pre- or post-should be conducted at all. But without such review there is no way to systematically check for non-discriminatory spending by state and local recipients of federal funds. In addition, post-award reviews mean that if discrimination is taking place, Title VI agencies must ask the recipients to return misused funds. This is practically impossible once expenditures have been made. Hence, the best that can be gotten in some instances is a mere promise that racially discriminatory expenditure of funds will not take place in the future. Pre-award reviews alleviate the problem, because expenditures that might have been made in a racially discriminatory manner can be prevented before hand.

All in all, at the departmental level personnel changes do occur, but because of the civil service nature of such jobs, the instability noted is not as significant as in the top administration levels. However, shifts in focus, functions, and program categories can take place rather rapidly and cause thereby significant instability in the regulatory thrust of the federal bureaucracy.

The Impact on Regulatory Activity

Because of decentralized responsibility, the creation of the new civil rights regulatory agencies occurred in a piecemeal and uneven fashion. This made the regulatory activity uneven at first. Secondly, due to this decentralized responsibility, the structuring of the new regulatory agencies resulted in different types of civil rights units in different departments. Some agencies had single offices and others had combined offices and this meant either single or dual focuses for these departments.

Substantial instability was found at the top administration levels—i.e., at the secretarial and Title VI levels. Some instability was found at the staff level, but not to the same degree; here it was principally in functional assignments. Staff often found themselves shifted around and, by the mid-eighties, the focus had changed from private and external programs to public and internal programs.

If comprehensive and continuous data on staffing and compliance resolutions had been kept, it would be possible to measure precisely how these instabilities, shifts, and changes impacted regulatory enforcements and effectiveness. Since there are significant gaps in the data reported in public documents, evaluation and assessments of this impact must rely mainly on inferential linkages.

The impact of creation on these agencies is clear. If the regulatory units did not exist, or if they did not come on line until several years after the enabling legislation was passed, then there was simply no civil rights regulatory activity undertaken by these agencies. Nothing could happen. This impact is clear—no regulatory units, no regulatory efforts.

On the matter of top administration one must be mindful of the responsibilities and duties of departmental secretaries. They run the agencies: they have *sign-off* authority on everything which leaves the department. Budgets, rules, regulations, personnel hiring, promotions, etc. take place only over their signatures. Secretaries of cabinet-level departments have full decision-making authority over the budgets and personnel sizes of civil rights regulatory units. They decide how much and what these agencies can get and spend and what size staff they can have. Hence, when secretaries come and go, so does commitment, emphasis, focus, and bugetary perspectives. For instance, in Table 2.15 data is presented on the Department of Transportation staff. Here we see staff positions that are funded and those that are filled for the Office of Civil Rights Compliance in each of the seven modal units. Where positions are filled but have not been funded, this authority can only be given by the Secretary of the Department of Transportation. No one else in the agency has the power to hire people for positions when no money is available. Generally, unless secretaries are committed to a program, they will not find resources elsewhere in the budget to fill unfunded positions. In this department alone nearly twice the positions are filled as are actually funded. Only 6.5 positions are funded, yet twelve positions have been filled.

The Department of Transportation's effort in staffing its Title VI office beyond what was authorized is truly the exception to the rule. Most departments with Title VI and VII agencies simply have not staffed their units anywhere near the limit. In Table 2.16, it is possible to see the authorized full-time permanent staff positions—and the actual positions from 1980-1983 for four cabinet-level departments and the EEOC.

In 1980 alone, between these four departments and the commission there were a total of 814 authorized positions that were not filled. This number declined to 388 in 1981. A year later there were more positions filled than were authorized, though this occurred in only two departments, Labor and Justice. The other three units showed an overall decline.

Moreover, when the data are analyzed by department and rank ordered,

EEOC lost 344, HEW 200, Labor 178, Health and Human Services 88, and the Justice Department 4 in 1980 alone. This trend would continue in 1982 for all of the departments with the exception of Justice and Labor. The other startling and most revealing trend in the data is the number of authorized positions that were lost from 1980 through 1983. Here, the impact of budget cuts by the Reagan administration can clearly be seen. Between 1980 and in 1983, (1981 and 1982 for some departments), four departments and the commission alone lost some 1,510 permanent full-time civil rights staff positions for a mean of 322 positions per department.

Table 2.15   Civil Rights Staff Positions Funded and Filled, Department of Transportation, 1980

	Positions Funded	Positions Filled
Office of Civil Rights	0.0	4
FRA	2.0	2
FAA	0.0	1
UMTA	0.0	2
NHTSA	2.5	2
FHA*	1.0	0
U.S. Coast Guard	1.0	1
Totals	6.5	12

*These figures do not include clerical positions.
Note: FHA sent EEOC an A-11 report during FY 80 which included external programs not covered by Justice. These were: 504, Contract Compliance, Support Services, External Youth Opportunity Program, and the State Highway Agency Employment Program.
Source: Data supplied to the author by the Department of Transportation.

In actual totals by department, the Labor Department had the greatest losses with 503 positions, followed by EEOC with 499, HEW with 488, HHS with 66 and Justice with 54. This data corroborates earlier findings in that it shows that the departments with the biggest losses in their civil rights regulatory staff were also those departments (Labor, EEOC, HEW) which had the greatest impact on the private sector. The least active private sector departments (HHS and Justice) saw the smallest permanent staff losses.

In the final analysis, once the positions have been authorized by Congress, it must be remembered that it is clearly up to departmental secretaries and Title VI and VII agency heads to fill these positions. And what the data reveals is that, although there was a steady decline in authorized positions, there was also a consistent policy per department not to fill the full number of authorized positions. The will on the part of some administrators was clearly missing. Yet, there are other ways that the "bureaucratic will" can be expressed.

At the level of Title VI and VII agency heads, instability has had nearly the same effect. These heads have *in-house sign-off authority*. A civil rights head signs-off on the number of complaints, which will be pursued, and the degree and level of vigor in pursuit. He recommends raises, promotions, hirings, and determines overall strategy for the office. He decides the rules and regulations that will be drafted and sent forth as proposed regulations. And he communicates directly to the cabinet secretary the goals and objectives for the agency each year. When there is frequent turnover in positions and/or the position is vacant, regulatory procedures and enforcement are effected. For instance, when the director of the Office of Civil Rights Compliance in the Law Enforcement Assistance Administration (hereafter LEAA) was forced to resign because of pressure from several police groups—which argued that he was not resolving racial discrimination complaints emanating from the Chicago Police Department and the Los Angeles Police Department—the head of LEAA let the

Table 2.16   The Number of Authorized and Actual Full–Time Permanent Civil Rights Staff Positions in Selected Departments and Commission: 1980–1983

Department of Education: Office for Civil Rights		
Fiscal Year	Authorized	Actual
1980 (HEW)	1,514	1,314
1980 (Education Department)	1,181	1,048
1981	1,098	1,055
1982 (Original Request)	1,070	1,025
1982 (Revised Request)	1,026	995
1983 (Department Request)	1,026	—
1983 (Foundation Request)	1,003	—

Department of Health and Human Services: Office for Civil Rights		
1980	590	502
1981	590	496
1982 (Request)	524	—
1982 (Continuing Resolution)	524	479
1983 (Request)	524	—

Department of Justice: Office for Civil Rights		
1980	436	432
1981	436	436
1982 (Request)	385	436
1982 (Continuing Resolution)	436	390
1983 (Request)	385	—

Department of Labor: Office of Federal Contract Compliance Program

Fiscal Year		Authorized	Actual
1980		1,482	1,304
1981		1,482	1,283
1982	(Original Request)	1,264	1,183
1982	(Revised Request)	979	1,194
1982	(Continuing Resolution)	1,008	985
1983	(Request)	979	—

The EEOC

1980		3,777	3,433
1981		3,468	3,416
1982	(Request)	3,468	—
1982	(Continuing Resolution)	3,316	—
1983	(Request)	3,278	—

Source: Commission on Civil Rights, *The Federal Civil Rights Enforcement Budget: Fiscal Year 1983* (Washington, D.C.: Government Printing Office, 1982) p. 14 for HEW, p. 26 for HHS, p. 33 for Justice, p. 43 for Labor, p. 54 for EEOC.

position stay vacant until the Ford administration left office. The civil rights director resigned in April 1976, and the administration left office in early January 1977. In the absence of the director, there was no one to approve office travel, to assign complaints, to monitor in-house progress, to work on regulation handbooks, to assign staff to tasks, etc. For all practical purposes, for nearly nine months the office simply drifted. Regulatory activity simply ceased or became minimal.[17]

The impact of functional changes on regulatory efforts is also clear. The switch from private to public function is also clear and precise. A shift in the functional assignments of staff means a change in regulatory emphasis and focus. In the case of civil rights regulatory activity, it means a *reduced* effort to follow political entities that receive federal funds, to see to it that these funds are not spent in a discriminatory manner. It means that those who do spend such funds in a discriminatory manner, run small risk or chance of getting caught.

Overall, then, the regulatory efforts of these civil rights agencies have been significantly influenced by when they were created, how they were structured, and the degree of stability in their top administrations as well as the functions assigned to their full-time permanent staff members. It is these insights that current civil rights implementation studies seem to have missed.

3. THE POLITICS OF BUDGET AND FINANCE

The preceeding chapter analyzed and evaluated the creation, structures, and staffing of the new civil rights regulatory agencies. The purpose of this chapter is to explain the financing and budgeting of these new agencies as best as the publicly available data will allow. There are two problems with the federal data. Financial and budgeting data for civil rights activity was reported by the Office of Management and Budget (hereafter OMB) from 1971 until the publication of the budget for fiscal year 1985, which carried actual figures for 1983, estimates for 1984, and proposed figures for 1985.[1] By 1986—with actual data and figures for 1984—OMB under the Reagan administration *stopped* reporting the civil rights budgets for *all* of the departments and independent agencies and provided data for only *"Principal"* federal departments. The reduction was from seventeen departments to eight. Thus budgetary data disappeared during President Reagan's first term for half of the federal agencies charged with civil rights regulatory activities. Midway into his second term the proposed 1988 budgetary data for *all* civil rights agencies in federal departments disappeared from OMB's special analyses of the budget. For the first time in fifteen years, OMB reported *no* data on civil rights budgets, staff, etc., in its *Special Analysis* reports.

If sketchy and incomplete data is the first problem, then the second one is that budget requests are not made in terms of Title VI activities, but in the form of salaries and expenses. Thus, it is difficult to track over time the financing of Title VI activities and budgetary data for their operation vis-a-vis other civil

56

rights responsibilities. The refusal of OMB to now publish even limited data makes a comprehensive and systematic analysis near impossible. Therefore, a different type of analytical and evaluative strategy had to be pursued, given the vagaries of the budget data, so that some sense of the degree of financial support for Title VI efforts could be gained.

Because there exists in the literature no significant treatment of civil rights financial and budgetary support,[2] this chapter begins with a broad and descriptive look at the total civil rights budget over time in both totals and departmental figures. This data is evaluated then on the basis of patterns and trends in the data itself—rather than on some externally imposed pattern or model.

Following this general perspective, the budgeting data is analyzed and evaluated from the standpoint of program categories. This approach permits the analyst to see the relationship between support for external (Title VI) programs and the internal (Title VII) programs which was discussed in the section on departmental staffing. By disaggregating the general principal data to program categories, it is possible to see support for Title VI efforts that could not readily emerge from the general treatment.

Once the broad perspective has been broken down it is then possible to see what percentage of the civil rights budget actually goes to Title VI activities. With such data one can see the relationship of the total civil rights budget to Title VI efforts.

At this point, the chapter takes up an analysis of specific Title VI activities, and compares exactly and precisely which Title VI activities the federal government has financed over time. Here one can determine if the government has given support to only compliance reviews, investigations, legal enforcement, or conciliations. Then all of the changes and shifts and patterns in these budgeting trends are examined in terms of particular presidents and the actions of OMB.

Thus, the next topic treated in the chapter is the departmental budgets and the role that Congress plays vis-a-vis presidential requests. Does Congress approve, enlarge, or reduce the budget requests that it receives from the president and OMB? Again, this section starts with a broad perspective and then breaks out the departmental data; the monies that each appropriated for Title VI enforcement efforts and activities. The point here is that even though Congress may approve exactly what the president through OMB requests, departmental secretaries and/or Title VI departments may decide not to expend all the funds appropriated.

Finally, an analysis of this budgetary and financial data is made in view of the impact that it can have on regulatory activity and effort. Again, because of the nature of the data, the linkage or impact is made in essentially inferential terms.

To recapitulate, this chapter begins with a look at the entire civil rights budget and then breaks down that budget so that Title VI budgetary and financial data are available. In addition, it relates changes in the data to different presidential administrations first, and then later analyzes those budgets in terms of what Congress did with the budget requests and finally, it looks briefly at what cabinet secretaries and Title VI departments do with the funds that have been appropriated. Finally, there are reflections on what budgetary change means for regulatory impact.

The Federal Civil Rights Budgets

The civil rights budget "indicates in concrete and specific terms the choices that have been made as to which types and levels of governmental activity will occur and, by implication, which activities will not occur."[3] Thus, one of the major functions of budgeting "is to generate a statement of *financial intent*, constructed on the basis of anticipated income and 'outgo'. A closely related function is to indicate *programmatic intent*, showing both preferences and (more important) priorities in deciding what to do with available funds. This suggests still another function of budgets, intentional or not. They reflect the political priorities of those who formulated them."[4]

In the civil rights area, final budget authority rests with the president and OMB. Cabinet secretaries and Title VI and VII heads may propose, but it is the president and OMB who formulate the final budget, based on the political priorities of the president. Hence, when one analyzes and evaluates the federal civil rights budget, it must be kept in mind that one sees *programmatic intent* as developed by the president through OMB.

A report on federal outlays for civil rights has been prepared each year since 1971 by the OMB and has been presented in a special section of the federal budget since 1973. In 1973 OMB *estimated* the cost of civil rights enforcement activity for 1969 and 1970. In the early years of reporting this sort of activity, OMB combined the amount of money spent for various minority assistance programs with the expenditures for civil rights, making the total sum appear huge. Data on federal outlays for civil rights activity for fiscal years 1969 to 1975 is presented in Figure 3.1. The amount of money spent for enforcement is indeed very small when compared to the total spent for minority assistance and civil rights. (Minority assistance includes the many efforts of federal agencies to foster minority business enterprise and to increase minority bank deposits; education programs to expand assistance to minority institutions; and federal expenditures to improve the living conditions of American Indians.)[5] For instance, civil rights enforcement outlays in 1971 were only twelve percent of the total; in 1972, only fifteen percent; and in 1973, twelve percent. In 1973 OMB stopped combining the totals in its civil rights analysis section of the budget.

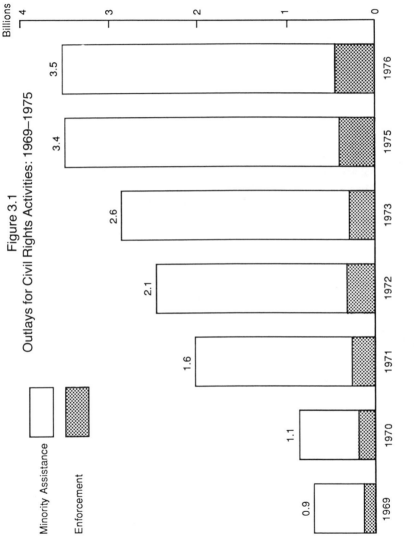

Figure 3.1
Outlays for Civil Rights Activities: 1969–1975

Billions

Minority Assistance

Enforcement

3.5 1976
3.4 1975
2.6 1973
2.1 1972
1.6 1971
1.1 1970
0.9 1969

Source: Office of Management and Budget, Special Analysis L: Civil Rights Activities, 1975

Clearly, this form of reporting the information exaggerated the amount of money the government was spending to enforce provisions of the 1964 Civil Rights Act.

Figure 3.2 shows the civil rights enforcement expenditures by the federal government over a seventeen-year period, 1969 to 1985. There were years of sharp increases, notably 1971, 1972, 1980, and 1982, and two years of sharp decline, 1974 and 1981. Overall, the pattern has been one of a steady increase in expenditures. The Nixon years showed strong increases followed by a decline in the final year of his second term, 1974; increases marked the brief Ford years (1974–1976). A sharp rise began during the Carter administration, particularly the last year in his term of office, 1980, an election year. Expenditures fell sharply during Reagan's first year, 1980, and rose slowly thereafter. In short, although all of the presidents budgetarily expanded their civil rights enforcement effort, the Republicans alone made cuts in enforcement budgets.

If the total outlay each year is broken down into the amount spent by each department and federal agency, another aspect of enforcement-related activity emerges. In Table 3.1 the amount of money spent by each cabinet-level department over a thirteen-year period is shown. What we see is that some departments spent large sums for enforcement while others spent small sums. No federal agency except Labor and the Civil Rights Commission itself received steady increases over the entire period. The money made available for civil rights enforcement fluctuated for nearly all the departments during this time. One reason for this is, of course, changing presidential priorities.

Of the new departments (Education, Energy, and Health and Human Services), only Education received continual increases over a four-year span from 1978–1984 (see Table 3.2). Moreover, the combined outlays made by the new departments of Education and of Health and Human Services are significantly higher than the amount spent by HEW before it was dissolved. In 1979, for instance, HEW spent $50.4 million for civil rights enforcement, whereas in 1980 the two departments created from HEW spent a total of $73 million. In fact, the Department of Education alone in 1980 nearly matched the old HEW outlay.

When the data in Tables 3.1 and 3.2 are rearranged by rank order, i.e., by the amount each agency spent by fiscal years of civil rights enforcement activity, other factors come to the fore. Using 1971 as the base year, the data in Table 3.3 shows that there are three categories of cabinet-level departments in terms of federal outlays for civil rights enforcement. First, there are three that consistently have spent more than $10 million a year in the administration of civil rights programs: HEW, Justice, and Defense. The second category is that group that has spent between $1 and $9 million per year: HUD, Labor, Agriculture, Transportation, and (after the first year) Interior. Departments in the third category are those spending less than $1 million each year during the early 1970s: Commerce, Treasury, and State.

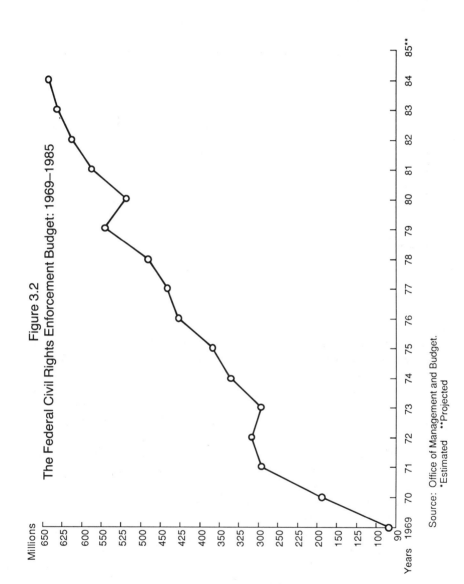

Figure 3.2
The Federal Civil Rights Enforcement Budget: 1969–1985

Source: Office of Management and Budget.
*Estimated **Projected

From 1971, the base year, to 1984 some categories increased to five departments and continued at this level until 1978, when the number fell back to four and remained there through 1979. In 1980 the number grew to eight (the newly created departments account for two),[6] and in 1982 grew again, to nine.

Table 3.1   The Federal Civil Rights Enforcement Budget, by Federal Agency: 1971-1977 (in millions of dollars)

	1971	1972	1973	1974	1975	1976	1977
Agriculture	3.60	9.18	9.43	9.96	5.30	6.00	7.9
Commerce	0.80	0.89	0.91	0.84	1.00	1.03	1.1
Defense	11.00	37.14	44.24	51.54	53.72	51.89	48.9
HEW	78.30	105.10	62.34	13.66	17.69	23.71	26.9
HUD	6.08	6.52	8.40	8.45	10.91	10.58	12.8
Interior	0.82	1.27	1.51	1.54	1.65	1.64	2.0
Labor	5.02	7.31	7.37	8.23	10.63	11.57	14.6
State	0.02	0.07	0.07	*	*	*	*
Transportation	2.07	2.17	2.76	2.94	3.55	3.97	4.1
Treasury	0.25	0.31	0.79	0.76	.95	1.36	2.3
Civil Rights Commission	3.17	3.64	4.62	6.06	6.92	7.89	9.5

*Not listed by OMB.
Source: Office of Management and Budget, *Special Analysis J: Civil Rights Activities, 1971–1985.*

In the intermediate category, departments spending less than $10 million per year but more than $1 million for civil rights enforcement, the number held at four or five through the end of 1978, thereafter drifting lower, between two and four. As for the lowest category, the departments spending less than $1 million for civil rights enforcement, the number steadily shrank from four in 1971 to zero in 1976 and after, with the single exception of Commerce, in 1979.

Thus, although civil rights enforcement budgets show an overall steady increase in dollar amounts, some of the gain must be attributed to inflation. The apparent shrinkage at the lower end should not be allowed to obfuscate the fact that consistent support by the president for civil rights enforcement simply did not exist across all departments, nor even, at times, within a department. For instance, if we take two departments from the top category (HEW and Justice) and one each from the other two categories (Agriculture and Commerce) and plot their spending on civil rights activity over time, fiscal uncertainties experienced by all in this particular policy area become clear (Figure 3.3). Especially dramatic are the fluctuations that occurred in HEW's budget. The Department of Justice enjoyed a relatively stable funding pattern of gradual increases after one precipitous drop in 1973, but Agriculture and Commerce struggled with constant shifts of funding levels that—to put it mildly—contributed little to the stability of their programs.

Table 3.2   The Federal Civil Rights Enforcement Budget, by Federal Agency: 1978–1985 (in millions of dollars)

	1978	1979	1980	1981	1982	1983	1984	1985
Agriculture	7.9	6.5	15.0	7.9	15.30	12.60	NR	NR
Commerce	1.4	.1	6.2	4.6	3.70	3.51	NR	NR
Defense	37.4	47.0	127.6	94.8	117.00	118.30	NR	NR
HEW	36.9	50.4	0.0	0.0	0.00	0.00	0.0	0.0
HUD	8.4	5.2	16.8	15.2	24.60	30.00	28.2	32.4
Interior	0.0	0.0	11.2	10.3	10.30	9.50	NR	NR
Justice	30.5	32.2	33.0	38.2	39.90	39.10	21.0	22.6
Labor	46.3	47.0	56.6	52.4	52.60	53.50	43.9	45.4
State	*	*	1.6	.8	.30	.70	NR	NR
Transportation	2.2	2.0	9.6	11.1	13.90	15.10	NR	NR
Civil Rights Commission	10.4	10.2	11.6	12.1	11.89	11.50	12.0	12.9
Treasury	0.0	0.0	9.7	8.6	11.20	11.50	NR	NR
Education	*	*	40.5	43.8	45.30	46.10	44.4	45.0
Energy	*	*	3.9	2.3	3.10	24.50	NR	NR
Health and Human Services	*	*	32.5	32.9	22.10	28.20	21.3	20.2
EEOC							154.0	163.7

NR = Not Reported
*Not Listed by OMB
Source: Office of Management and Budget, *Special Analysis J: Civil Rights Activities, 1971–1985*.

Nixon dramatically reduced, because of pressures from southerners, the enforcement budgets of HEW and Justice in 1974.[7] Ford increased them only modestly, but significantly reduced Agriculture's budget. He also modestly increased Commerce's budget. Carter, on the other hand, modestly increased the HEW and Justice budgets, slightly increased Commerce, but reduced slightly the budget for Agriculture. In 1979, Carter raised nearly every civil rights enforcement budget. Reagan lowered the majority of the civil rights enforcement budgets in his first year in office but thereafter began to slightly raise most during his first term in office.

An analysis by program category provides other important insights not available in the more general data.

There are nine program categories for civil rights enforcement in the federal government. The first six categories—Federal Service Equal Employment Opportunities (FSEEO), Military Service Equal Opportunities (MSEO), Private Sector Equal Employment Opportunities (PSEEO), Equal Educational Opportunity (EEO), Fair Housing (FH), and Enforcement and Investigation

Table 3.3 Civil Rights Enforcement Budgets, 1971-1985 (in millions of dollars)

							Departments as of								
	'71	'72	'73	'74	'75	'76	'77	'78	'79	'80	'81	'82	'83	'84	'85
HEW	78.3	105.1	62.34	13.66	17.69	23.71	26.9	36.9	50.4	NR	NR	NR	NR	NR	NR
Justice	28.7	38.8	37.42	18.65	20.61	23.87	22.0	30.5	32.2	33.0	38.2	39.9	39.1	21.0	22.6
Defense	11.0	37.14	44.24	51.54	43.72	51.89	48.9	37.4	47.0	127.6	94.8	117.0	118.3	NR	NR
HUD	6.08	6.5	8.40	8.45	10.91	10.58	12.8	8.4	5.2	16.8	15.2	24.5	30.0	28.2	32.4
Labor	5.02	7.31	7.37	8.23	10.63	11.57	14.6	46.3	47.0	56.6	52.4	52.6	53.5	43.9	45.4
Agriculture	3.6	9.1	9.43	9.96	5.3	6.00	4.2	7.9	6.5	15.0	7.9	15.3	12.6	NR	NR
Transportation	2.06	2.17	2.76	2.94	3.55	3.97	4.1	2.2	2.0	9.6	11.1	13.0	15.1	NR	NR
Interior	.82	1.27	1.61	1.54	1.65	1.64	2.0	NR	NR	11.2	10.3	10.3	9.5	NR	NR
Commerce	.80	.89	.91	.84	1.00	1.03	1.1	1.4	.1	6.2	4.6	3.7	3.51	NR	NR
Treasury	.25	.31	.79	.76	.95	1.36	2.3	NR	NR	9.7	8.6	11.2	11.5	NR	NR
State	.02	.07	.07	NR	NR	NR	NR	NR	NR	NR	NR	NR	NR	NR	NR
						New Departments as of 1980									
Education										40.5	43.8	45.3	46.1	44.4	45.0
Energy										3.9	2.3	3.1	2.45	NR	NR
HHS										32.5	32.9	27.1	28.2	21.3	20.2

NR = Not Reported

Figure 3.3
Civil Rights Enforcement Budgets for Four Departments: 1971–1983

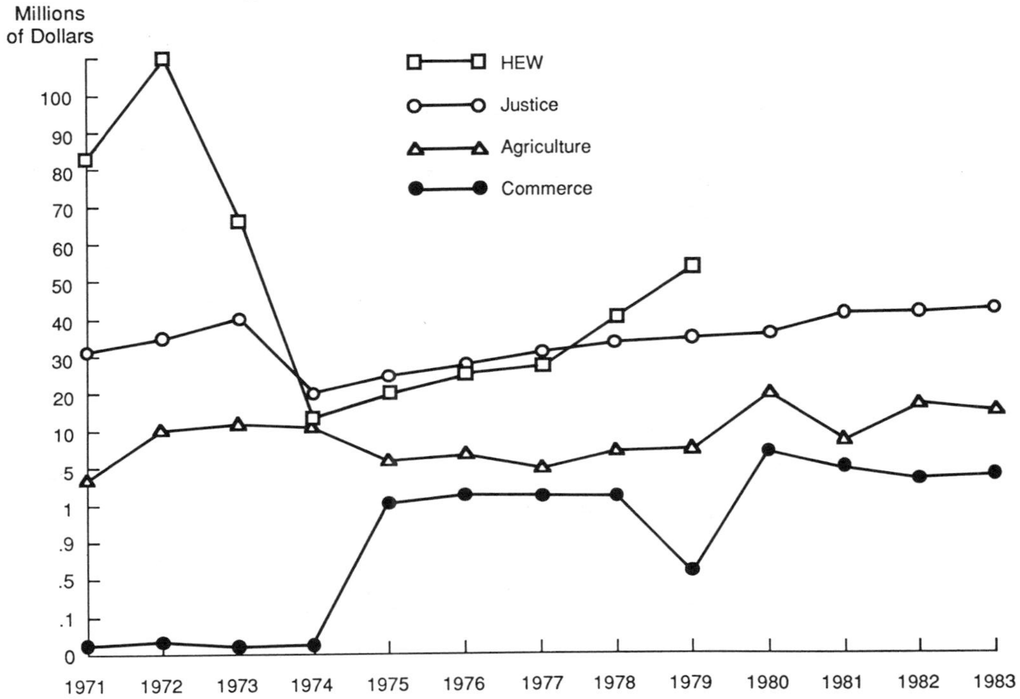

Millions
of Dollars

HEW
Justice
Agriculture
Commerce

Source: Office of Management and Budget, Special Analysis: Civil Rights Activity, 1971-1983.

(EI)—represent the expenditures of departments or agencies in the executive branch for the establishment and maintenance of an affirmative program of equal employment opportunity, equal educational opportunity, and fair housing. The next program category, Program Direction, Research and Information Dissemination (PDRID), is a catch-all. Everything not covered in other categories, plus federal research and information dissemination, is accounted for here. As new initiatives are introduced, they are included under this designation. Civil Rights Conciliation and Prevention of Disputes (CRCPD) refers to the money spent by the Community Relations Service of the Department of Justice, to provide assistance to a community in resolving difficulties arising from discriminatory practices that disrupt or threaten to disrupt peaceful relations among citizens. This unit of Justice Department was created by Title X of the 1964 Civil Rights Act and placed in the Commerce Department but later shifted to Justice. The ninth category, Indian programs (IP), involves money spent by the federal government to aid native Americans. The Bureau of Indian Affairs (BIA) of the Department of Interior uses some of this money to support the economic and social development of native Americans on reservations.

In Table 3.4 are data on the outlays covered within eight of the nine program areas for the years 1971 to 1979.[8] No data are available for 1980, 1981, and 1982, when OMB budget analyses did not report separate figures for the programs. Partial reporting by program areas was resumed in 1983 but stopped again in 1986. Fluctuation in expenditure levels is apparent in programmatic categories, and again, stability is clearly absent from the overall pattern. For example, the EEO programs grew significantly between 1971 and 1972 but declined drastically during Nixon's second term and in Ford's term. They rose slightly during Carter's early years but dropped significantly again near the end.

The enormous expenditures for FSEEO and PSEEO[9] during all these years indicate that both within the federal establishment and in the public sector, a major part of the government's focus has been concentrated on achieving equal employment opportunities. Increases are greater in the private than in the federal sector during Reagan's first term, and it is projected that PSEEO expenditures will be the largest of all in 1985. These two top categories are followed by expenditures in the military services and in the enforcement and investigation of Title VI concerns.

The most surprising figures are those for the equal educational opportunity (EEO). Apparently, none of the presidents since 1972 have been willing to push for the elimination of discrimination in the schools.

The other unexpected figures concern the money spent for Title VI enforcement. When one combines the funds spent for fair housing with the funds spent for enforcement and investigation activities (these two categories being basically the money spent in connection with Title VI), and examines the percentage that this combined figure represents over time, one can see how much

Table 3.4 Federal Civil Rights Budget Outlays by Program Category: 1971-1985 (in millions of dollars)

	'71	'72	'73	'74	'75	'76	'77	'78	'79	'80	'81	'82	'83	'84*	'85**
FSEEO	27.80	55.50	95.89	117.83	145.12	160.80	189.7	188.4	170.4	NR	NR	NR	180.7	203.9	209.6
MSEO	5.95	26.16	32.91	37.78	37.50	38.33	37.7	32.9	39.7	NR	NR	NR	NR	51.8	54.6
PSEEO	34.43	46.67	58.63	73.10	94.07	104.38	111.4	117.1	135.5	NR	NR	NR	173.0	211.5	215.9
EEO	70.30	96.43	61.67	11.89	16.64	19.64	27.7	38.5	14.8	NR	NR	NR	NR	NR	NR
FH	7.55	11.83	12.63	13.50	16.78	16.71	12.5	14.4	15.2	NR	NR	NR	13.1	28.4	31.5
EI	34.15	43.71	36.72	24.12	22.25	22.18	32.7	38.8	76.7	NR	NR	NR	75.2	94.2	94.0
PDRID	4.96	6.17	7.38	9.02	9.05	9.07	11.7	11.4	11.5	NR	NR	NR	15.2	NR	NR
IP	.40	.75	.71	.41	NR	NR	NR	NR	NR	NR	NR	NR	NR	NR	NR
CRCPD	4.20	5.51	6.64	3.79	3.54	4.09	9.4	6.5	5.3	NR	NR	NR	NR	NR	NR

Note: Data for 1980, 1981, and 1982 were not reported (NR)

*Estimated

**Projected

Source: Office of Management and Budget, *Special Analysis J: Civil Rights Activities, 1971–1985.*

of the federal budget for civil rights has not actually been spent on Title VI, but on equal job and employment opportunities. Enforcement and investigation expenditures for Title VI began in 1971 (under the Nixon administration) at twenty-two percent of the total federal civil rights budget, but then dropped each year through the Nixon and Ford administrations, when such expenditures bottomed out at ten percent (Figure 3.4). Beginning with the first year of the Carter administration, this figure rose slowly until it reached twenty percent in 1979. However, in 1983, the third year of the Reagan administration, it had declined again; a new rise is projected for 1984 and 1985.

The mean percentage for the twelve years in 15.66 percent. In other words, the federal government has spent on the average only fifteen percent of its civil rights budget on investigating complaints of discrimination and enforcing the law regarding the nondiscriminatory use of federal funds. Efforts in this area pale beside the money the government has spent on other areas of its civil rights program.

What this analysis of the budgetary data reveals is that amongst the four presidents—Nixon, Ford, Carter and Reagan—the funding of Title VI enforcement efforts, with the exception of one year, 1979 in the Carter administration, has not been a major political priority. Instead of cutting off federal funds to state and local agencies that discriminate, the *programmatic intent* of these presidents has been to emphasize civil rights expenditures in the area of equal job and employment opportunities—especially in the federal and military sectors. Expenditures and regulatory efforts in these areas would not have the impact and generate the political heat and upheaval that might come if funds were cut off or if the private sector instead was targeted for regulatory activity.

But this isn't all that can be seen in regard to the bugetary and financial support for Title VI regulatory agencies. All Title VI civil rights regulatory agencies have developed six major techniques or procedures which they can use to get recipients of federal funds to comply with the 1964 civil rights law. Therefore, further analyses of the civil rights budget by these six procedural categories will be even more revealing in terms of *programmatic intent* and thrust of the Title VI agencies. But first of all let's define and describe these six techniques and procedures. They are: (1) complaint conciliation, (2) compliance investigation, (3) compliance review, (4) legal enforcement, (5) research, and (6) technical assistance. Of these, the first four are the most important and used regulatory procedures. *Complaint conciliation* is designed to work out problems between two or more contending parties when federal funds are an issue. *Compliance investigation*, on the other hand, occurs when an agency or department responds to complaints that discrimination has been a pattern in the past. If the demand for investigations exceeds the budgetary limits, the agencies and departments may conduct investigations on a selective basis to achieve the maximum benefit for the least cost.

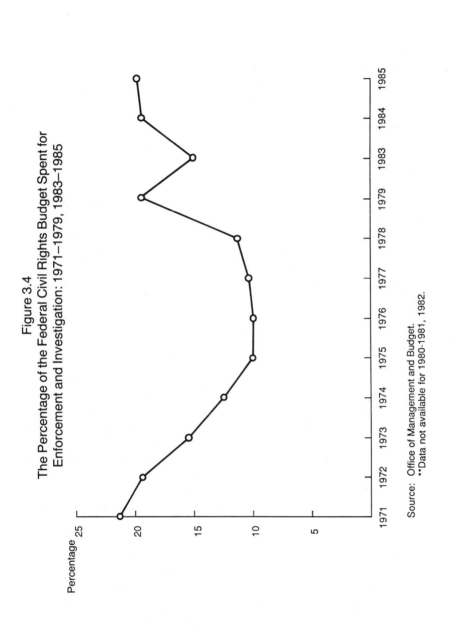

Figure 3.4

The Percentage of the Federal Civil Rights Budget Spent for Enforcement and Investigation: 1971–1979, 1983–1985

Source: Office of Management and Budget.
          **Data not available for 1980-1981, 1982.

Compliance review by federal agencies and departments may occur before federal funds are awarded or afterward. In an attempt to ensure that there is no discrimination on the part of state and local recipients of federal funds, these recipients are periodically monitored by their federal funding sources. A serious constraint for these new civil rights regulatory agencies is that limited funding and budgets prevents the periodic monitoring; therefore, it has to be done on a selected basis. The Offices of Civil Rights in LEAA, for instance, used an arbitrary cut-off point; only those recipients receiving more than $25,000 were monitored for civil rights compliance.

Legal enforcement must be resorted to when voluntary compliance and conciliation cannot be achieved. If recipients of federal funds are found to be in noncompliance and cannot be persuaded to comply, or if a conflict between a recipient of federal funds and the group or individual discriminated against cannot be satisfactorily resolved, then legal enforcement by the Justice Department must be pursued. The Justice Department is authorized to file suit on behalf of the discriminated party.

Program direction and research refers to expenditures made for the direction and management of civil rights activities that are not counted elsewhere as well as federal research and information dissemination efforts. New proposals are undertaken with this money. For instance, the cabinet Committee on Opportunities for Spanish-Speaking People received $1.1 million in 1975, and the Council of Economic Advisers spent $100,000 in 1976 on its advisory committee which was examining the economic role of women.

Finally, funds are budgeted for *technical assistance* that the federal government gives to state and local agencies who wish to comply but need help in doing so. Under this category state and local agencies can hire experts, contract for studies and services, and monitor other agencies that have successfully carried out their Title VI obligations. Many critics have argued that local governments use this money simply to buy time to put off compliance under the guise of learning how to do it. Others see it as "bribe" money given to reluctant agencies that might not comply unless this carrot were given.

Together, these various activities theoretically should ensure an orderly, balanced, uniform, comprehensive, and systematic civil rights enforcement procedure for the entire country. What patterns can be discerned in the funding for enforcement activities since 1971? Graphic presentation of the funding of activities reveals no overall trend (Figure 3.5). As one president left office and the next entered, spending patterns changed. Under nearly all of the presidents, the largest expenditures were for compliance review. Spending for this activity peaked during 1973 under Nixon, fell and then rose slightly under Ford, rose dramatically under Carter, only to decline significantly in the Reagan administration. The second largest budget activity was complaint investigation. Spending in this activity fluctuated during Ford's last year, rose dramatically during

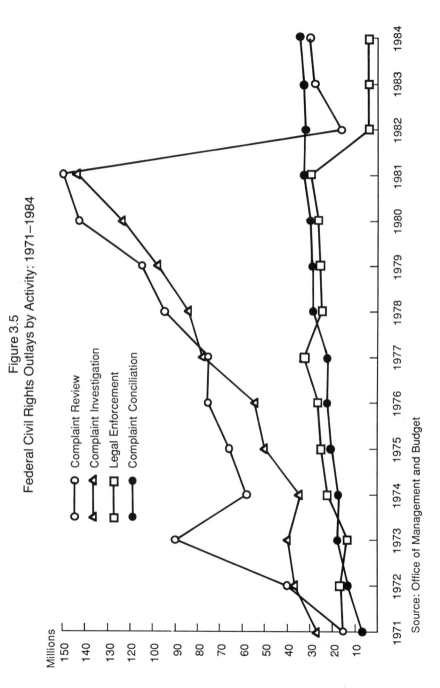

Figure 3.5
Federal Civil Rights Outlays by Activity: 1971–1984

○—○ Complaint Review
◁—◁ Complaint Investigation
□—□ Legal Enforcement
●—● Complaint Conciliation

Millions
150
140
130
120
100
90
80
70
60
50
40
30
20
10

1971 1972 1973 1974 1975 1976 1977 1978 1979 1980 1981 1982 1983 1984

Source: Office of Management and Budget

the Carter years, and became nearly nonexistent during the Reagan years. Legal enforcement had a modest beginning under the Nixon administration and declined shortly thereafter, but rose slightly during the Ford years. When Carter took office, it peaked at $30.2 million in 1977 and then began a modest descent that accelerated to a steep decline in the Reagan years.

Complaint conciliation has seen gradual increases over the years, even under the Reagan administration. Still the federal government has devoted very little to getting contending parties to reconcile their civil rights differences.

It appears that the federal government has reviewed recipients of federal funds to investigate complaints and has done some very modest legal enforcement, but conciliation has been the least of the government's concerns. Little has been spent in trying to obtain voluntary compliance—that is, negotiating the resolution of discriminatory issues. In this area, the government has spent little.

Technical assistance reached a high in 1974 and then stabilized at somewhat lower levels until the final Carter years, when it nearly reached the 1974 high. When the Reagan administration took over, spending for this activity was nearly phased out. Spending for program direction and research was modestly supported in the Nixon years, sagged during Ford's administration, and rose rapidly under Carter, to be dropped early in the first term of the Reagan administration.

Seeing Title VI budgeting support and spending from the standpoint of procedural categories, several additional points became clear. First of all, here we can see the impact of cabinet secretaries and Title VI department heads. Significant funds have been spent on compliance review and compliant investigation, but little on legal enforcement and next to nothing on conciliation. This suggests that even with reviews and investigation, Title VI regulatory agencies might be funding discrimination—yet they are spending little if anything in terms of cutting off federal funding to discriminatory recipients because there is little money spent on legal enforcement. Third, since next to nothing is spent on conciliation, one can assume that not only is the federal government funding discrimination and not reducing it, it is making little or no attempt at even voluntary compliance. If the discriminatory use of federal funds is found, it simply goes unregulated; since fund termination and voluntary compliance might ruffle feathers at the state and local levels, the entire matter is simply kept as an in-house secret.[9] Findings from this analysis of the budget corroborate the earlier finding that little is being done budgetarily for Title VI agencies. And of the little that is being done, little is being spent on controversial areas like enforcement and voluntary compliance. *The majority of Title VI funds are spent on review and investigation.*

Yet when the Reagan administration arrived, Figure 3.5 shows that even these funded efforts of review and investigation dropped to very low funding levels indeed. George Gordon writes:

> Ronald Reagan, from the very start of his term in the White House, used a comprehensive assault on the national government budget as the key to his attempt to reshape the national buraucracy and the programs it operates. Reagan demonstrated convincingly that the most direct way (if not always the easiest, politically) to control an agency is to cut—or increase—its budget.[10]

The president, through OMB and his department heads, influences enormously the programmatic thrust of these new civil rights regulatory agencies. Thus, President Reagan's political priorities severely restricted the regulatory impact of Title VI agencies.

At this point, let's pause for a moment and reflect not on the civil rights regulatory priorities of these presidents but on their concern with simply getting the facts. Let's explore how well the Civil Rights Commission was supported between 1971 and 1983. The commission is an independent watchdog, a fact-finding agency. This agency has enjoyed only a very modest budget each year, with small increases except in 1979, 1982, 1983, and 1984 (Tables 3.1 and 3.2). Its budget in short, rose under Carter and declined significantly under Reagan. The mean for thirteen years stands at two percent of the federal civil rights budget. Overall, the percentage of the budget for the Civil Rights Commission has been erratic. Under Nixon, the commission had the lowest percentage of the total civil rights budget, rising under Ford and Carter, and beginning a new descent under Reagan.

Thus, not only has fact finding not been a major presidential budgetary priority, only certain types of civil rights regulatory efforts have been supported and even that has dramatically declined in the Reagan administration. First, federal expenditures overall have been slowly increasing since 1971. However, expenditures by department show wide fluctuations, as do expenditures by program category and by activity. One pattern is characteristic of all: the three Republican presidents cut expenditures whereas the Democratic president increased the federal civil rights budget. Although regulatory agencies and their budgets are supposed to be "nominally bipartisan and thus seemingly removed from party struggle, the fact remains that business and corporate interests generally have their own partisan leanings. It follows that there might well be partisan undercurrents in regulatory politics, partly depending on which party follows the White House—and on individual presidential preferences."[11]

Leon Panetta, (now Congressman D-Calif.), who headed the Office of Civil Rights Compliance in HEW during President Nixon's first term, described in great detail how southern Democrats and Republicans who had supported Nixon's presidential election in 1969 expected the administration to slow, if not stop, school desegration in the south. Specifically, these southerners of both parties, wanted HEW's Title VI unit not to cut off funds to school districts that were not complying with the law or had spent funds in a discriminatory manner.

Panetta describes a White House meeting with Presidential Assistant John Ehrlichman on what to do about strong enforcement of Title VI regulatory efforts in the face of southern pressures. In the course and aftermath of that meeting, Ehrlichman described the partisan nature of the White House's decision:

> "Well, for one thing, hundreds of blacks are already beginning to demonstrate, there's a potential for trouble, and it would help restore some needed confidence in the Administration that the law will be enforced."
>
> Ehrlichman's retort: "Well, haven't we got some pressure on this from Thurmond? You know, Jack*, the blacks aren't where our votes are."
>
> "John, I think I know something about politics, too, and I don't read it that way. Somebody'd better start worrying about the North."
>
> When Jack relayed this to me, I could hardly believe it. It was the first time I had heard the Southern strategy blown out in the open by two high-level Administration officials over a direct policy decision. While it was obvious that it always was a factor, never had it become so clear as when Ehrlichman repeated, "The blacks aren't where our votes are." In one brief phrase, he had cut off over twenty million Americans from their Government because a model political debt was not involved.[12]

The point here is that partisanship does play a role in both regulatory politics and in the funding of regulatory agencies. Black support for the Republican party during these years had been rather small though stable, while black support for the Democrats had been very high and fairly stable. Hence, civil rights budgetary shifts can be explained in part by partisan presidential decisions.

Sharp cuts, when they occurred, obviously affected the viability of civil rights enforcement programs. For instance, in 1972 HEW was spending more than $105 million for civil rights enforcement, but two years later, in 1974, it was spending only $13.5 million. Such a drastic cut, reflecting the impact of the constituency of southern white Republicans and Democrats upon the Nixon administration, obviously severely lowered the enforcement power of the civil rights office in HEW. By 1979, the department's civil rights budget was only

---

*Jack Venernon was Under Secretary in HEW.

half of what it had been in 1972. In another instance, by 1973 the Department of Transportation budget had been cut in half—reduced from $4.1 million to $2.2 million, while Agriculture's budget was increased from $4.2 to $7.0 million. Changes on such a scale surely impair enforcement effectiveness and deny programmatic objectives and goals.

Abrupt increases, ironically, can also be a problem. Huge shifts upward can mean that a department suddenly has more money and resources than it can put to effective use. The Department of Defense in 1971 had $11 million to spend; the next year it had $37.14 million—nearly a three hundred percent increase—but had the problem of civil rights in the military grown so much in one year that it needed such a massive increase? The Department of the Interior offers another example. In 1977 it had a $2 million budget, yet in 1980 it had $11.2 million. Had the civil rights issues faced by Interior increased by nearly five hundred percent?

The failure by the federal government to establish any semblance of fiscal stability in the area of civil rights enforcement has sent two signals to friends and foes of this controversial public policy activity. First, that fiscal support for this policy area has not been a high priority and second that over time the federal government has had no consistent plan for program enforcement.

This is the budgetary picture when one looks at the entire federal budget and specifically at the Title VI programs. This perspective includes only the president and OMB; however, a new, different, but similar portrait emerges when one looks at the departmental civil rights regulatory budgets and the role that Congress plays in the budgetary process vis-a-vis the president.

The Departmental Civil Rights Budgets

Although, as had been shown in the previous analysis, there is a significant relationship between presidents and unusual changes in budget amounts, presidential politics is not the entire story. Congress appropriates the monies for agencies. The agencies must first submit their budget requests, (1) to their departmental budget office,[13] (2) then to OMB, and, finally, (3) to the congressional appropriations committees. *At each level cuts can be made.*

First, we need to determine if the amount approved by OMB, the president's budget agency, is the amount that Congress appropriates, or if Congress either lowers the amount further or raises it. In the area of civil rights, budget requests to Congress are made in terms of salaries and expenses, not in terms of Title VI activities.[14] This is a well-known and much-used bureaucratic budget technique to assure that unpopular or potentially troublesome programs can get support without a political struggle.[15] Of course, not all of the money granted a department for "salaries and expenses" in civil rights program really go for Title

VI enforcement. Much of this money goes for salaries, expenses, and other overhead, not directly connected to advancing the national mandate—the enforcement of civil rights.

The data in Table 3.5 illustrates the civil rights budget requests to Congress

Table 3.5 The Budget Requests of and Congressional Appropriations to HEW and Education: 1970–1982

	Budget Request	Appropriation
1970	$ 5,259,000	$ 5,259,000
1971	8,581,000	8,581,000
1973	11,061,000	12,518,000
1974	14,161,000	15,077,000
1975	15,521,000	16,301,000
1976	18,094,000	18,356,000
1977	21,954,000	23,310,000
1978	30,737,000	30,081,000
1979	48,238,000	44,245,000
1980	45,847,000	45,847,000
1981	46,915,000	46,915,000[1]
1982	50,971,000	NA

[1]The Senate did not enact an appropriations bill for FY81. Instead, the Congress enacted three continuing resolutions—Public Law 96–369; Public Law 96–536; and Public Law 97–12.
Source: Office of Civil Rights; Annual Report to Congress: U.S. Department of Education (copy of the report sent to author by Dale Pullin, Special Concerns Staff, Office for Civil Rights, December 7, 1981), p. 18.

made by HEW (and later the Department of Education) and the amounts ultimately approved by Congress between 1970 and 1982. In five instances, nearly half of the time, Congress increased the department's request, most of this coming during the years 1973 through 1977. And in four other instances, Congress approved exactly the amount requested. Once, in 1978, Congress cut the department's budget request.

The pattern in the case of HUD is altogether different (Table 3.6). In six instances, or more than half of the time, Congress cut the civil rights budget request of HUD. In four instances Congress approved exactly what the department requested. Only once, in the election year of 1974, did Congress increase the initial request made by the department. In the remaining instances, there is no data to determine what Congress did.

In Table 3.7 we see that the Department of Labor received exactly what it requested in seven of the eleven years for which data is available. In four instances, all of them during Nixon's tenure (1971, 1972, 1973, and 1974), Congress cut the requests of the department. This is strange behavior for a Democratic Congress. (Only once did Labor request less than it had the preceding year—in 1976. HUD submitted reduced budget requests twice, in 1970 and 1972, all during the Nixon years).

Table 3.6 The Budget Requests of and Congressional Appropriations to the HUD (Fair Housing) Equal Opportunity Office: 1969–1980

	Budget Request		Appropriation
1969	$11,100,000		
	8,000,000	(1st Supp.)	$2,000,000
	2,000,000	(2nd Supp.)	
1970	10,500,000	(1st Supp.)	6,000,000
	412,000		391,000
1971	11,000,000		8,000,000
1972	9,254,000		8,250,000
1973	9,489,000		9,546,000
1974	9,580,000		9,546,000
1975	11,900,000		11,735,000
1977	13,003,000		13,003,000
1978	13,500,000		13,500,000
1979	14,500,000		14,500,000
1980	15,000,000		15,000,000

Source: Augustus Jones, Jr., *Law, Bureaucracy and Politics* (Washington, D.C.: University Press of America, 1982), p. 101.

Taking the pattern of all three departments together, we find that in fifteen instances Congress approved exactly what was submitted; on eleven occasions Congress cut the budgets requests; only seven times did Congress raise the submitted budgets. Indications are that Congress on the whole has tended to support departmental requests. These facts tend to support the earlier contention that it was the president's action through OMB that had the greatest negative impact on budgets for civil rights compliance.

Not all of the money appropriated for civil rights enforcement actually goes for enforcement work. The data in Table 3.8 reveals how little of its total civil rights budget the Department of Defense spent on Title VI activities. For five years, less than one percent actually went into Title VI enforcement and activities. In 1981 the Agriculture Department spent only thirty-three percent of its total civil rights budget on Title VI efforts. Putting more into the civil rights budget, in short, will not ensure that money will end up paying for Title VI enforcement. These findings corroborate those earlier in the chapter concerning expenditures for activities, which revealed that only a very small portion of the budget went toward enforcement.

Budgetary information from the Department of Transportation for 1980 supports the same conclusion: only $1,918,000, of the overall civil rights budget of $11.1 million, went into the enforcement of Title VI (Table 3.9). The departmental budgets reveal in finer detail what was indicated from the overall federal budget, that the proportion of funds devoted to efforts to sustain Title VI is very small indeed.

Table 3.7   The Budget Requests of and Congressional Appropriations to the Investigation and Compliance (or Equal Opportunity) Office of the Department of Labor: 1970–1980

Fiscal Years	Investigation and Compliance's Budget Requests	Congressional Appropriations
1970	$ 700,000	$ 700,000
1971	725,000	723,000
1972	797,000	795,000
1973	815,000	814,000
1974	893,000	891,000
1975	1,810,000	1,810,000
1976	1,809,000	1,809,000
1977	1,890,000	1,890,000
1978	2,001,000	2,001,000
1979	2,410,000	2,410,000
1980	2,800,000	2,800,000

Source: Augustus Jones, Jr., *Law, Bureaucracy and Politics* (Washington, D.C.: University Press of America, 1982), p. 228.

What is more, not every division spent all of its civil rights enforcement funds. The National Highway Traffic Safety Administration did not spend $13,000 of its budget. Put differently, it made use of only eighty-seven percent of its Title VI enforcement budget. Bureaucrats can and do refuse or fail to spend all of the money provided them to carry out their mandates. It is a discretionary matter that is left up to individual dictates and personal whim.[16]

No cost overruns seem to have occurred. In all likelihood, enforcement activities are suspended when the budget limits are reached, and work undone is carried over for next year. The data in the next chapter on the carryover of compliance speaks clearly to this matter.

The Impact on the Federal Civil Rights Regulatory Effort

It is difficult to escape one overriding conclusion: presidential budgetary priorities do impact civil rights regulatory programs. An analysis of the entire federal civil rights budget clearly illustrates that the budget permits a wide range of program options to be supported. Of all the programs available, four presidents have decided to give the Title VI regulatory programs a little over fifteen percent of the budget.

Table 3.8   The Department of Defense Title VI and Total Civil Rights Budget Spent on Title VI

Fiscal Year	Estimated Funds Spent on Title VI Activity	Title VI Expenditures as % of Total Departmental Civil Rights Budget
1973	$123,000	.003
1974	315,000	.006
1975	344,922	.006
1976	477,410	.009
1981	387,000	.004

Source: Department of Defense, *The Department of Defense Title VI Enforcement Efforts and Related Matters 1964–1980*, Volume 1 (booklet sent to author by Claiborne D. Haughton, Jr., Director, Equal Opportunity Programs—Civilian), p. 11.

In addition, when one explores the funding of Title VI regulatory procedures and techniques, it is found that support has been primarily in the area of review and investigation, little has been spent on enforcement and voluntary compliance. This was the situation under three of the four presidents analyzed. Under the Reagan administration significant reductions have been made in each procedural category, with support for legal enforcement practically disappearing.

At the cabinet and agency levels, there is some budgetary discretion and these individuals can spend or withhold the spending of appropriated funds for Title VI activities. A cabinet secretary can withhold some of the Title VI agency funds. He can also help decide on programmatic direction and legal enforcement.

A Title VI head can deny funds for investigation, for travel, for review, and for assistance in getting voluntary compliance. And both administrators can do this in light of the nature of partisan support and the concerns of the president. One participant observer put it thus:

> Every agency, big or small, needs friends. If it is a pork-barrel outfit like the Army Corps of Engineers, no worry, because every Congressman loves to announce money coming in. If you can get industry lobbyists or professional groups like the American Medical Association on your side, they have campaign contribution leverage over Congressmen and Presidents. Civil rights units, however, have a

tough problem. They have no natural allies with money or influence. They have to count on Congressmen with a big constituency of racial minorities, some eloquent lawyers, a President when he's in the mood or position to help, and a few rare birds who seem to be acting out of conscience alone and who have some power.[17]

Beginning with the Nixon administration at least, those who had voted against the 1964 Civil Rights Act could now extract revenge by urging the Republican president to spend little for Title VI enforcement. Thus, if budgetary supporters were few in the early Republican administrations, by the time of the Reagan administration and the onset of fiscal conservatism budgetary friends had all but vanished.

Table 3.9   The Civil Rights Budget for Headquarters and Each Operating Element, Department of Transportation: 1980

	Obligations (in thousands)	Outlays (in thousands)
The Departmental Office of Civil Rights	$ 216.1	$ 216.1
Federal Railroad Administration	170.3	170.3
Federal Aviation Administration	346.0	346.0
Urban Mass Transportation Administration	523.6	523.6
National Highway Traffic Safety Administration	97.0	84.0
Federal Highway Administration	510.0	510.0
United States Coast Guard	55.0	55.0
*Research and Safety Programs Administration Total Budget for the Department	$1,918.0	$1,905.0

*The Research and Special Programs Administration (RSPA) administers the state gas pipeline safety grant program, which is an activity covered by Title VI of the Civil Rights Act of 1964. In 1980, 48 states were granted a total of $3,141,052. The RSPA does require grant recipients to comply with Title VI, although no staff time or funding is provided to ensure compliance. The Title VI requirement is emphasized in the grant program's procedural guide, which has been distributed to the 53 state jurisdictions eligible for grant funding. The grant-in-aid program has never been the object of a Title VI discrimination complaint.
Source: Data supplied the author by the Department of Transportation.

David Stockman, the OMB director during the Reagan administration's first term, explains that even congressional friends were unimportant and of little consequence. He writes:

Just before the inaugural, the President had approved, in principle, a series of symbolic "first day" directives designed to show that we would "hit the ground running" and come out slugging the federal monster. Among these were an across-the-board hiring freeze, a 15 percent cutback in agency travel budgets, a 5 percent cutback in consulting fees, and a freeze on buying any more furniture, office machines, and other such equipment.[18]

The point here is that even if the program has allies, there are still things that the presidents, cabinet secretaries and Title VI agency heads can do to impact Title VI regulatory agencies if public opinion has been manipulated to view affirmative action and civil rights enforcement in a negative or biased manner.

There is one final reflection on how budgetary priorities of presidents can shape the programmatic efforts of the civil rights agencies. In the entire previous discussion in this chapter, the civil rights budgetary data has been described and evaluated without any compensation for inflation.

Again, using 1971 as the base line year point, let's compensate for inflation for the beginning of the constant dollar analyses. The findings are indeed startling. Clearly Table 3.10 illustrates the failure of the civil rights enforcement budget to keep pace with inflation. No president from Nixon through Reagan compensated for the inflationary spiral. No matter the amounts that the civil rights enforcement budgets were raised, they were *never* raised high enough by any president to account or compensate for inflation. And even when inflation reached double digits under the Carter administration, the budget expenditures for civil rights regulatory enforcement activity didn't keep pace. Thus, all during the seventies and into the mid-eighties, these agencies had only about half the purchasing power and support of the actual dollars amounts indicated, once the budget is adjusted for inflation. Put another way, these Title VI agencies got only half the money they needed to fulfill their normal civil rights enforcement efforts. And receiving so little support obviously meant a ceasing of their regulatory reach.

Moreover, when this same data is plotted over time (see Figure 3.6), another perspective emerges. The overall trends and patterns show the civil rights enforcement budget to be steadily increasing, while in terms of constant dollars the same budget has essentially reached a plateau and leveled off (1972–1980) and in the Reagan years (1982–1985) began to decline.

That is the portrait in terms of the entire budget. Turning to the departmental level and looking at the data for five departments (Education, Health and Human Services, Justice, Labor, and the EEOC) and using 1980 constant dollars, as shown in Table 3.11 the inflationary impact on these individual departments, while it is less, it is still significant, given the much lower inflation rate during the first term of the Reagan era.

Table 3.10 The Federal Civil Rights Enforcement Budget: 1971–1985. A Comparison of Acutal Dollars and Constant Dollars (amounts in millions of dollars)

Years	Actual Dollars	Constant Dollars (Adjusted for Inflation)
1971	189.74	156.42
1972	292.73	233.62
1973	313.08	235.22
1974	291.43	197.31
1975	345.54	214.35
1976	375.20	220.05
1977	427.80	235.70
1978	448.00	220.27
1979	469.10	215.78
1980	552.80	223.99
1981	567.60	199.58
1982	567.60	199.45
1983	589.80	197.65
1984	633.10	203.50
1985	643.30	199.65

Source: For Enforcement dollars, OMB, Special Analyses: 1971–85; for constant dollars in terms of adjusting for inflation, calculations were made by Professor Johnny Campbell—Savannah State College's School of Business. In making his calculations Professor Campbell used the Consumer Price Index with 1967 = 100 as the base year.

Table 3.11 The Departmental Budgets for Selected Title VI and Title VII Agencies in Actual and 1980 Constant Dollars: 1980–1983 (in thousand of dollars)

Fiscal Year		Appropriation (annualized)	In 1980 Constant Dollars
Department of Education: Office for Civil Rights			
1980	(HEW, Estimated)	53,953	53,953
1980	(Education Department)	45,847	45,847
1981		46,915	42,884
1982	(Request)	49,396	41,885
1982	(Continuing Resolution)	45,038	38,189
1982	(Permitted Spending Level)	43,468	36,858
1983	(Request for Foundation)	43,999	34,770

Fiscal Year		Appropriation (annualized)	In 1980 Constant Dollars
Department of Health and Human Services: Office for Civil Rights			
1980		19,651	19,651
1981		17,420	15,923
1982	(Request)	17,063	14,468
1982	(Continuing Resolution)	19,319	15,381
1983	(Request)	19,163	15,144
Department of Justice: Civil Rights Division			
1980		15,145	15,145
1981		16,515	15,096
1982	(Budget Request)	17,139	14,533
1982	(Continuing Resolution)	16,515	14,004
1983	(Budget Request)	18,822	14,874
Department of Labor: Office of Federal Contract Compliance Programs			
1980		50,962	50,962
1981		49,318	45,080
1982	(Original Request)	48,309	40,963
1982	(Revised Request)	39,289	33,771
1982	(Continuing Resolution)	41,415	35,117
1983	(Request)	42,614	33,676
Equal Employment Opportunity Commission			
1980		124,562	124,562
1981		137,875	126,028
1982	(Budget Request)	140,389	119,041
1982	(Continuing Resolution)	139,889	118,617
1983	(Budget)	144,937	114,536

Source: U.S. Commission on Civil Rights, *The Federal Civil Rights Enforcement Budget: Fiscal Year 1983* (Washington, D.C.: Government Printing Office, 1982) p. 11 for Education; 24 for Health and Human Services; 32 for Justice; 42 for Labor; and 52 for EEOC.

Using the last year, and rank ordering these five departments by the size of the loss, EEOC had a thirty million dollar drop in purchasing power, Education a nine million drop, Labor 8.9 million drop, Health and Human Services, a four million drop, and Justice with a 3.9 million drop. These departments are the most active in pursuing civil rights enforcements, yet inflation reduced their total budgetary purchasing power in one year by more than fifty-six million dollars.

Thus, whether by design or by happenstance—and the former seems more realistic—presidential budget priorities have permitted inflation to stall and reduce the dollars that Title VI agencies have had to carry out their enforcement of the 1964 congressional mandate. When the marching stopped, presidents used inflation as a battering ram to lessen the achievements of the grand civil rights coalition.

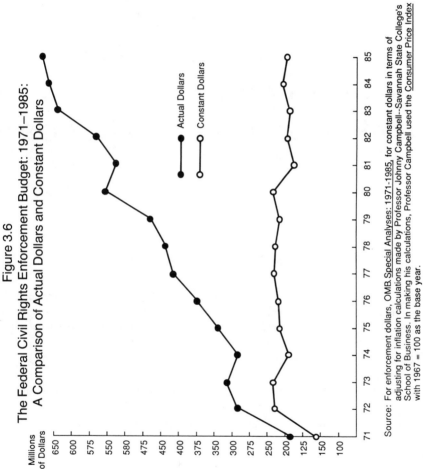

Figure 3.6
The Federal Civil Rights Enforcement Budget: 1971–1985:
A Comparison of Actual Dollars and Constant Dollars

Source: For enforcement dollars, OMB, Special Analyses: 1971-1985, for constant dollars in terms of
adjusting for inflation calculations made by Professor Johnny Campbell--Savannah State College's
School of Business. In making his calculations, Professor Campbell used the Consumer Price Index
with 1967 = 100 as the base year.

4. THE POLITICS OF CIVIL RIGHTS ENFORCEMENT: REGULATORY RULEMAKING AND ACTION

Professor Jeffrey M. Berry writes: "Few aspects of American society have been left untouched by the regulations of federal administrative agencies. There are regulations to cover everything from day care centers to funeral homes. Most of the regulations that come out of Washington each week have little impact on the consciousness of the general public. Yet regulations affect the quality of life of ordinary citizens."[1]

Although governmental "regulatory activity dates back to the 1800s and was aimed essentially at the economic sphere, beginning in the sixties and seventies, new 'social' regulations began to appear and these social policy rules were aimed at society and various segments in it." One observer put it thus:

> Economic ("old") regulation focuses on markets, rates, and the obligation to serve. Social ("new") regulation affects the conditions under which goods and services are produced, and the physical characteristics of products that are manufactured. Social regulation also differs from economic regulation in the wider scope of its im-

pacts. Social regulation arose out of a concern for reducing public involuntary (and voluntary) exposure to risk.[2]

However, it must be said that while nearly every student of the regulation process acknowledges the existence of these "new" social regulatory agencies, few, if any, included these new civil rights regulatory agencies either in their discussion or in the definitions. The current definitions of the new social regulatory agencies completely eliminate or omit from their definitional frameworks the focus and concern of the civil rights regulatory agencies, i.e. agencies designed to minimize or eliminate racist and discriminatory behavior by those state and local agencies that use federal funds. These agencies involve much more than a mere concern with *risk*. Yet, in one of the pioneering books on the new social regulatory agencies, the author observed that currently, "regulation by the federal government encompass a far wider range of activities than determining standards, rates, and fair practices for different segments of the economy. It is important to extend research on the regulatory process to such nonmarket policy areas as nutrition, mental health, job training, community development, cash assistance, and social insurance."[3] He continues: "of course, the agencies that regulate economic interests differ significantly from those that have responsibility for social welfare programs. Social welfare agencies do not divide up markets among competitors; they are not structured as independent commissions; and they do not appear to have well-organized clients. Still, there is one basic similarity between social and economic regulatory agencies that must not be overlooked: Both types of agencies have been given authority by Congress to allocate goods and services among the American people."[4]

Here is another example of how the conceptual definition of social regulatory agencies has completely omitted the new civil rights regulatory agencies. But, if the scholars and academicians have overlooked them, the newspapers, journal articles, and the intellectual magazines are filled with discussions of how these civil rights agencies are engendering bad race relations as well as being a drag on the economy, big business, and state, local, and federal bodies.

This chapter, in order to deal with this problem of pressure groups attacking and criticizing a political entity that doesn't exist in the academic and scholarly definitions of social regulatory agencies, begins first by focusing upon the reasons why government develops regulations in the first place.

"Government regulations have developed, in large part, as a result of decisions designed to show compassion for the individual and to maintain representativeness and fairness in governing. Compassionate motives have included protecting people from each other, alleviating distress, and preventing major systemic disruptions. Steps aimed at representativeness and fairness include requirements of procedural fairness and public participation, limitations on dishonesty and corruption, and tax laws."[5] Understood in this fashion, blacks have experienced so much racially discriminatory behavior in this society that it has become necessary for the group to seek laws and regulatory agencies to protect them from such evils and the many ills that such evils cause within the black community. Hence, as Chapter One illustrates, these new civil rights regulatory agencies have "been fostered by a desire—and a willingness—to have government protect" blacks as groups and individuals from the discriminatory expenditure of federal funds by state and local bodies. This is what the rulemaking efforts of these agencies is supposed to address.

"Every agency that has been given rulemaking powers must interpret congressional intent and then make discretionary decisions as to what policies best serve the public's need."[6] In fact, "each agency must use its regulatory powers to transform statutes into practical rules for program implementation." In regard to the new civil rights regulatory agencies, they had to take the broad, vague, and general mandate of Title VI and develop rules, regulations, and guidelines so that recipients of federal funds would know whether they were complying with the laws of the land.

Anticipating resistance or at least reluctance from some recipients of federal funds, Congress provided the Title VI agencies with the means to assure uniform compliance with the laws of the land. Public Law 88–352, the Civil Rights Act of 1964, empowered Title VI agencies to enforce compliance by terminating funds or "by any other means authorized by law." That phrase has been interpreted to mean the deferral of funds or referral of non-compliant behavior to the Justice Department for legal or other appropriate action. Enforcement techniques, then, in order of increasing severity, are (a) fund-deferral, (2) fund termination, and (3) referral to Justice for legal action. Before such sanctions can be applied, federal agencies must *first must tell the recipient of federal funds what to do so as to comply with the law.*

This chapter, therefore, will explore how each cabinet-level department with a Title VI civil rights regulatory agency went about its rulemaking process, looking specifically at how and when each department developed "proposed" rules and the time between the "proposed" rules and the "final" regulations as they appeared in the *Federal Code*. Next the chapter will analyze the various techniques available to Title VI agencies in determining racially discriminatory behavior and, once that behavior has been determined, exactly what the agencies did to eliminate such behavior.

Finally, this chapter will assess how well the federal government coordinated the regulatory efforts of the Title VI units. Since each unit or agency is located within a specific cabinet department, and each department has its own focus and concerns as well as each department being separate and equal, Title VI units of different departments do not work in unison, ever though such coordinated effort might prove more effective with a recalcitrant recipient. Thus, this section explores both the legal environment for coordination as well as the success of the coordinating efforts.

Beyond creation, structure, staffing, and budgets, there is the matter of civil rights rulemaking: the basis upon which these new social regulatory agencies operate. That is the concern of this chapter.

Rulemaking in the Civil Rights Regulatory Agencies

Although "procedures used by regulatory agencies fall into two broad categories: rulemaking and adjudicating proceeding,"[7] Title VI procedures rest mainly on rulemaking. Thus, "agencies are empowered under the Administrative Procedure Act of 1946 to engage in rule making, an action quasi-legislative (in the manner of a legislature) in nature. Rule making involves issuing a formal rule that covers a general class of happenings or enterprises. It has about the same effect as a law passed by Congress or another legislature."[8] Finally, "rule making is characterized by its general applicability and by its uniformly affecting all within a given category."[9]

Therefore, those who receive federal funds have to wait until each federal agency (hereafter: the grantor) develops its own guidelines for dissemination to the public. Only when recipients have the guidelines in hand and have an opportunity to implement them can an agency judge whether they are in compliance. Recipients must have received guidelines and submitted an "assurance of compliance" form to the grantor before these agencies may exercise their power to enforce compliance (see Appendix B). Each agency has two means of disseminating guidelines. First, all rules and regulations (or their revisions) of executive branch agencies are supposed to appear in the *Federal Register*. The city, time, and date for public hearings concerning such rules and rules changes are to be announced in the *Register*, along with information about how the public can reach the agency to get additional information about the hearing, the proposed rule and regulations, how to submit comments if one cannot attend the hearing, and how to obtain transcripts of the hearing. Second, agencies issue manuals, handbooks, secretary's orders, memoranda, and digests of significant case-related memoranda to the recipients of funds and to other divisions and bureaus. Subtleties of the interpretation of the law notwithstanding, the purpose of all of these devices is to provide the recipients of federal funds with an understanding of the basic parameters within which they must act in order to be in compliance with the law. Such guidelines also provide the agencies with a yardstick by which to judge what is and what is not compliant behavior.

How quickly did Title VI agencies develop their rules and regulations, their manuals and handbooks for the recipients of federal funds? For some agencies, the promulgation of the rules was all that was done to carry out the civil rights mandate—at least for some time. For instance, the Department of Interior issued its compliance manual on May 10, 1966, two years after the Civil Rights Act was passed, but years before an office was created to run the program. (It issued a second manual on May 10, 1974, to update the old one.) Other departments simply never issued a manual or a code book, particularly if Title VI activities were under a program chief instead of an administrator. Program chiefs tend to see their first priority as one of getting the funds to the recipient and compliance with civil rights requirements as obstacles.

HUD, created in 1965, did not issue its Title VI regulations until June 23, 1973. Apparently moving more quickly, the Department of Defense sent its regulations to the president for approval on December 19, 1964, and published them in the *Federal Register* on December 31, 1964. But, as we have seen in the previous chapter, as late as 1979 the Department had only a part-time staff working on Title VI activities, despite its disbursing approximately $2.5 million in funds through twenty-three different federal assistance programs.

The Department of Transportation put its rules and regulations into the *Federal Register* on June 18, 1970, but it was not until January 21, 1977 that it issued order number 1000.12, effective February 18, 1977, implementing Title VI of the Civil Rights Act of 1964. Nearly seven years elapsed between the time that the regulations and rules were promulgated and the time that this department moved to implement them.

Like Defense, the Agriculture Department moved quickly —in publishing its rules and regulations in the *Federal Register* on December 4 and 11, 1964. But an office within this cabinet-level agency to carry out these rules did not emerge until 1972. The Department of Labor, on the other hand, did not create its Office of Civil Rights until October 23, 1980, though it had published rules and regulations in the *Federal Register* on December 4, 1964. Labor, in short, had rules and regulations in place fully sixteen years before it created an office to implement them.

It is clear that although the various departments acted fairly quickly—in some instances, less than six months after the law was passed—to put forth rules and regulations, they were less-than-speedy in designing an organizational mechanism for putting the rules and regulations into effect. Some departments may have delegated the authority to enforce the rules to the program-officer level, but such means for implementation lacks the force and effectiveness that an official office, bureau, or division has, for it has the sole function of handling the Title VI mandate.

After a department first places its rules and regulations in the *Federal Register*, there follows a specified period when comments and criticisms can be made about them, after which the proposed "regs" are revised and then placed in the *Code of Federal Regulations*. Once they enter the *Code*, they become part of the law of the land. An agency or its components may continue to amend these regulations. As a result, those who receive federal funds can be faced with having to comply with hard-to-follow fluctuations in the rules. Table 4.1 shows

Table 4.1   Delays between Proposed and Codification of Title VI Regulations

Agency	Date Place in Fed. Reg.	Date Proposed in Code	Citation	
ACTION	1983	01/26/74	74	*Code* pt. 1203
Agriculture	1984	12/04/64	7	*Code* SS 15.1-.12, 60.143
CAB	1984	12/31/64	14	*Code* pt. 379
Commerce	1984	07/05/73	15	*Code* pt. 8
Defense	1983	12/31/64	32	*Code* pt. 300
Education	1984	06/13/80	34	*Code* pt. 1040
EPA	1984	01/12/83	40	*Code* pts. 7 & 12
REMA	1983	01/09/65	44	*Code* pt. 7
	1983	01/20/75	44	*Code* pt. 307
GSA	1983	12/04/64	SS	101-6.2
HHS	1983	12/04/64	45	*Code* pt. 80
HUD	1983	07/05/73	45	*Code* pt. 1
IDCA/AID	1983	01/09/65	22	*Code* pt. 217
Interior	1983	12/04/64	43	*Code* pt. 17
Justice	1983	07/29/66	28	*Code* SS 42.101-.112
Labor	1983	12/04/64	29	*Code* pt. 31
NASA	1984	01/29/65	14	*Code* pt. 1250
NEA	1983	07/05/73	45	*Code* pt. 1110
NEH	1983	07/05/73	45	*Code* pt. 1110
NRC	1984	03/06/80	10	*Code* SS 4.11-.93
NSF	1983	12/04/64	45	*Code* pt. 611
OPM	1984	07/05/73	5	*Code* SS 900.401-.412
SBA	1984	01/09/65	13	*Code* pt. 112
State	1983	01/09/65	22	*Code* pt. 141
TVA	1983	01/09/65	18	*Code* pt. 1302
DOT	1983	06/18/70	49	*Code* pt. 21
Treasury (ORS)	1983	09/30/81	31	*Code* pt. 51
USIA	1983	01/09/65	22	*Code* pt. 141
VA	1983	12/31/64	38	*Code* SS 18.1-.13

Source: Civil Rights Forum, Spring, 1984, p. 2.

that it usually took several years, and in some instances two full decades, for proposed regulations to become the law of the land when they became a part of the *Code*.

Most agencies began proposing regulations to carry out their Title VI mandate as early as 1964. All of the agencies formalized these proposed regulations and placed them in the *Code* in 1983 or 1984. Why the concentration occurred in those two years is not clear. Seemingly, the heavy emphasis on "regulatory relief" that President Reagan committed his office to, forced the cabinet secretaries and Title VI agency heads to finalize their lingering *proposed* rules and regulations because once the Reagan administration began its policy of deferring, revising, and rescinding regulations, these new civil rights regulatory agencies had nothing to "defer," "revise," or "recind." Ironically, the administration that was most opposed to these social regulations made their final adoption possible.

Figure 4.1 graphically portrays the pace at which regulatons were proposed in the *Federal Register*. A clear pattern emerges between 1964 and 1984. The years when the greatest number were proposed were 1964, 1965, 1973, and 1980, in descending order. There seem to be seven-year cycles for proposing regulations that do not follow presidential or congressional election patterns of change or reflect the appointment of a department secretary.

Interpretation of Table 4.1 and Figure 4.1 is somewhat limited by the fact that not all of the federal agencies included in the table and the figure existed in 1964. To compensate for this time lag factor, in Table 4.2 only those depart-

Table 4.2   Cabinet-Level Departments Ranked in Order of Time Taken to Promulgate Final Title VI Rules

	Rules Proposed	Rules Codified	Time Elapsed (in years)
Agriculture	1964	1984	20
Defense	1964	1983	19
Interior	1964	1983	19
Labor	1964	1983	19
State	1965	1983	18
Justice	1966	1983	17
Transportation	1970	1983	13
Commerce	1973	1984	11
HUD	1973	1983	10
Treasury	1981	1983	2
Mean Years			14.8

Source: Adapted from *Civil Rights Forum* (Spring, 1984) p.2.

ments that existed in 1964 are listed (the exception is the Department of Transportation). They are ranked according to the total number of years each department took to promulgate its final rules. Of the nine departments that existed in 1964 when the Civil Rights Act was passed, only four developed proposed regulations that year—forty-four percent of the total. Two of the nine departments issued such regulations in 1973, while in 1965, 1966, 1970, and 1981 one department issued regulations in each of these years. The Treasury Department,

Figure 4.1

Proposal Cycle: Title VI Regulations in the *Federal Register* 1964–1984

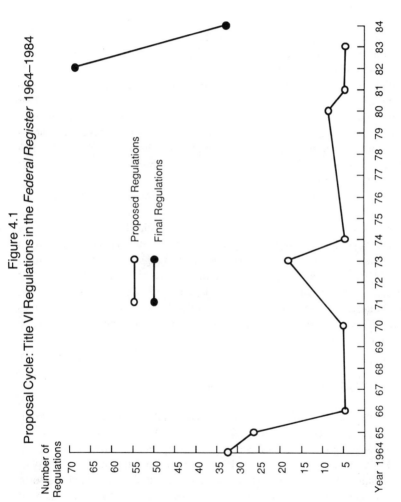

Source: <u>Civil Rights Forum</u> (Spring, 1984) p. 2.

which existed in 1964, took seventeen years before it issued even proposed regulations but only two years before it codified them.

Usually much more time elapsed between the development and the finalized rules. Again, the data in Table 4.2 reveals that for the nine cabinet-level departments that existed in 1964, it took, on the average, almost fifteen years for proposed Title VI rules and regulations to become codified into law. At the extreme, the Department of Agriculture took twenty years—a period covering five presidencies—before it completed this process. Overall, federal departments have taken their time putting in place regulations requiring the recipients of federal funds to be in compliance with Title VI. In the interim, each recipient of federal funds had considerable leeway for bargaining with the federal government about complying with the law.

What is also clear is that, despite journalistic and academic arguments to the contrary, the government did not quickly thrust upon the states and their agencies new rules and regulations. The federal bureaucracy moved most guardedly in carrying out its congressionally imposed civil rights mandate— much more so than it did to regulate compliance with section 504 of the Rehabilitation Act of 1973, which forbids nondiscrimination in use of federal funds for handicapped people.[10]

Agencies have enjoyed considerable latitude in the way they may carry out their Title VI responsibilities. First, they devise their own regulations (which at first were approved by the president, later by the Justice Department, and now by OMB.) Second, the promulgation of rules and regulations is divorced from an administrative vehicle to carry out such rules or regulations. Third, the rules exist on paper several years before the administrative vehicle to carry them out is formed. Moreover, most agencies took years to bring their rules into final form. Finally, in each case the agency writing the guidelines also determines who is and who is not in compliance. Determining compliance without final regulations is indeed a complex matter.

The Determination of Discrimination

Once the rules and regulations are proposed and codified, Title VI units within agencies can proceed along two paths in their implementation activity. First, they may wait until a complaint is brought, either from an individual or from a group. In response, these units may then investigate to determine the validity of the complaint, and then act to enforce the law. Second, these units may perform reviews of any or all award of federal funds, before or after an award has been made, or both. If any discrimination is found, agencies may begin the four-step process described below to ensure compliance and nondiscrimination in federally assisted services and benefits.

In short, there are two triggering mechanisms—those who feel discriminated against may act, or the government itself may take the initiative. In either case, if discrimination is found, the agencies may then seek (1) voluntary compliance, (2) fund deferral, (3) fund termination, or (4) referral to the Department of Justice to ensure enforcement of the act.

How have the various executive departments responded to complaints and handled pre- and post-award reviews? The record keeping by federal agencies involved in Title VI enforcement leaves much to be desired; consistent, comprehensive, and accurate records of complaints have not been kept. Disaggregation of data by race is rare. For example, the director of the Civil Rights Office in HUD stated that prior to 1974 "inadequate and sometimes no Title VI data files had been kept by HUD officials."[11] Coupled with this problem of poor records is the problem of political sensitivity. William T. Harris, deputy director of the Office of Civil Rights of the Department of Labor, in responding to a written request for copies or summaries of Title VI compliance findings, wrote that the "Office of Civil Rights policy is not to make this kind of information public due to its sensitive nature. Please understand that we are not denying you this information for any personal reasons. This kind of information has not been sanitized and often it is used later for litigative purposes."[12] Harris provided only the most general information. The Agriculture Department responded to a similar inquiry by indicating that such a request would have to be made under the Freedom of Information Act—in which case information would be sent only to the department's Freedom of Information Officer and that it would include only previously published data, not detailed unpublished material.[13] Most irritating of all is that data is not reported the same way each year.

From the limited data that does exist it is possible to describe what the federal agencies have done in response to complaints regarding Title VI funds. For instance, HUD's *Statistical Yearbook* from 1969 through 1979, in its section on Fair Housing and Equal Opportunity, provides data on the number of Title VI and Title VIII complaints received each year. HUD however is exceptional among the federal agencies in doing this.[14] (Title VIII is part of the Civil Rights Act of 1968; it prohibits discrimination in the sale or rental of housing, and in real estate, advertising, financing, brokerage services, and blacklisting.)[15]

HUD's records reveal that the number of Title VI complaints have steadily declined while those filed under Title VIII rose steadily from 1969 and then leveled out beginning in 1974 (Table 4.3).[16] Two-thirds of the complaints under each category have been made by black people. What did the agency do about these incoming complaints?

Figure 4.2 shows the percentage of Title VI and Title VIII complaints that were investigated by HUD each year between 1969 and 1979 and, of those actually investigated, those that were conciliated and ended. As the graph shows, this data was available for Title VIII only until 1979. The reader should bear in mind that after the initial years of these programs each title had substantial numbers of carryover complaints that were added to the incoming new ones. For instance, in 1970 there were 1,025 new complaints, but 301 old complaints carried forward from 1969 and 103 complaints that had been referred to the states where the complaints originated for resolution but recalled during 1970. Hence, there was an actual total of 1,429 complaints in 1970. The percentages in the figure are based on these grand totals not on the number of new complaints each year.

Table 4.3 New Title VI and Title VIII Complaints Received by HUD: 1969–1981

Year	Title VI	Brought by Blacks (%)	Title VIII	Brought by Blacks (%)
1969	NA	NA	979	NA
1970	240	NA	1,025	NA
1971	437	NA	1,570	NA
1972	345	NA	2,562	NA
1973	236	NA	2,684	NA
1974	238	73.3	2,752	74.5
1975	225	60.4	3,130	68.7
1976	93	60.2	3,336	61.6
1977	91	44.0	3,323	68.7
1978	98	79.6	3,120	67.2
1979	86	81.7	2,833	65.3
1980	73	NA	NA	NA
1981	.56	NA	NA	NA
Mean	185	66.5	2,483.9	67.7

Source: HUD, *Statistical Yearbook* (1969–1979). Data for Title VI in 1979, 1980, 1981, were received from Lawrence D. Pearl, director, Office of HUD Program Compliance, November 19, 1981, p. 2.

The number of investigations fluctuated from year to year, with a mean investigation rate of 48.7 percent. HUD did not investigate quite half of its complaints under Title VIII. Its record for Title VI is even lower; only 37.6 percent of all complaints were investigated. The agency stopped reporting Title VI complaint data after 1975.

Of the Title VIII cases that were investigated, only 29.4 percent were conciliated and resolved. The HUD *Yearbook* reports data for only three years—1969–1971. According to the *Yearbook*, HUD referred 12.7 percent in 1969, 2.1 percent in 1970, and 1.1 percent in 1971 to the Justice Department for action. Obviously, HUD was having some difficulty responding to complaints as a part of carrying out its Title VI and Title VIII mandate. A substantial backlog was occurring each year, and the department maintained only a moderate rate of

Figure 4.2

The Investigation, Conciliation, and Referral to State of Complaints Received and Carried Forward by HUD: 1969–1979

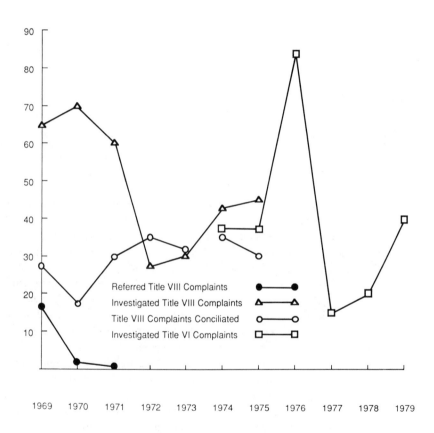

Source: HUD. Statistical Yearbook, (1969-1979).

investigation, a low rate of conciliation, and a very low rate of referral.

What was HUD's record with regard to its own efforts to initiate investigations of recipients of federal funds? The number of compliance reviews HUD performed during the 1970s reveals a tendency to forge ahead for several years and then to fall back to lower levels for several years (Table 4.4). More recently

Table 4.4   Compliance Reviews Initiated by HUD 1970–1977, 1979–1980

Year	Number	Change
1970	72	
1971	142	+70
1972	158	+16
1973	100	−58
1974	94	−6
1975	125	+31
1976	108	−17
1977	219	+111
1979	180	−39
1980	196	+16
Mean	130.4	

Source: Data supplied the author by the Department of Housing and Urban Development.

the department has seemed to increase its compliance reviews. The mean number of reviews per year is 139.

In sharp contrast to the pattern at HUD, which saw a decreasing number of Title VI complaints over time, the number of Title VI and Title VII complaints at the Department of Agriculture steadily increased each year between 1973 and 1981 (Figure 4.3). Not only did more complaints come into this department, these complaints tended to come to specific program areas within the agency. The data in Table 4.5 reveals that two agencies, the Farmer's Home Administration (FmHA) and the Food and Nutrition Service (FNS), consistently received the lion's share of the complaints—an average of about ninety-six complaints per year for the three years. Of these two agencies, the complaints received by the FmHA accounted for nearly two-thirds of the complaints.

In Table 4.6 we can see the specific FmHA loan programs that generated complaints. In the three years for which data were obtained (1978, 1979, and 1980), the housing farm operating loans, and farm ownership loan programs generated the greatest number of complaints. Many of the investigations of these complaints resulted in the finding of discrimination, and some corrective action was proposed and taken. For instance, one of the complaints dealt with a county supervisor who had refused to process the loan application of a black who had previously complained about racial discrimination by the supervisor.

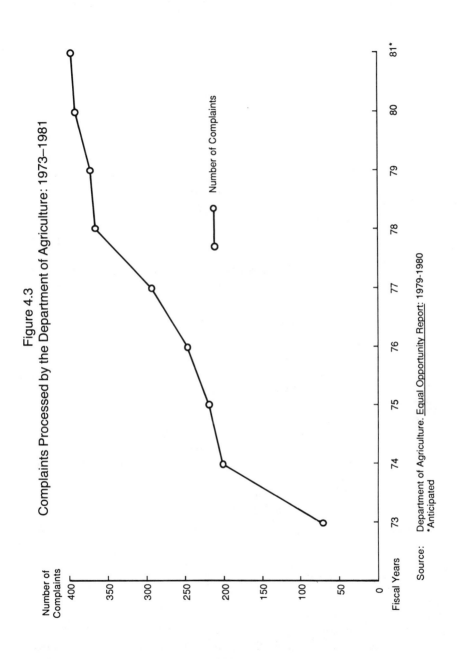

Figure 4.3

Complaints Processed by the Department of Agriculture: 1973–1981

Number of Complaints

Number of Complaints

Fiscal Years

Source: Department of Agriculture. Equal Opportunity Report: 1979-1980
         *Anticipated

Table 4.5 Complaints Received by the Department of Agriculture, by Program Area: 1978–1980

Agencies	1978	%	1979*	%	1980*	%
Farmer's Home Administration (FmHA)	183	59.2	188	61.2	202	59.8
Food and Nutrition Service (FNS)	116	37.5	109	35.5	122	36.1
Science and Education Administration (SEA)	1	.3	0	0.0	2	.6
Agricultural Stabilization and Conservation Service (ASCS)	3	.9	2	.7	5	1.5
Rural Electrification Administration (REA)	3	.9	2	.7	4	1.2
Forest Service (FS)	0	0.0	3	1.0	3	.9
Extension Service (ES)	2	.6	3	1.0	0	0.0
Federal Crop Insurance Corporation (FCIC)	1	.3	0	0.0	0	0.0
Total	309	99.7	307	99.7	338	100.1

*Not all complaints coming into the department each year fell under its jurisdiction; thus, of 375 overall in 1979, only 309, and of 392 in 1980, only 338 came under its jurisdiction. It was the smaller number that was used to calculate the percentage.

Source: Department of Agriculture, *Equal Opportunity Report, 1978, 1979, 1980* (Washington: D.C.: Government Printing Office, 1979, 1980, 1981), pp. 10, 12, 5. Although the department has been printing this annual report for nearly ten years, it was only for these three years that it provided complaints by program category.

Table 4.6 Title VI Complaints Received by the Farmer's Home Administration Loan Programs: 1978–1980

Type of Program	1978	%	1979	%	1980	%
Rural Housing Loans	94	51.4	103	54.8	110	54.5
Operating Loans	47	25.7	45	23.9	48	23.8
Farm Ownership Loans	36	19.7	35	18.6	37	18.3
Sewer and Water Loans	4	2.2	3	1.6	0	0.0
Emergency Loans	2	1.1	2	1.1	0	0.0
Unknown					7	3.5
Total	183	100.1	188	100.0	202	100.1

Source: Department of Agriculture, *Equal Opportunity Report, 1978, 1979, 1980* (Washington, D.C.: Government Printing Office, 1979, 1980, 1981), pp. 10, 12, 5.

The investigation resulted in the processing of the complainant's application and the recommendation that disciplinary action be taken against the supervisor for not processing the loan application. Generally speaking, "the most common complaints of alleged discrimination against FmHA are based on race, sex or ethnic origin in denying loan approval for FmHA's housing and farm loans. The second most frequent complaint involves alleged discrimination in the leasing interaction between contractor and FmHA borrowers, and housing contractors and FmHA officials. The more complex cases involved alleged discrimination in sewer and water project loans, farm labor housing, and rural rental housing programs."[17]

The second largest number of complaints in the Agriculture Department concern the Food and Nutrition Service (FNS). The majority of civil rights complaints were filed by potential or actual food stamp recipients; these complaints dealt with alleged discrimination based on race or ethnic origin in the application for, the servicing of, or the denial of food stamp benefits.[18] The department concluded in its investigation of these charges, that "numerous complaints filed in the Food Stamp Program were a result of the lack of sensitivity on the part of food stamp personnel toward program beneficiaries, and the lack of knowledge by food stamp applicants of the Food Stamp Program's rules and regulations."[19]

As an example, one food stamp case involved a complaint of "rude and discourteous treatment by food stamp personnel against food stamp recipients. The investigation disclosed that there were three workers who were regularly rude and discourteous to food stamp recipients. Since they treated all clients in this fashion, no discrimination was proven, but corrective action was taken to correct this serious problem. The Food Stamp Supervisor was reprimanded and cautioned to improve her attitude toward recipients or face severe disciplinary action." In addition, "the Director of the office was counselled as to her responsibility toward the Food Stamp Program." And "the state agency responsible for the successful implementation of the program" was instructed to establish a complaint procedure that "would provide for the receipt, recording, investigation and disposition of such complaints."[20]

How many complaints like these has the Department of Agriculture been resolving each year? The annual reports of the department do not answer the question, but the Freedom of Information Officer did provide the author with figures concerning the resolution of complaints in 1981. The department received 405 complaints and resolved 283, or 69.9 percent of them. In 1981, then, the Agriculture Department was much more successful than HUD in dealing with its Title VI obligations.

In initiating its own investigations, the department undertook compliance reviews (both before and after awards) in two areas: in direct assistance programs and in federal funds and grants programs. The total number of reviews ranged from a high of 32,566 in 1975 to a low of 15,048 in 1976. The mean stands at 19,909. The reviews have shown that about ninety-two recipients per year have not been in compliance when they received federal funds.

For instance, during 1980, the department conducted thirteen compliance reviews of programs administered by the Food and Nutrition Service (FNS) program to determine if FNS recipients were operating in compliance with Title VI and departmental rules and regulations. Reviews covered the Food Stamp Program, the Commodity Supplemental Food Program (CSFP), and the Special Supplemental Food Program for Women, Infants, and Children (WIC), and it included "onsite observations of certification and issuance facilities, examinations of household case files and outreach files, and interviews with participants and minority community leaders."

The figures shown in Table 4.7, a tabulation which is a composite and does not cover all sites, shows the distribution of the types of deficiencies found.

Table 4.7   Findings in Thirteen Compliance Reviews of FNS Programs by the Civil Rights Division, OEO

Findings	Instances
Need for expansion of outreach program and referral system	10
Failure to include nondiscrimination statements in public notices and announcements	9
Minority representation in staff not proportionate to area population	4
Racial participation data not maintained and/or reported	2
"And Justice for All" or "Food Stamp Rights" poster not displayed in all offices	6
Compliance reviews not conducted or documented by agency administrators	8
Lack of specific civil rights training for employees	13
Lack of bilingual staff members to handle non-English speaking participants	3

Source: Department of Agriculture, *Equal Opportunity Report: 1980* (Washington, D.C.: Government Printing Office, 1981), pp. 27–28.

In the same year, twenty-four compliance reviews were conducted of the Farmer's Home Administration (FmHA) district and county offices in eight states (California, Florida, Louisiana, Maryland, Ohio, Pennsylvania, Tennessee, and Texas). Included in these reviews were examinations of "loan files and application for Title VI and direct programs, reviews of program items and outreach files; interviews with district and county FmHA personnel, grassroots organization officials, minority program borrowers and beneficiaries; and onsite inspection of rural rental housing units and FmHA financial subdivisions."[21] The composite results, summarized in Table 4.8, show the distribution of deficiencies that were found.

A more precisely-targeted compliance review undertaken in May, 1980 of the FmHA office in Winston County, North Carolina, which also serves Gates and Hertford counties, reveals staggering problems affecting black farmers.

Table 4.8 Findings in Twenty-Four Compliance Reviews of FmHA Programs by the Civil Rights Division, OEO

Findings	Instances
Lack of regular, systematic outreach program efforts	12
"And Justice for All" poster not displayed in county and district offices.	7
Equal Employment Opportunity (EEO) posters not displayed in Title VI recipients' facilities	6
Civil rights training not provided to county and district personnel	9
Equal Credit Opportunity Act (ECOA) training not provided to county and district personnel	5
Compliance reviews not conducted of Title VI programs	3
Lack of nondiscrimination statement in news items of public interest.	24

Source: Department of Agriculture, *Equal Opportunity Report: 1980* (Washington, D.C.: Government Printing Office, 1980), p. 29.

The review analyzed only the farm loan program; it lasted four days and covered all loan processing work for three years, examining selected case files of farm borrowers. The review revealed much about what was happening to the black farmers in that one area of North Carolina:

(1) Few blacks received loans where payments were deferred over a period of years.

(2) There was a disparity in the number and amount of Economic Emergency Loans to minorities.

(3) Equal Credit Opportunity violations were applicable to all borrowers who were required to have their spouses sign instruments of indebtedness for chattels where no evidence was given that the spouse giving the signature had signed the original instrument of indebtedness.

(4) On two occasions, at least, minortiy borrowers were required to agree to voluntary liquidation as a condition before they could secure a loan.

(5) Minorities waited inordinate periods between application and loan approval for the 1980 crop season, especially in Gates County.

(6) There were irregularities concerning the processing of a black borrower's 1979 loans:

    a. Acceleration of an emergency loan payment from 7 years to 1 year.

    b. The county supervisor's decision that FmHA would not secure a first lien on a combine if he paid off the existing first lien.

(7) There was no folder containing civil rights directives and news releases of program availability.

(8) There were irregularities concerning the processing of a black applicant's loan request.

Such broad based reviews are helpful not only in uncovering invidious discrimination and in instigating corrections of individual violations but also in revealing institutional patterns in the administration of federal assistance that perpetuate discrimination in clear violation of the law and that individual compliants for one reason or another might not reveal. In short, the two types of compliance work reinforce each other and work best in combination (individual compliance and compliance reviews). Nevertheless, the compliance reviews that have been done are only a small portion of the number that should be conducted.

In the Department of Defense one can see another pattern. This department's responses to a General Accounting Office (GAO) questionnaire about its compliance activities for the years 1971–1977 indicated that among 25,563 Title VI program recipients, not one was found to be in noncompliance (Table 4.9). Moreover, only eight compliants were received and investigated during

Table 4.9   The Defense Department's Report of Perfect Compliance: 1971–1977

Fiscal Year	Number of Recipients	On-Site Compliance Reviews	Number of Recipients in Compliance	Number of Complaints Received	Number of Complaints Where Discrimination Was Not Found
1971	4,973	6,462	6,462	1	1
1974	5,030	4,168	4,168	2	2
1975	5,124	7,676	7,676	4	4
1976	5,194	5,338	5,338		
1977	5,242	7,226	7,226	1	1

Source: The data for this table was compiled from responses to a 1978 GAO questionnaire "Survey of Federal Agency Enforcement of Title VI of the 1964 Civil Rights Act" by components of the Defense Department.

this period, and in all eight cases no discrimination was found. Findings of such perfect compliance aroused the suspicions of the deputy assistant secretary for equal opportunity; not only was the validity of the report questioned, but new guidelines were issued when it was learned that most of the "on-site reviews consisted merely of an examination of the recipient's signed assurances (letter of assurance) of nondiscrimination."[22]

This criticism led to the issuance of a new report in 1979 on 2,053 recipients, 1,149 (or fifty-six percent) of whom were reviewed for compliance. The data issued since this time has been far more reliable than earlier reports, which were deliberately distorted to show a perfect conformity of behavior with the regulations.

Another agency that claims to have a perfect compliance record is the Department of the Interior. In 1981 the department's Title VI assistant director wrote: "approximately twenty (20) complaints regarding Title VI are received and processed by our office each year. Generally, the same number of complaints are investigated and resolved each year. Since the inception of the Act, this office has never initiated administrative proceedings against a recipient, i.e., fund termination, hearings, etc."[23] By its own evaluation, the Interior Department is completely effective in carrying out its Title VI mandate. Because the department has released no other information whereby the claim can be checked, it is necessary to take its conclusions with some skepticism.[24]

The Department of Transportation released compliance data only for 1980. It had received 127 new complaints during the year and had a carryover of 224 unresolved complaints from 1979, for a total of 351 complaints. Of that number, 233 or sixty-six percent were left unresolved at the end of the year.[25] The determination of emphasis, i.e. whether things will be reviewed, investigated, resolved, or legal enforcement, is made primarily by the cabinet secretary in consultation with his Title VI agency head. And as the budgetary data revealed in Chapter 3, most of the emphasis was upon review and investigation—not upon *resolution of complaints*. This data from the Department of Transportation simply highlights that reality.

The response of the Department of Labor was similar. It provided information only for the year 1980. The deputy director of Labor's Office of Civil Rights wrote that the number of complaints coming into the office each year was approximately 1,000 and that "approximately one-third of those received, for which OCR had jurisdiction, were resolved."[26] However, because OMB included some of the Labor Department's data in its budget report, it is possible to throw more light on the Labor Department's compliance efforts (Table 4.10). Comparison of compliance activity in 1980 and 1983 indicates a substantial improvement in each category by the Office of Federal Contract Compliance Program. But because OMB does not reveal how many complaints DOL received and how many reviews actually took place, there is no way to measure the effectiveness of the department's compliance administration.

Data for 1975 to 1980 obtained from Labor's Compliance and Investigation Office paints another picture of the agency (Figure 4.4). The data reveals the trend in the department's investigative practices. The Labor Department investigated only a very small number of complaints each year, new and backlogged complaints. Only in 1979 did the department's effectiveness rise to as much as one-fourth of all the complaints it had in-house.

The record for *compliance review* is even bleaker. The department has

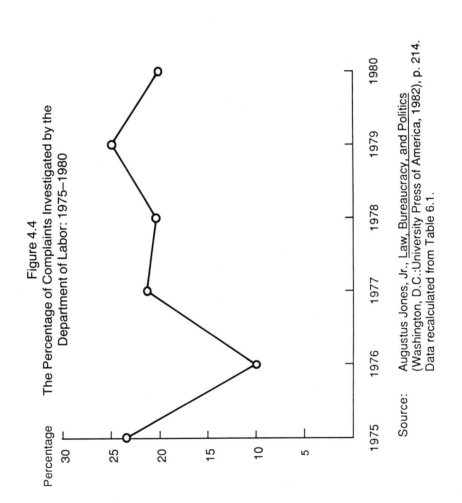

Figure 4.4
The Percentage of Complaints Investigated by the
Department of Labor: 1975–1980

Source: Augustus Jones, Jr., Law, Bureaucracy, and Politics
(Washington, D.C.:University Press of America, 1982), p. 214.
Data recalculated from Table 6.1.

some 20,000 recipients of federal funds, but over a six-year period concluded compliance reviews of only 1.2 percent of all its recipients. With such an extremely low review rate, Labor cannot possibly determine if its recipients are violating Title VI rules and regulations. Those who receive funds from Labor obviously run very little risk of being checked or called into question in regard to discriminatory practices. Again, we can see the role that the cabinet secretaries and Title VI agency heads can play in the enforcement process. It is up to these individuals to decide how much, if any, compliance review will take place. They can provide the funds, personnel, and direction on this matter. In the Department of Labor, such decisions were simply not made. A major reason for that is that the Title VI office wasn't created until 1981.

Table 4.10 Compliance Activity of the Office of Federal Contract Compliance Program, Department of Labor: 1980 and 1983

	1980	1983	Difference
Complaint investigations completed	1,726	2,375	+ 33
Compliance reviews completed	2,632	4,295	+ 63
Total employment of re-reviewed establishments (millions)	1.05	3.15	+ 300
Total compliance reviews in which discriminatory practices were identified and corrected	113	1,740	+ 1,440

Source: Office of Management and Budget, *Budget Report, 1985* (Washington, D.C.: Government Printing Office, 1985).

HEW's track record provides yet another perspective of federal civil rights enforcement regulation. In the seven years between 1974 and 1980 HEW investigated on the average forty-two percent of all the complaints in-house each year; the range ran from a high of fifty-three percent in 1977 to a low of thirty-five percent in 1980 (Figure 4.5). The overwhelming majority of these complaints were made by black people. For example, eighty-six percent of the complainants in 1974, and in 1980, ninety-nine percent of the complaints filed were by blacks.

HEW conducted compliance reviews of only 4.2 percent of its 31,000 recipients in 1977, seven percent in 1978, 6.4 percent in 1979, and 6.5 percent in 1980. Consistently, HEW has reviewed under ten percent of all of its recipients of federal funds to determine if they were following departmental Title VI regulations. In sum, HEW has been more vigorous about investigating individual complaints than it has been about *reviewing* recipients' compliance with Title

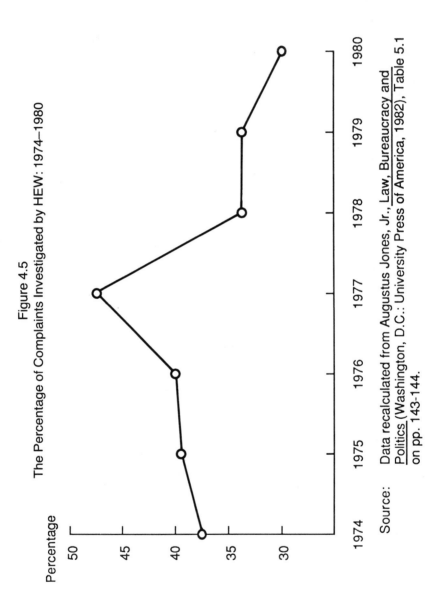

Figure 4.5
The Percentage of Complaints Investigated by HEW: 1974–1980

Source: Data recalculated from Augustus Jones, Jr., Law, Bureaucracy and
           Politics (Washington, D.C.: University Press of America, 1982), Table 5.1
           on pp. 143-144.

VI. Once again, one can see the influence and policy priorities of cabinet secretaries and Title VI agency heads. The decision to pursue individual complaints vis-a-vis compliance reviews is solely a discretionary matter that administration officers can decide on depending on the political cost and pressures
in the environment. Politically, it was less costly to resolve a single individual
complaint, than it was to cut off funds to entire school districts. Hence, HEW
took the path of least resistance, but one that was more expensive financially. It
is not cost-effective to pursue numerous *single* individual complaints. Yet, this
is what HEW did.

To summarize: analysis of all the cabinet-level departments to determine
how well they have investigated individual complaints of discrimination and
how thoroughly they conducted compliance reviews shows that they are doing
at best only a *modest* job. Having now seen the nature and scope of the federal
effort to determine discriminatory behavior among the recipients of federal
funds, we can now look to see what the civil rights regulatory agencies did once
they found cases of noncompliance with the law.

The Impact of Civil Rights Regulatory Agencies on Noncompliance

Violation of the rules, guidelines, and regulations of the Title VI agencies
means noncompliance with the law. When noncompliance is found, Congress,
in the enabling legislation, provided each Title VI and Title VII agency with
specific techniques and procedures to ensure compliance. Both the Title VI and
VII agencies and the recipients of federal funds know what the procedures are
for ensuring compliance. However, the foregoing analysis has shown that recipients of federal funds are indeed found to have violated Title VI rules and regulations (Table 4.11). The findings are: (1) Many participants in federally
funded programs are discriminating on the basis of race. (2) The larger the
agency and the greater the number of its recipients of federal funds, the greater
the number of violators. (3) Even though two decades have passed since the
passage of the Civil Rights Act, many state and local agencies continue to discriminate on the basis of race. (4) With the exception of HUD and HEW, most
of these reports of noncompliance were found during the Carter administration.
What is more, one must keep in mind that these findings of discriminatory activity are based upon the most *modest* efforts of the government to investigate
noncompliance. It is possible that more vigorous investigation would find more
cases of noncompliance.

OMB, in a special budget report, took a position on this very matter. Using
both pre-award and post-award noncompliance findings, OMB concluded: "in
1981 only 2% of the pre-award reviews conducted by all agencies resulted in

Table 4.11 Recipients of Federal Funds Found in Noncompliance under Title VI, by Department: 1973–1981

Department	1973	1974	1975	1976	1977	1978	1979	1980	1981	Total
Agriculture	NA	NA	NA	64	121	42	140	NA	0	367
Defense	NA	NA	NA	0	0	1	NA	NA	NA	1
Interior	NA	NA	22	44	27	10	NA	NA	NA	103
Labor	NA	NA	220	40	30	27	23	20	NA	360
State	NA	NA	NA	NA	NA	NA	NA	NA	NA	NA
Justice	NA	NA	NA	NA	18	39	NA	NA	NA	57
Transportation	NA	NA	NA	24	179	224	NA	NA	NA	427
Commerce	NA	NA	NA	NA	5	8	NA	NA	NA	13
HUD	NA	48	42	16	6	3	4	3	NA	122
HEW	NA	74	132	130	115	122	140	179	NA	893
Treasury	NA	NA	NA	NA	NA	NA	NA	NA	NA	

Source: Table is a composite of data found in various issues of *Title VI Forum* and data supplied the author by the various departments. Where discrepancies appeared, data from the departments was used.

NA = Not Available

finding any deficiencies requiring correction before assistance could be awarded—and fewer than 3/5 of 1% of these activities resulted in identifying and correcting any discriminating practices. In 1982, which saw substantially more pre-award review activity, the percentage of noncompliance findings of all kinds fell to 1.8% and the percentage resulted in correction of discrimination practice in only 1/5 of 1%."[27] As for post-award reviews, OMB felt that the "rate at which even routine reviews resulted in the correction of illegal discrimination was a disappointing two percent."[28] Thus, in OMB's view, the low levels of noncompliance discovered coupled with the rather high cost of conducting reviews raised "serious questions of cost-effectiveness." The implication throughout OMB's 1984 budget analysis is that these procedures should be dropped or greatly modified.

However, seen from another perspective, finding a low incidence of noncompliance after conducting a very limited search is hardly surprising, particularly given the poor quality of: (a) record keeping and (b) the data that does exist; indeed, it may be inevitable. As has been shown thus far, most of the federal agencies are reviewing less than ten percent of their funding recipients; a finding of only one or two percent noncompliance is fairly predictable. OMB's concerns about cost effectiveness, particularly given the methodology it has used, i.e. simple desk audits which merely involve reviews of written material submitted by the applicant for federal funds, are an over reaction that fit the ideology of the Reagan administration. Thus, the argument "that this is a particularly questionable use of resources" provides the administration with the rationale for cutting expenditures in the area of civil rights enforcement.[29]

Once they determine that discrimination has taken place, how do federal agencies get compliance? Which of several legal procedures at their disposal do they choose to use? The data currently available reveals that legal sanctions to ensure compliance are used very sparingly, if at all. Reliable data for 1976, 1977, and 1978 reveals that many recipients of federal funds were violating antidiscrimination rules (Table 4.12). Although the incidence of reported dis-

Table 4.12 Recipients of Federal Funds, by Departments Awarding Funds, Found in Violation of Title VI Regulations[1]

	1976	1977	1978	Changes 1976-1978
Agriculture	68	121	61	− 7
Commerce	2	5	8	+ 6
CSA	29	20	28	− 1
Defense	0	0	1	+ 1
Energy			0	
EPA	1			
HEW			296	
HUD	49	16	48	− 1
Interior	44	27	10	− 34
Labor	113	220	202	+ 89
LEAA		18	39	
SBA	57	3,116*	259	+ 202
Transportation	24	179	224	+ 200
VA	11	24	1	− 10
Others		1	0	
(N = 19)				
Total	398	3,747	1,177	

*An anomaly of reporting procedures.
[1]Discrepancies between this table and Table 4.11 are due to my use of recent departmental data for Table 4.11. Here I used *Forum* data as reported.
Source: *Title VI Forums*, 1977, 1978, 1979.

crimination rose and fell in this three-year period, the data suggests that as America prepared to enter the 1980s, some of the users of federal financial assistance were still spending these monies in a discriminatory fashion.

The Federal Program Section of the Department of Justice sent questionnaires to all federal agencies administering domestic assistance asking how many times over a five-year period these agencies had initiated procedures to terminate funding (Table 4.13). Follow-up telephone calls were made to those

Table 4.13   Federal Agencies Terminating Funds under Title VI: 1971–1976

ACTION	0
Agriculture	2
CSA	0
CSC	0
Defense	0
EDA	0
EPA	0[1]
ERDA	0
HEW	86[2]
HUD	1[3]
Interior	0
Labor	0[4]
NEA	0
NSF	0
NEH	0
NRC	0
SBA	0
Transportation	3
VA	0
Total	92

[1] Data supplied by Sid Green, chief Title VI officer, EPA, in telephone conversation on May 8, 1977.
[2] Data supplied by Frank Druger; 83 of these proceedings have been against local school districts.
[3] Data supplied by Larry Pearl, director of the Office of Program Compliance, HUD, in telephone conversation on May 8, 1977.
[4] This figure is for 1975 and 1976 only. Data supplied by William Harris, director of the Office of Investigation and Compliance, Department of Labor, in telephone conversation May 8, 1977.
Source: Title VI Forums

agencies that did not respond to the questionnaire. It was found that nineteen federal agencies had initiated a total of ninety-two termination proceedings between 1971 and 1976. Of this number, over ninety percent of the termination proceedings has been launched by a single federal agency, HEW. Given the large number of findings of noncompliance, as detailed in Table 4.12, it appears that those who used federal monies in a discriminatory manner knew they had little to fear; the federal government had been terminating only a very small percentage of those recipients who were in noncompliance. Most escaped notice entirely or were simply asked to voluntarily comply. Moreover, only HEW was actually doing anything concrete, the facts suggest. However, as data below reveals, this performance record by HEW is misleading.

In 1979 the Civil Rights Division of the Justice Department decided to see how well the various federal agencies were carrying out their Title VI enforcement responsibilities. The division compared the resources, workload, and effectiveness of the agencies over time, taking into account their various sizes (Table 4.14). Justice found that although "more than one half of all the work years devoted to Title VI enforcement are expended by Department of HEW, an agency which received more than one half of all the Title VI complaints filed in FY 1978, and was responsible, in the same fiscal year, for administering the distribution of nearly one half of all Title VI covered assistance dollars, that agency did not rank in the top five under any of the three measures of effectiveness."[30]

Effectiveness of the agencies reviewed varied widely. Despite the fact that HEW was found to terminate awards far more often than other agencies, it was still quite *ineffective* in assuring that federal funds were not spent in a discriminatory fashion. Even with its large staff, generous budget, and record for frequent terminations, this agency was found to be only partly fulfilling its Title VI responsibilities. Discrimination continued at the state and local level, even as these levels of government continued to use federal funds. During its first term the Reagan administration retreated from strong Title VI enforcement in the educational sectors and proposed to withdraw even further by relying almost totally on voluntary compliance.[31]

To summarize: throughout the 1970s, when a Title VI agency determined that discrimination had occurred, it relied most heavily on voluntary compliance by recipients for resolution. In the main, only HEW took significant steps to stop discrimination under its Title VI mandate. Moreover when the Reagan administration took over, it took the position that too much enforcement had taken place in the 1970s and that a reduced federal role was called for. Federal agencies, it said, needed to rely more on voluntary compliance by recipients of federal aid. The administration stood firm, despite the fact that even the strongest methods used by HEW had not proven to be effective. Enforcement of civil rights rules was not as strong as many in the minority community had hoped it would be. In addition, this administration has not released any data about the results of this shift in emphasis; chances are, current efforts are even less effective than past ones.

In short—the research indicates that an official finding of discrimination by the federal government does not necessarily lead to the elimination or even the diminution of discrimination.

The Politics of Coordination

Federal enforcement of civil rights legislation is not left just to each agency and department. Within a year of the enactment of the Civil Rights Law of 1964 the

Table 4.14 Federal Agencies Ranked by Performance of Title VI Enforcement, 1976–1978

	Dollar Amount	Work Years	Dollar Amount of Covered Programs	Number of Recipients	Number of Complaints Received	Complaints Received to Complaints Investigated	Ratio of On-Site Reviews to Work Years Available	Ratio of Pre-award Review to Primary Recipient
1	HEW	HEW	HEW	USDA	ETA	VA	VA	DOT
2	USDA	USDA	ETA	VA	HEW	HUD	USDA	EDA
3	HUD	HUD	USDA	SBA	LEAA	SBA	SBA	CSA
4	DOT	DOT	DOT	HEW	USDA	USDA	DOT	VA
5	ETA	ETA	HUD	HUD	CSA	Interior	DSA	ETA
6	SBA	SBA	VA	ETA	DOT	CSA	Interior	HEW
7	EDA	EDA	SBA	EDA	HUD	ETA	ETA	HUD
8	CSA	CSA	Interior	EDA	SBA	LEAA	LEAA	USDA
9	LEAA	VA	LEAA	LEAA	Interior	DOT	HUD	LEAA
10	Interior, VA	Interior, LEAA	CSA, EDA	CSA Interior	VA, EDA	HEW, EDA	HEW, EDA	Interior SBA

*Represents FY 1978 only: data for previous fiscal years is not available.

Source: Title VI Forum, (Fall, 1979), p. 4.

Justice Department was given powers to assist in the enforcement of civil rights regulatory policies. Then, "because of diverse agency performance in enforcing Title VI and the evolution of different standards and approaches to its implementation," President Johnson issued Executive Order 11247 in September 1968, authorizing the attorney general "to coordinate federal implementation of Title VI: so to ensure uniform and effective implementation of the Title. But even with this specific directive, the attorney general's authority remained largely unused until 1974, during which period Title VI received uneven and generally weak enforcement."[32] This problem surfaced repeatedly in reports of the Commission on Civil Rights, in testimony during congressional hearings, and in the protests of several public interest groups.

Therefore, to rectify the problem, in 1974 Attorney General Elliott Richardson sought and President Nixon signed Executive Order 17764.33, This executive order provided "the Department of Justice with the authority necessary to effectuate its coordination responsibility." Shortly thereafter the department promulgated the regulations in the United States Code that prescribed the general standards and procedures that all federal departments and agencies were to abide by in enforcing Title VI.[34]

Among the regulations was a provision that required that all Title VI regulations of each agency and department be approved by the Department of Justice before being put into effect.[35] In order to be certain that each agency and department adhered to the new standards, the Justice Department's Civil Rights Division devised four ways to monitor Title VI operations:

1. The Civil Rights Division of the Justice Department assigned selected members of its staff to act as lead coordinators and attorney/advisors to all Title VI agencies to "develop contacts," "maintain close liaison," and acquire a "working knowledge of that agency's Title VI program";
2. Each lead coordinator had the sole responsibility of evaluating and examining the enforcement efforts of the agency;
3. Each lead coordinator identified the deficiencies and problems in those programs that they surveyed, and those agencies that agreed to rectify such problems would sign a Memorandum of Understanding with the attorney general; and
4. The Justice Department would provide technical assistance and legal opinions to agencies at their request.

In addition, the Civil Rights Division also conducted special projects to ensure coordination and standard operating practices. Some were one-time projects that addressed the overlapping enforcement issues of several offices; some were projects concerning Title VI matters of continuing concern to all agencies. A prime example of the latter is the informative newsletter initially entitled *The Title VI Forum* and renamed the *Civil Rights Forum* by the Reagan administration in 1982. It is published quarterly and sent to all concerned federal offices and outside groups and individuals. It is not, however, sent to the Library of Congress.

The Nixon administration had no sooner issued the executive order giving the Justice Department responsibility for coordinating Title VI enforcement, however, than that administration cut the civil rights budget, and these cuts were apparently sustained by Congress. Faced with limited resources to implement its mandate, the department decided to focus on only a few Title VI programs, selecting only fourteen agencies, or forty-five percent of the agencies it had previously monitored. It produced an Interagency Survey Report on twelve, or thirty-nine percent of these agencies; it signed memoranda of understanding with four agencies (thirteen percent), and completed a follow-up review of one of the agencies that had signed memoranda—to ensure that implementation plans were being followed.

The period from 1964 to 1974 saw little or no coordination; the years 1974 to 1977 were not much better. Reduced civil rights budgets forced the Justice Department to severely restrict its role in coordinating enforcement. As a consequence, some of the departments and agencies not reviewed and evaluated by Justice continued to carry out Title VI mandates in a very circumscribed manner.

Faced with the lax Title VI enforcement of his predecessor, President Jimmy Carter issued a memorandum on July 20, 1977, to the heads of all executive departments and agencies formally committing his administration to the enforcement of Title VI.[36] Carter also reminded agency heads that Title VI required them to "exert firm leadership" so that each agency or department indeed enforced the law. Finally, the memorandum reaffirmed the responsibility for coordination set forth in Executive Order 11764, and further stated:

> The Department of Justice will shortly be contacting each department and agency to determine what action has been taken to comply with the Attorney General's Title VI regulations. You should insist that your staff cooperate fully with the Department of Justice staff as they carry out this task and their other responsibilities under the Executive Order.[37]

Then, in closing, the directive stressed the need to use sanctions provided in the law, sanctions such as fund termination, to ensure "equal treatment in federal programs."[38]

To facilitate this directive, the black assistant attorney general Drew S. Days on April 9, 1979 "reorganized the Civil Rights Division of the Justice Department" and created a unit called "the Office of Coordination and Review." It was to be responsible for "coordinating and reviewing the enforcement by federal departments and agencies Title VI programs, policies and regulations."[39] A woman, Stewart B. Oneglia, was named director, and a black, Ted Nickens, was named deputy director. Prior to this reorganization, the responsibility for coordination had rested with the Federal Programs Unit of the department, which had numerous other responsibilities — a structural placement that, like the budget reduction, sharply hampered its effectiveness.

However this reorganization by Drew Days only placed responsibility for Title VI and IX of the education amendment of 1972 in this new unit. Within a year of its creation the new unit identified "seven major problem areas in federal Title VI enforcement efforts":

1. Agencies have not vested Title VI Offices with the authority necessary to administer their Title VI enforcement program.

2. Agencies have placed Title VI Offices in their organizational structures in positions subordinate to the agency components which administer the program they are responsible for monitoring. This has compromised the operational integrity of these offices.

3. Agencies have not allocated enough staff resources to the Title VI function to cope with Title VI enforcement workloads.

4. Agencies do not provide for the collection of sufficient data to permit Title VI Offices to accurately determine the compliance status of their recipients; in many cases, even where such data are being collected, the data are inaccessible to Title VI compliance officers.

5. Title VI Offices often focus their enforcement efforts on non-Title VI issues (e.g., the internal staffing practices of grant recipients) to the detriment of ensuring nondiscrimination in services.

6. Agencies, especially those with field components, are not exercising good management over their Title VI enforcement programs: Title VI Offices are particularly deficient in their planning.

7. Agencies have not kept their "paper compliance systems (e.g., Title VI regulations, enforcement manuals, procedures, guidelines, etc.) up-to-date; consequently, the structure upon which their Title VI enforcement program is founded is unsound.

With these initiatives, it appeared that serious coordination of Title VI programs was finally under way. But this promising start was to come to an end in little over a year because in the fall of 1980 the Carter administration lost its bid for reelection. The Reagan administration came into office with a new philosophy of deregulation and an ideology of conservatism. Reagan moved swiftly to put his stamp on the regulatory policies of the civil rights agencies.

The Impact of the Reagan Administration on the Coordination of Civil Rights Regulatory Agencies

One observer has described the Reagan administration in the following terms: "The Reagan program of regulatory relief involved reviews of existing rules, a slowdown in issuing major new regulations, relaxing enforcement of existing rules, and making significant reductions in regulatory agency budgets. President Reagan also sought to establish more centralized control over new and existing regulations, and mandated the use of cost-benefit analysis in assessing regulations."[40] Moreover, in another, less visible undertaking, top presidential aides began to explore possible ways of transferring regulatory authority from the national government to state governments, consistent with the president's intentions both to ease regulatory requirements and to shift responsibilty to the states, in the spirit of "New Federalism."[41] However, Reagan's overall regulatory program would have considerable impact and influence on the coordination efforts of Title VI civil rights regulatory agencies.

His first year in office in 1981, President Reagan issued Executive Order 12250, charging the attorney general with the responsibility "to coordinate the enforcement of Title VI of the Civil Rights Act of 1964, Title XI of the Education Amendment of 1972, Section 504 of the Rehabilitation Act of 1973, and the nondiscrimination provisions of various program statutes that prohibit discrimination of the basis of race, color, national origin, handicap, religion or sex."[42] The new order enlarged and expanded the Justice Department's coordinating authority beyond Title VI and superseded Executive Order 11764 issued by Jimmy Carter in 1976. Under Executive Order 12250, the assistant attorney general for civil rights was delegated the authority for carrying out coordinating responsibilities. It also changed the title of the newsletter to the *Civil Rights Forum*, to "reflect the expanded authority" expressed in E.O. 12250.

Shortly thereafter, the Justice Department began to revise its coordination regulations, but "copies of several drafts of the regulations and comments by OMB" that were leaked to the press "generated an avalanche of mail and telephone calls to congressional offices, OMB and the Civil Rights Division, from concerned citizens, recipients and advisory groups."[43] This reaction slowed the department's efforts, and in the spring of 1983, after a review of the coordination regulations with the Presidential Task Force on Regulation Relief, the department still had not issued a revised set of coordination regulations.[44]

However, the assistant attorney general for civil rights, William Bradford Reynolds, did shift the department's priorities. The new emphasis—though it was not explicit[45]—was on the coordination of Title VI regulations with section 504 complaints—i.e., the concern with nondiscrimination in federally funded programs was shifting toward the concerns of handicapped people.[46] In November 1983, Reynolds reorganized the Civil Rights Division. He expanded the Coordination and Review Section Unit by adding to its duties oversight functions in regard to section 504.[47] Thus, the responsibilities of the Justice Department for coordination of Title VI enforcement underwent a major transformation during the Reagan administration. In effect its focus was enlarged and its emphasis was significantly changed.

Additionally, the Reagan administration cut the budget of the civil rights office, cuts that strained the outreach power of the coordination section to a breaking point, at the same time that its responsibilities were increased. Consequently, new priorities arose and a trade-off was made, as the division turned away from Title VI coordination to center its attention on coordinating issues of concern to the handicapped. Coordination by the attorney general that was intended to resolve the lack of uniform enforcement of Title VI rules by the departments and agencies, had run into severe difficulty. The Justice Department was severely hampered, first, by its lack of "bureaucratic will." It had also endured several internal reorganizations. Finally, it saw a change of emphasis and suffered a rash of budget cuts instituted during the Reagan administration. The Justice Department has not yet achieved what it was expected to do under the original orders from the Johnson White House.

Summary

The federal government's apparatus for enforcing civil rights regulations essentially involves a variety of administrative procedures. First, the government, through its Title VI agencies, is supposed to resolve individual complaints about discrimination as they are brought to the sundry offices of civil rights compliance. Second, these agencies are supposed to conduct pre- and post-award compliance reviews of state and local agencies that receive federal funds, to ensure that those funds are not spent in a way that discriminates on the basis of race. Third, the Justice Department is supposed to coordinate and oversee the various civil rights regulatory agencies to ensure as much standardization as possible, so that the procedures, guidelines, regulations of different agencies are comparable, to improve efficiency, productivity, and performance, and to make certain that each agency carries out its Title VI mandate, not assigning it a low priority.

This research has revealed that enforcement procedures are inconsistently defined and implemented. There is no agreement within the federal government about the proper way to implement these procedures. There is no agreement about the proper way to determine when the procedures have been successful. Most importantly, there is no agreement about the proper way to determine the cost effectiveness of these procedures. Because there are no agreed-upon definitions and standards, each president, each cabinet and agency head, each assistant attorney general for civil rights, and each director of a Title VI unit within a federal department must individually *shape* and even *reshape* enforcement procedures from his or her own ideological and social perspectives. It is little wonder that there have been wide fluctuations and virtually no uniformity in the application of the law.

Analysis of the enforcement done by federal departments and agencies shows them to have vacillated in the level of enforcement as different presidents, cabinet heads, and agency personnel have come and gone. The differing priorities of public officials have had an unsettling impact on enforcement, as have differing budget outlooks and ways of assessing cost effectiveness.

However, before closing this summation section, a word should be said about the difference between *voluntary* and *involuntary* compliance. Voluntary compliance simply means that federal agencies do little more than to ask noncomplying state and local federal agencies for letters of assurance that they will abide by Title VI regulations in the future. If a state or local agency indicates that it wants to comply but does not know how, the federal departments and agencies can then use funds from their technical assistance budgets to help these noncomplying public officials to adjust their actions to meet the requirements of Title VI. Voluntary compliance, in short, is the acceptance of *a good faith promise* that noncomplying agencies will finally do their duty and abide by the law.

Involuntary compliance, on the other hand, requires the federal department and agencies to force resistant state and local agencies to abide by the law. When state and local agencies refuse to comply, the federal agencies are required under Title VI to either defer funds or terminate funds. Cases may be finally referred to Justice for legal action.

The Justice Department may sue a noncompliant recipient of federal funds and the courts may then direct the noncomplying agency or department to carry out its duties and responsibilities under the law.

Hence, one must be careful to distinguish *compliance procedures* which determine whether the law is being violated from *enforcement procedures* which determine that the law is indeed being carried out. This chapter has shown that most federal agencies have relied on promises of voluntary compliance when they have discovered that recipients of federal funds are reluctant to adhere to the law. Involuntary compliance techniques have only been used a very small percentage of the time, despite the picture given in some media reports and in the conservative political literature. The federal government has constantly been criticized for only forcing compliance when in fact it has sought in the majority of cases only voluntary compliance.[48]

To a mishmash of enforcement procedures, the Justice Department has been able to bring only minimal order. Clearly, political pressures and a variety of internal governmental factors have seriously eroded effective enforcement of Title VI rules. Federally funded, illegal discrimination has continued largely unabated, even after the marching stopped.[49]

5. THE POLITICS OF PRESSURE GROUPS

As we have seen in Chapter Four, internal factors are not the only forces seeking to shape civil rights enforcement and regulatory activity. External forces, pressure groups, constantly try to alter compliance and enforcement procedures as well. Regulatory activity takes place in a political arena where those who strongly oppose and those who strongly support civil rights enforcement vie for dominance. The offices of civil rights compliance must contend with these external forces and their pressure politics. These new regulatory offices are facing nothing different from what the old regulatory agencies had to face. American politics is made up of contending and competitive interest groups, and no federal agency can escape this reality as it seeks to carry out its mandate.

However, before we proceed with this chapter's analysis of civil rights interest groups and pressure politics, it is necessary to reacquaint the reader with the leading theoretical perspective that dominates the political science and, to some extent, the journalistic literature about interest group politics in Washington. But not only do we want to call the reader's attention to these realities, it is likewise necessary to inform the reader of the nature and scope of our approach and the justifications for the deviations from the standard interest group perspective.

The key assumptions behind the leading and dominant theoretical perspective is that in Washington: (1) a political subsystem exists; (2) that it operates like an "iron-triangle", i.e. a cozy relationship between three partners; and (3) that these three political entities operate on a consensual basis. One observer of a new social regulatory agency described it thus:

> In its simplest form, a policy subsystem consists of a congressional committee or subcommittee, an administrative agency, and relevant interest groups. The terminology has frequently changed, but whether they are called "subgovernments," "iron triangles," or "cozy little triangles," such subsystems are based on the same idea: Agency administrators, lobbyists from client groups, and congressmen with committee jurisdiction over that agency work together continuously to formulate policy.[1]

He continues:

> The policy making in a subsystem is held to be consensual. Each side of the triangle can be helped by working cooperatively with the other two. Congressmen look for political support and campaign contributions from the interest groups. Agency administrators want to protect their budgets and otherwise enhance their programs. Finally, client groups want to make sure that their interests are furthered by government policies. Over time, close working relationships develop, and individuals may even move from one point in the triangle to another, such as the agency official who later takes a job with a client group. It is a "mutual self-help arrangement" where policies are formulated with the needs of all partners in mind.[2]

Another analyst of the administrative and policy system describes the same phenomena in similar fashion. "A . . . major source of (political) support," he writes, for administrative agencies (i.e. regulatory agencies) in national politics," which is carefully cultivated, "is constituent or clientele groups that look to the agency for satisfaction of their policy demands."

> Such groups come under the heading of interest groups, as that term is commonly used, and represent an organized expression of political opinion by a portion (usually a small portion) of the general adult population. They tend to be groups affected directly by the agency's operations, and therefore they have a tangible stake in its programmatic output and impact. The political relationship which usually develops between an agency and such a group is one of reciprocity, where each has some political commodity from which the other can benefit. The agency's greatest strength is its expertise and the con-

trol it exercises over particular government programs that it makes available to the agency in return for agency attention to its needs and desires. The group may provide channels of communication to other influential individuals and groups in the political process, help the agency sell its program to Congress and the president, or aid the agency in anticipating changes in the political environment that would present problems or provide opportunities.[3]

Although this theoretical perspective has come under substantial criticism and scrutiny and has been found to have limited value, recent analyses and research have renamed and redefined the "political subsystem" or "iron triangle" as *Issue networks*.[4] And while this concept and theoretical perspective is supposed to be superior to the earlier ideas, "there is still a certain amount of vagueness to the whole idea and little concrete knowledge about how issue networks behave." The concept of issue networks evolved from the work of Hugh Heclo.

Therefore, the crucial question to be raised at this point is the relevance of these limited and incomplete theoretical ideas and concepts for pressure and interest group politics around the new civil rights regulatory agencies.

Elsewhere, it has already been argued that many of the concepts, theories, models, and presuppositions of academic political scientists *cannot* be readily and functionally applied to matters involving the black political experience in America.[5] And here is another example of that situation. The ideas of the subsystem and its key assumptions, the concept of "iron triangle" and "consensual agreements," as well as the new device of issue network have marginal, if any, utility or explanatory value in understanding interest and pressure politics for the new civil rights regulatory agencies.

First of all, the assumption and idea of a Washington-based political subsystem does not hold in terms of civil rights policy and regulatory behavior. Racially discriminatory behavior has been pervasive throughout the country and particularly in the South for well over a century. And as numerous monographic case studies of Title VI efforts in sundry school districts have uncovered, the national capital and its administrative agencies are only one of the many battlefields.[6] Secondly, the assumption and idea that there exists a cozy iron triangle defies the truth. Civil rights politics in this country generates intracongressional clashes, and even intraparty clashes in Congress, as well as intrabureaucratic clashes and, most assuredly, inter-pressuregroup clashes. Moreover, one director of a Title VI office in HEW has described in his memoirs how President Nixon, under pressure from southerners, deliberately placed in each cabinet-level department an informer, whose sole purpose and task in the department was to undermine and sabotage Title VI regulatory efforts.[7] Thus, the relationship between these triangle components was anything but "cozy" and, as noted, with the president involved it was much more than a three sided figure.

Finally, the assumption of a consensual arrangement and approach surely needs reworking and rethinking in civil rights regulatory politics. The law itself engenders conflict. It was borne out of a need to provide protection and assistance to a racial minority from a racial majority. Hence, various parts of the country not only disagree with the law, but openly defied and used all of their political capital and connections to neutralize the law and/or its effects. Therefore, the law and the effort exerted by Title VI civil rights regulatory agencies to enforce the law, run into, from the outset, conflictive, combative, and oppositional behavior. A retreat from enforcing the law means then that the individual or group that is discriminated against is asked to continue to bear their burden until the majority accepts the law—which may be never.

Therefore, this chapter on interest and pressure group politics tries to move around the weaknesses and limitations of the dominant theoretical perspective in political science literature by focusing instead on the inside and outside pressure groups involved with these new civil rights regulatory agencies. First, there is an extensive discussion on when and where the inside pressure groups are, and secondly, there is a similar discussion about the external groups. Finally, there is a brief look at how the relationship between these groups impacts the regulatory efforts of the Title VI and VII agencies.

The Pressure Groups in Civil Rights Enforcement and Regulation

The pressure put on civil rights regulatory agencies tends to come from two directions. The first comes from *inside* forces—institutional forces inside the government itself, like the White House domestic staff and the president, the OMB, the federal regional councils, the federal executive boards, the Commission on Civil Rights, the GAO, and congressional oversight committees. Any or all of these can affect civil rights enforcement and regulations. The *outside* forces include civil rights organizations, the Congressional Black Caucus, individual civil rights leaders, anti–civil rights organizations and their leaders—anyone, in short, who might influence the way any of the agencies or their offices of civil rights compliance enforce civil rights regulations.

Both the insiders and the outside pressure groups can, of course, change public opinion, affecting what Americans deem essential for an American society of equal justice under the law.

Before we can discuss the way pressure groups have affected the enforcement of Title VI and, to some extent, Title VII of the 1964 Civil Rights Acts, we need to examine the way the enforcement process and apparatus is perceived to work in this country. The typical textbook explanation of the federal enforcement process assumes that the president and his domestic staff members monitor cabinet-level departments and agencies to ensure that all actions mandated by congressional legislation are faithfully executed (Figure 5.1). But this simply is not the case. First, the federal enforcement process has become exceedingly complex (Figure 5.2). The president is given recommendations by the (1) Civil Rights Commission, (2) his domestic advisors, (3) OMB, (4) the attorney general, and (5) electoral and financial support groups. Then acting upon this information, on his own initiative, or both, he gives directives to these various political entities for action, all of which falls to the individual cabinet and agency leaders. Once it gets to this level, executive enforcement in some instances can be mixed with legislative enforcement efforts coming through congressional oversight committees that have been advised by the GAO through independent studies requested by those committees. And at this point, both executive and legislative enforcement efforts are passed on to the national offices of civil rights compliance, and they in turn move to the regional offices of civil rights compliance. At this point both the federal regional councils and the federal executive boards can get into the local implementation process. With all of these players in the enforcement process, the reality is a tangled mosaic, a cumbersome and unwieldy mechanism.

If all of the players carried out their specific functions and roles, the problem would consist merely of complexity. But they do not. The truth of the matter is that these players do not carry out their assigned enforcement roles. In the real enforcement process, each group or political entity operates as an advocate or inside pressure group rather than an enforcement body or apparatus (Figure 5.3). This is because, first, it is much easier to play advocate or critic to get something done than it is to move the whole cumbersome process. Secondly, many other goals and objectives of each job in the system are much more important than policy oversight, implementation, and evaluation. For instance, one scholar in assessing the functional roles of the presidency showed that policy oversight, implementation, and enforcement are its lowest priorities. At the top of the list are crisis management and symbolic leadership.[8] Another group of scholars said, "Most domestic programs give out funds or services to state, local, or private groups. This makes it physically impossible or politically unfeasible for the president to keep up supervision." In addition, they write, "Following through on programs is unglamorous and politically risky. Presidents are rarely inclined to have time to pursue it."[9] Oversight and supervision are low-priority matters because "the benefits are scattered and all but invisible."[10] Such work by the president will not generate much positive publicity and national support. Therefore, the president usually plays an advocacy rather than an enforcement role.

Most of the federal establishment, in other words, does not perform an enforcement role. Instead, it performs the function of internal pressure groups. In this chapter we will explore this unrecognized role of the president and the

Figure 5.1
The Textbook Model of the Federal Enforcement Process

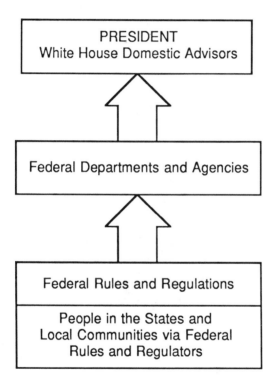

PRESIDENT
White House Domestic Advisors

Federal Departments and Agencies

Federal Rules and Regulations

People in the States and
Local Communities via Federal
Rules and Regulators

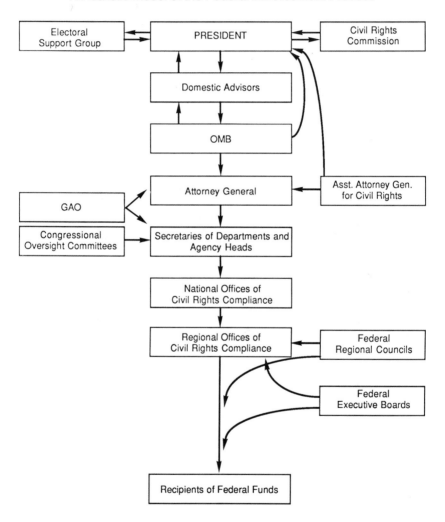

Figure 5.2
A Realistic Model of the Federal Enforcement Process

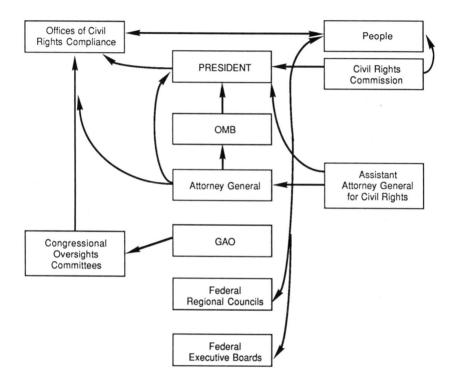

Figure 5.3
Government Insiders as Pressure Groups: Another Realistic Model

White House staff, the OMB, the GAO, the Civil Rights Commission, congressional oversight, and the federal regional councils and executive boards. It is hoped that this type of analysis will provide clear insight into the way internal governmental bodies can shape civil rights regulation and enforcement. At the same time, it will reveal the many access points that various external groups can reach in their efforts to change policy and the vast difficulty that any group can have in truly altering policy.

The Inside Pressure Groups

The president is served both by the White House staff and the Domestic Council. "Although the Domestic Council has a separate budget from that of the White House Office, its staff is generally regarded as an adjunct of the White House Office staff."[11] In 1973 the White House Office Staff employed 510 people and the Domestic Council, seventy-five. However, "despite the size of the White House staff, there was no White House official whose exclusive concern was the oversight of Federal civil rights enforcement. There was also no office in the White House responsible for a broad spectrum of civil rights concerns" during the Nixon and Ford administrations. For instance, "in the summer of 1973, four persons performed civil rights functions on a full-time basis for the White House. At least one of these was actually on the staff of another agency." In addition to these four individuals, "eight other persons directed 25 percent or more of their time to civil rights and when not working on civil rights carried out a variety of other responsibilities."[12]

One of the members of the White House staff who had these responsibilities was black—Stanley S. Scott, the special assistant to President Nixon. This seems to be something of a tradition that goes back to the one black in the Eisenhower administration, E. Frederic Morrow. It continues in the second Reagan administration with Mel Bradley.

The White House staff has scattered its civil rights personnel among at least five different organizational units within the White House. This structure creates "competition among constituent groups, sometimes focusing attention upon status within the White House rather than upon the resolution of" civil rights enforcement concerns.[13] Such a structural arrangement, as was noted in Chapter Two, is highly inefficient, fragmenting a "weak civil rights program with inconsistent oversight of civil rights enforcements." An example of this occurred in December 1972, when the attorney general sent President Nixon a set of revised federal agency regulations implementing Title VI of the Civil Rights Act of 1964. The regulations were not filed by the White House for publication in the *Federal Register* until July 3, 1973.[14]

What caused this six-month delay? President Nixon had signed these regulations on January 27, 1973. They were sent to the files by mistake, rather than to the *Federal Register*, and the error was not detected for six months. Scattered responsibilities and a diverse structure explain this breakdown.

This awkward structure for civil rights regulation continued into the Ford years, with one new factor. The White House staff under President Ford made no attempt to investigate the civil rights backgrounds of individuals being considered for presidential appointment. Members of the Congressional Black Caucus had to offer to assist the president in these areas.

When the Carter administration took office, with its numerous black appointees, civil rights functions were still scattered, but they rested primarily with a black advisor, "Bunny" Mitchell. Her inability to get things done led to an uprising by several civil rights organizations, who publicly criticized her. President Carter responded by removing her to the Small Business Administration and bringing in special advisor Louis B. Martin, a black newspaperman who had worked in several Democratic administrations since the 1940s. When Martin's office was asked about the offices devoted to civil rights compliance in the federal government, one of his assistants replied that they had no such knowledge at their fingertips.[15]

In Reagan's first term, blacks on the White House staff indicated that no one among them was assigned to handle civil rights. That issue, they argued, was dead and did not need any more attention.[16] But by midterm the administration had endured so much criticism that senior advisor, Mel Bradley, decided to become the key staff man concerned with civil rights matters. This arrangement would change before the end of Reagan's first term, when he appointed a controversial black, Clarence Pendleton, to head the reconstituted Civil Rights Commission.[17] Pendleton became the spokesman who articulated the president's anti–civil rights politics during the last stages of his first term and in the four years of the second term. Behind all of Pendleton's bombastic rhetoric, the White House staff remained divided over civil rights.

The Domestic Council was even less organized about carrying out civil rights responsibilities. On July 1, 1970, the reorganization plan that created the OMB created the Domestic Council. Its purpose was to coordinate the formulation of domestic policy and to concern itself with what the government should do, as opposed to OMB's mission, which was to determine how the government should act.

Within the Domestic Council committees are established to conduct methodical analyses of specific issues. "Once a domestic policy issue was passed, a Committee was . . . established" to deal with it. Thus, in April 1971, the White House announced the establishment of a committee on civil rights enforcement.[18] But the committee never met more than three or four times, and each of those was at the request of its chairman, George D. Schultz. Because the committee had never been given specific duties, it ceased to function when

Shultz left in 1973 to become secretary of Treasury.

Under the Ford administration, three members of the council's staff were given permanent civil rights assignments. The first such assignment was in April 1976. These members were to review the reports sent to the White House by the Civil Rights Commission. In so using its council, the Ford administration became the *first* to regularly review the commission's reports. The council staff prepared series of memoranda to the president with recommendations to improve federal civil rights enforcement. Most of these memoranda were responses to major crises or to external deadlines, and not regularly scheduled, routine reports.

Under the Carter and Reagan administrations the council continued its rather negative policy of having to react to a crisis to take action at all. The Reagan administration council makes recommendations not only in terms of a crisis but with the cost-benefit approach in mind. Two important exceptions are the renewal of the Voting Rights Act and enactment of the King Holiday bill. In short, the council does not enforce; it simply pressures the system by making recommendations during a crisis. The same description applies to the council's counterpart, the White House staff.

Another major inside pressure group is OMB. The civil rights responsibilities of OMB include (1) the budgeting of resources, (2) the assessment of the effectiveness of civil rights programs, and (3) the setting of statistical policy in regard to all governmental forms that collect racial, ethnic, and sex data from more than ten individuals.

To carry out these duties, the first director of OMB, George Schultz, in February 1972, "announced that the Associate Director of OMB would monitor and coordinate the overall OMB civil rights efforts."[19] On March 25, 1971, a Civil Rights Unit was established within the General Government Programs Division of OMB, with a staff of two individuals. But in April 1973, that staff was transferred to the Community and Veteran Affairs Division and was eventually phased out. Several staff members with civil rights responsibilities did remain at OMB.

Even though no formal unit of any size existed within OMB, the agency still had certain civil rights functions. Through its budget examination, review, and hearing process, OMB could greatly affect civil rights efforts and protection. "If an OMB budget examiner believed, for example, that an agency program was ineffective or did not produce the desired results or that a proposed agency initiative within that program was inconsistent with administration policy or objectives, then the budget examiner might recommend to senior officials in OMB that the funding for that program may be reduced."[20] Likewise, an examiner might recommend an increase, though in the absence of a meaningful civil rights structure, OMB rarely if ever fulfilled such a function.

OMB could pressure the departments and agencies through program evaluation and assessment. To carry out this responsibility OMB at first developed a Performance Management System but later in 1973 changed that to Management by Objectives (MBO). Under these systems, OMB developed lists of objectives "which they believed to be of priority interest to the president. . . . In order to measure progress toward these objectives, tracking systems were designed and progress reports were to be submitted to OMB for review by management analysts."[21]

Two things happened. First, of the 172 presidential objectives in 1975, three, or 1.7 percent, dealt with civil rights goals; over the years the number has remained quite small. Reagan's first-term objectives were to eliminate as many civil rights regulations as possible. Moreover, no one from OMB ever contacted any staff member with civil rights responsibilities to get his or her insight. No proper assessment and monitoring by the OMB could have taken place.

Second, there is the matter of statistical policy in regard to data collection. OMB has failed to provide for standardized classification of ethnic and racial groups and for standardized forms. "In the absence of such guidance" from OMB, "federal agencies continue to use a variety of identifiers, often collecting data that were not comparable with other agencies and therefore of limited utility." To put it bluntly, without standardization, federal agencies have had to act independently to collect racial, ethnic, and sexual data, and they have cross-classified data as they saw fit.

As if that were not enough, the Reagan administration during its first term urged that OMB not only stop collecting such data but stop using it to determine discrimination.[22] EEOC chairman Clarence Thomas, a black Reagan appointee, told a House Subcommittee on Employment Opportunities that "statistics have been misused to charge discrimination against employers." Thomas testified that "differences between the proportion of blacks, Hispanics or women at a work site and their proportion in the total work force are not proof of discrimination," and he urged the government to stop using statistics as an indicator of possible discrimination.[23]

One final note about OMB's function should be made. Its Legislative Reference Division (LRD) clears "all draft legislative proposals, comments, and testimony transmitted by Federal agencies and Departments to Congress." In addition, it also collects "agency views on enrolled bills, that is legislation awaiting Presidential signature or veto."[24] But throughout its history OMB has not developed a systematic and comprehensive mechanism for seeing to it that all legislation conforms with civil rights laws.

OMB can influence the enforcement process by making budget recommendations, by making program assessments, and by commenting on legislation and shaping statistical policy. Because of its structure and the political concerns of its directors, it has moved from one area to the other, making an impact but inconsistently. One area where it has been consistent is in the budgetary process. The agency has seen many significant drops in the civil rights budget from the earlier years of the Nixon administration to the first term of the Reagan administration. Like the White House staff and the Domestic Council, OMB usually refrains from exerting pressure until an issue has become very heated and controversial. But it has helped to perpetuate confusion because of its lack of standardization in the collection of data, data needed to discern exactly what the government is doing in civil rights regulation.

OMB's rule-making function, however, has been upgraded under Reagan. Prior to 1981, rule-making in the federal government was an essentially decentralized process. Historically, most of this function has been delegated to governmental agencies, not to the president; final discretion as to the shape of such rules was vested in the leaders of the agencies. This power was essentially provided by the Administrative Procedure Act in 1946.[25] Starting in the 1970s several presidents moved to enhance the chief executive's role in the rule-making process. Executive Order 11821, issued by President Ford, required all executive agencies to assess the inflationary impact of proposed regulations; President Carter's Executive Order 12044 required all agencies to anticipate the impact of certain rules and provide several alternatives.

President Reagan in 1981 issued Executive Order 12291, which required that all proposed "major" rules be subject to a cost-benefit analysis before the rules could be implemented and enforced. The measure was part of President's Reagan's promise to eliminate burdensome and unnecessary governmental regulations.

Very shortly after his second term started, President Reagan issued Executive Order 12498.[26]

On January 4, 1985, the President further extended his control over the agency rulemaking process by the issuance of E.O. 12498. Under this new Order, agencies each year are required to establish a regulatory agenda which is subject to review by OMB. The agenda must detail every agency regulatory activity planned or under way, 'including the development of documents that may influence, anticipate, or could lead to the commencement of rule making proceedings at a later date.' The annual agency submissions must 'explain how they are consistent with the Administration's regulatory principles.' If OMB decides that a proposed action is not consistent with those principles, it may not be pursued by an agency. If during the year an agency wants to undertake an activity that was not part of the approved regulatory program, it must seek OMB approval. Thus an agency may not engage in a regulatory activity not approved by OMB unless it is so required by Congress or court order.[27]

After reviewing an agency submission, OMB determines whether a program is consistent with the administration's policies and priorities and may add further regulatory or deregulatory actions. No regulatory action that is materially different from those described in the program as approved may be undertaken by an agency without OMB approval, unless an emergency exists or a judicial or statutory deadline applies. Thus, all agency regulatory action is automatically stayed until OMB approval is received. OMB is authorized to take any actions necessary to implement Executive Order 12498, "to the extent permitted by law."

Under this order OMB enters the rule-making process in the *initial* stage. Executive Order 12291, requiring cost-benefit analysis, had provided OMB that right only in the *final* stage of the rule-making process. Thus, with these two orders President Reagan gave OMB the right to *review* and to *control* agency rule-making from initial formulation to final promulgation.[28] OMB is no longer a mere pressure group in the civil rights regulatory process; it now determines how the rules and regulations covering civil rights compliance can be enforced. It can even kill them in the proposal stage. One environmental group is taking the administration to court to have this Executive Order 12498 declared inoperative. Civil rights groups may join in the litigation.[29]

The legal challenge notwithstanding, OMB, pursuant to Executive Order 12498, issued on August 8, 1985, for the first time ever, "a comprehensive program of regulatory policy to be carried out over the coming year"—(April 1985 - March 31, 1986).[30] This volume, the first in a planned annual series, "describes in detail all of the 'Significant Regulatory Actions' (SRAs) of the 17 agencies included in the Program in this first year. It includes the agency head's overview of the broad regulatory goals, objectives, and purposes of each agency for the forthcoming year, followed by a description of each 'Significant Regulatory Action' upon which one agency plans important actions during the Program year."[31]

In addition, this new document by OMB reveals three levels of regulatory rule-making activity, i.e. (a) a prerule stage (2) a proposed-rule stage and (3) a final-rule stage. The first stage, i.e. prerule stage, is the new and added component. Beyond these stages, each SRA is assigned a permanent Regulation Identifier Number (I.N.).[32] In Table 5.1 are listed all of the 17 departments and agencies included in this initial document and the number of SRAs that each one is contemplating for the first year. Also in the table is the number of SRAs that are devoted to civil rights regulatory practices, as well as the percentage this is to the total number of SRAs offered by the Department and agencies.

The findings are quite clear—of the total 537 SRAs for 1985–1986, only five or one percent are offered by the Title VI civil rights regulatory agencies. This is indeed small. And when this data is seen from the departmental level, only three of seventeen agencies and departments are involved. Both Labor and

EEOC have offered two rules each, while HUD offers only one rule. In terms of each department, a mere two percent of all their SRA deal with civil rights regulatory efforts. And of the EEOC—a surprising forty percent of their SRA deal with civil rights regulations efforts.

Table 5.1 The Number and Percentage of Significant Regulation Actions to Take Place by Title VI Regulatory Agencies – First Year

Agency/Department	Number of SRAs	Civil Rights SRAs	Percentage
Agriculture	34	0	0
Commerce	15	0	0
Education	15	0	0
Energy	5	0	0
Health & Human Services	88	0	0
Housing & Urban Development	42	1	2
Interior	46	0	0
Labor	100	2	2
State	3	0	0
Transportation	71	0	0
Treasury	14	0	0
Environmental Protection Agency	78	0	0
EEOC	5	2	40
General Services Administration	4	0	0
Office of Personnel Management	10	0	0
Small Business Administration	2	0	0
Veterans Administration	5	0	0
Total	537	5	44

SRA – Significant Regulatory Actions
Source: Adapted from OMB, *Regulatory Program of the United States Government April 1, 1985 — March 31, 1986* (Washington, D. C.: Government Printing Office 1985) pp. 3, 5 5–580)

Upon closer examination, the five SRAs include two regulations at the pre-rule stage, one at the proposed-rule stage, and two at the final stage. Hence, three of the five may never get to the final stage given OMB's new powers. Moreover, in terms of the sources and motivations for these new regulatory initiatives, HUD's single regulation is in the final stage and it evolves out of several court interpretations that were basically different. To resolve that problem, HUD offered a new regulation.

Labor's two regulations, one of which is in the proposed stage and one in the final stage, emerge for two different reasons. The proposed regulation is an in-house effort to deal with problems coming from new legislation, particularly the Job Training Partnership Act. The second regulation, which is in the final stage, is designed to revise existing regulations to make them more cost effective and in line with President Reagan's first Executive Order 11246. Although several pressure groups and congressmen opposed this, Labor has proceeded with it anyway.[33]

EEOC has two regulatory rules, both in the pre-rule stage. One emerges from in-house concerns, while the second one arose in response to a GAO report that revealed numerous problems in the commission procedure for "resolving charges of unlawful discrimination filed by federal employees or applicants for federal employment."[34]

In the final analysis then, this initial OMB regulatory document shows that three of these new civil rights regulations were derived from external pressures and only two came from agency initiatives. And in terms of an overall perspective, this new regulatory initiative by OMB seems to have slowed down the development of new civil rights regulatory rules. Whether this present trend will continue, it is difficult to say.

Two other types of federal agencies can pressure the process at the regional and state levels: the Federal Regional Councils (FRCs) and the Federal Executive Boards (FEBs). Executive Order 11647 established the FRCs in 1972. It provides for one of these councils in each of the ten federal regions functioning as an intergovernmental mechanism for eleven grant-making federal agencies. The councils are made up of the departments of Agriculture, Commerce, HEW, HUD, Interior, Labor, Transportation, EPA, Federal Energy Administration, and the LEAA of the Department of Justice. Council members are the senior regional officials of the member agencies. Being primarily responsible for conducting the activities of member agencies and developing "better ways to deliver benefits of Federal Programs over the short term," the councils can be said to have civil rights responsibility by general action rather than by specific statutory authority. Hence, not all of the ten FRCs have concerned themselves with civil rights policy.

In the grant-making process, where the FRCs as a whole can help implement programs, the FRCs as a whole have done very little to date. Only two or three regional offices have bothered to concern themselves with civil rights matters. Lacking the specific statutory authority to do so, the other councils have not ventured into the process. Thus, very little pressure on state officials to correct civil rights problems has come from the FRCs.

The FEBs were established in ten cities by President Kennedy in November 1961. They are the voluntary associations of top regional federal executives, who are instructed to convey presidential policies directly to "Federal agency field offices and to assure their implementation." Nixon changed the thrust of the boards by placing them under the direction of the Bureau of the Budget and later OMB. The Ford administration increased their number, locating them in twenty-six cities, and urged them to look into the energy shortage and the crisis of confidence in government. "FEB authority is limited to member agencies using their combined resources . . . for projects in personnel management or public relations, which individual member agencies could not afford to support alone."[35] FEBs have no independent authority and must "depend upon the voluntary cooperation of their members and guidance from lead agencies, as well as encouragement from the Office of Management and Budget."[36] The boards are traditional types of pressure groups that function at the local level in twenty-six major cities. They exert pressure by disseminating information and encouraging federal employees to work together to solve problems. Most of the FEBs have involved themselves with two civil rights issues: (1) equal employment opportunities for minorities and women, and (2) minority business opportunities. The boards have had difficulty reaching concerted goals in these two areas. "Each FEB conducted its activities through periodic meetings of the full Board, meetings of the policy committee, and meetings of permanent committees on such matters as community services, intergovernmental relations, minority business enterprise and equal opportunity." This meant that "such sizable groups of persons participating only on a voluntary part-time basis in such a loosely structured system resulted in a rather unwieldly organization which was not conducive to effective decision-making."[37] The FEB can at best exert pressure only through dissemination and persuasion and at only the local level in twenty-six cities—a very limited scope of action, considering the reach of the federal government.

Another federal agency considered to be important in the enforcement process is the General Accounting Office (GAO). The GAO was established in 1921 by the Budget and Accounting Act to (1) "assist Congress in carrying out its legislative and oversight responsibilites" and (2) to "recommend more efficient and effective government operations." The GAO investigates and recommends.[38]

Responding to a request from a congressional committee, a cabinet department, or a federal agency, the GAO can review civil rights enforcement and regulatory policies and report its findings and its recommendation. At the author's request, GAO did a bibliographic search of its data base in the subject area of civil rights and related matters from 1964–1984 and found that it had produced twenty-three reports after reviewing sundry federal civil rights programs. The GAO reports fall into two distinct categories—those reports dealing with specific federal agencies and those dealing with federal civil rights laws (Table 5.2). GAO was called upon continually to review the civil rights efforts of HEW. Its reviews of EEOC, another controversial agency, and of the Justice Department were also numerous. One request for a review came from Congressman G. V. Montgomery, who felt that the Justice Department was focusing unfairly on Mississippi, processing complaints in his state faster than in other states. The GAO review found otherwise. Another rather controversial agency was the Office of Revenue Sharing; many congressmen received complaints that revenue-sharing funds were being spent in a discriminatory fashion. GAO found that the agency needed to improve its enforcement, coordination and compliance review efforts.

Table 5.2   GAO Investigations of Federal Civil Rights Enforcement 1964–1984

Department & Agencies Investigated	Number of Reports	%
Reports Dealing with Departments		
HEW: Education; Health and Human Services	7	30.4
EEOC	4	17.4
Justice	3	13.0
Office of Revenue Sharing (Treasury)	2	8.7
Internal Revenue Service	1	4.3
Labor	1	4.3
Defense	1	4.3
Farmers' Home Administration (Agriculture)	1	4.3
Reports Dealing with Civil Rights Law		
Title VI	1	4.3
Voting Rights Act, 1965	1	4.3
Federal Laws and Executive Orders for Nondiscrimination Compliance	1	4.3
Total	23	99.6

Source: Abstracted from sixty-eight page GAO computer printout given to author on October 17, 1984. Later, at author's request, GAO furnished copies of most of the reports.

GAO was called upon early in 1980 by the House Committee on the Judiciary's Subcommittee on Civil and Constitutional Rights to assess the actions taken by various federal agencies to implement Title VI of the Civil Rights Act of 1964. GAO sent questionnaires to the agencies "to determine their perception of their Title VI responsibilities and how they ensure compliance." The response revealed that as late as March 1980 many federal agencies were unclear about which activities were covered by Title VI responsibilities and how they could ensure compliance. And in its report to the subcommittee "GAO recommended that the Attorney General direct Justice's Civil Rights Division to clarify criteria and cite examples for agencies to use in determining which federal assistance activities and programs are covered by Title VI and provide technical assistance to, and review the determination of, Title VI coverage of those agencies uncertain about Title VI."[39]

The GAO survey and the subsequent analysis of that material reveals that although each federal agency is required to develop guidelines for use in implementing and enforcing their Title VI responsibilities, the Justice Department up until early 1980 had simply "*Failed to insure that these requirements are being met.*" GAO, therefore, recommended that the attorney general or his staff ensure that requirements are implemented and that enforcement monitoring be improved. It recommended that the Justice Department's regulations be amended to: (1) provide for reviews and approval of agencies' Title VI guidelines, (2) require agencies to collect racial and ethnic data for their programs, and (3) develop criteria for agencies' use in conducting on-site compliance reviews.[40]

Another GAO report on civil rights laws came out in February 1978, this one on the Voting Rights Act. The GAO found that the enforcement of the act needed considerable strengthening. As GAO saw it, the purpose of the act had not been fully realized because: (1) the Justice Department had "not adequately monitored jurisdictions to determine whether they submitted their proposed election law changes for review," (2) there was no way to determine the effectiveness of the examiner and observer programs in the absence of sufficient data, (3) the litigative efforts had been limited, (4) the language provisions of the act did not cover all minorities needing assistance, and, finally, (5) vague guidelines and the department's failure to provide assistance had hampered the implementation of minority language provisions.

The weaknesses the GAO survey uncovered are readily observed in concrete cases. For instance, when the city of Savannah decided to annex part of the county and reduce black political strength in the city from more than fifty percent to below forty percent, the city fathers held a local referendum, but did not let citizens in the area to be annexed vote on their own fate. The newly-ratified city government had eight aldermen, two of them black; the old board had consisted of six aldermen, two being black. Blacks went from holding one-third of the aldermanic board to holding one-fourth. The formation of this new city government was submitted to the Justice Department as an accomplished fact, not for advance approval, which was in clear violation of civil rights rules and regulations.

Even though several national newspapers covered this violation, nothing was done. Columnist Jack Anderson suggested that the reason was that the attorney general, Griffin Bell, was from Georgia, and his son had been hired at a huge salary by the city to serve the school board as an attorney.[41] Despite these revelations, nothing was done; as of this writing the city remains as annexed. This is but one of a legion of examples of the Justice Department's failure to litigate in support of the Voting Rights Act.[42]

The last GAO report in Table 5.2 compiled federal laws and executive orders for nondiscrimination and equal opportunity programs, bringing together for the first time all of the various federal civil rights laws.[43] The Subcommittee on the Constitution of the Committee on the Judiciary of the United States Senate would follow suit four years later and publish its own list of laws.[44]

Overall, the GAO found several weaknesses in the structure, the enforcement, and the implementation and administrative procedures of the federal government's regulation of civil rights law. Yet all it could do was recommend, since it had no real jurisdiction over any of these federal agencies. The agencies could claim, as they usually did, that the GAO study was flawed, and they could continue functioning as usual. The best that GAO could hope for was that the congressional committees would follow through on some of its recommendations, which happened once, when the Voting Rights Act was renewed in 1982.

One final example will further highlight the role of the GAO.[45] On June 3, 1971, the chairman of the House Committee on the Judiciary, Emanuel Celler, requested in a letter to the GAO that the agency examine whether hospitals, extended care facilities (ECFs), and nursing homes, participating in Medicare or Medicaid were complying with Title VI of the Civil Rights Act.

By October 1971, the GAO had visited sixty-six hospitals, forty-one ECFs, and two nursing homes in Atlanta, Georgia; Birmingham, Alabama; Wayne County, Michigan; and Los Angeles County, California. In these four locations the GAO interviewed seventy-nine physicians, forty-eight nurses, eighty-nine patients, and representatives of seventy-three civil rights groups, medicaid societies, and community organizations. GAO found that "shortly after Medicare and Medicaid were enacted, HEW made extensive efforts to enforce Title VI compliance. . . .(but) now makes relatively few onsite visits to hospitals, ECFs, or nursing homes." Instead, HEW was relying more on information reported by institutions participating in Medicare and Medicaid.[46] The GAO also found that (1) there was a disproportionate use of government-owned hospitals by minority groups, and (2) minority group patients tended to cluster at certain health care facilities.

In its report GAO made certain recommendations to the chairman based on its findings, but it was nearly two years—(September 12, 17, 24, and October 1, 1973)—before the Subcommittee on Civil Rights and Constitutional Rights held a hearing on the GAO's findings. Even after four days of hearings that elaborated further on these findings, the committee did little more than accept the words of Peter Holmes, the director of the Office of Civil Rights at HEW, that he would improve the department's efforts in this area. "I think," he told the chairman of the subcommittee, Don Edwards, "you also will be interested to know that our office is preparing a brochure and a poster emphasizing the rights of recipients of care at Medicaid and Medicare facilities to be free of discriminating treatment. The subject also will be stressed by my staff at upcoming meetings with the National Urban League and the Leadership Conference on Civil Rights and we will make available the brochures and posters for distribution by these organizations."[47] The solution to the apparent maldistribution of care was simple; merely to get out more information and give some of it to civil rights organizations.

Commenting on a later GAO report that dealt with the health care of blacks, Professors Mitchell R. Rice and Woodrow Jones, Jr., stated that in terms of "compliants concerning hospitals' failure in meeting their free care obligation" and in terms of "community services," the Department of Health and Human Services had a poor and sorry performance record of enforcements and, "Blacks must utilize the courts and other avenues of enforcements" to address their problems.[48]

The point here is that whatever the GAO finds and recommends, Congress and the federal agencies and departments must be the ones to implement remedies and correct problems and inadequacies.

Another pressure group inside the government that must operate solely on the force of persuasion is the United States Commission on Civil Rights. Employing every type of persuasion known—telephone calls, letter writing, meetings, conferences, reports, investigations, news conferences, hearings, giving testimony, providing expert witnesses and materials, using connections, heaping praise, and issuing strongly worded verbal attacks—the commission has tried to use its extremely limited fact-finding mission to promote civil rights enforcement and effective civil rights regulation in America. Simply by using tactics of persuasion, the commission has attracted criticism from several presidents, many attacks from the bureaucracy, and nearly endless criticism from the right-wing conservative elements in American society.

Finally, during President Reagan's first term in office, he tried to fire the liberal members of the commission—the federal courts reinstated them—and proposed to completely reconstitute the commission more along the lines of his conversative views. In a letter of November 3, 1983, to Senate Majority Leader Howard H. Baker, Jr., President Reagan wrote: "The leading features of my proposal (are) a twenty-year extension of the Commission's life (the largest in history) and staggered, fixed terms for the members." However, the "House rejected the idea" and also adopted "a provision which stated that Commissioners could in the future be removed only for cause."[49] President Reagan eventually urged Senator Baker to pass the House bill.

However, the newly reauthorized commission created by Congress provided that the Congress and the president could each now choose one-half of the membership of the commission; earlier, the president appointed all the members of the commission. The chairman of the commission was to be selected by the president himself. Reagan appointed a black conservative, Clarence Pendleton, to head the new body. It was not long before Pendleton's savage attacks upon such civil rights programs as affirmative action goals, comparable worth, and civil rights enforcement led one black newspaper columnist, Carl T. Rowan, to call for the abolition of the commission. He wrote, "If Congress wants to show President Reagan that it is sincere about reducing spending and the federal deficit, it might vote swiftly to abolish the U.S. Civil Rights Commission." He continued: "Under the leadership of Clarence Pendleton, the Civil Rights Commission has become an arrogant enemy of the most abused, most miserable, most helpless people in the land." As Rowan saw it: "Pendleton, his deputy Morris Abrams and a majority of the Commission are waging war on the civil rights movement."[50]

"Pendleton," argued Rowan, "labels blacks of the NAACP, the Urban League and other groups—people who endured cattle prods, fire hoses, police dogs, jail terms and more—the 'new racists.' He has given great comfort to those whites who recoil at any suggestion that white racism is still rampant in America."[51] Rowan felt that Congress had created the commission to be an ally of the civil rights movement but that now the commission was being turned against its own friends.

Rowan was not alone in being enraged by Reagan's new chairman. *The Washington Post* editorialized: "If the Reagan administration has any hope at all of improving its relationship with blacks, something is going to have to be done about the prose of Clarence Pendleton, Jr., Chairman of the United States Commission Civil Rights. If the Commission as an institution wants to maintain any credibility as an independent body exploring and seeking to remedy problems of racial conflict, individual commissioners are going to have to speak quietly to the chairman or speak out loudly to counter some of his assaults."[52]

President Reagan not only selected a chairman who took an unprecedented position on civil rights on the commission's behalf, he created a new leadership position for the commission, one that changed the direction of the commission itself. He let it be known that the commission under Pendleton would cease investigating racial and sexual discrimination and stop studying and issuing reports on the same. Thus, in the early days of his second term, Reagan reversed the thrust of this governmental pressure group. In fact, this commission redefined the problem and the solution: civil rights leaders, it has said, are the problem, and they must be pressured into silence, or pushed out of leadership roles in the black community.

Before the commission was reconstituted along conservative ideological lines, it issued volume VI of its Federal Civil Rights Enforcement Effort in 1974, dealing specifically with Title VI agencies. The report offers the most comprehensive and systematic history of the evolution of Title VI agencies.

The Commission also made recommendations to the president, his White House staff, the Domestic Council, and OMB that the coordination and direction of civil rights enforcement be moved up to the executive suite, specifically, to OMB.[53] The commission felt that pressure tactics were ineffective and that the president and his executive staff would have to move to take full control of an enforcement process that was drifting, with only a hit-or-miss record of achievement. Needless to say, the recommendation was not followed.

Another category of internal pressure groups that has exerted some influence on the federal civil rights bureaucracy is the congressional committees that exercise legislature oversight. "Legislature oversight," according to Morris Ogul, "is behavior by legislators and their staff, individually or collectively, which result in an impact intended or not, on bureaucratic behavior."[54] He continues: "Congress oversees essentially through its committees and subcommittees." Subcommittee Five of the House Judiciary Committee has responsibility and broad jurisdiction for civil rights bills and oversight investigations.

Despite the fact that this subcommittee has jurisdiction and it can impact bureaucratic behavior, oversight does not routinely occur. Why? One scholar has written: "Policy oversight requires disciplined analysis, hard work, perspective, time to reflect, and detachment from the agency one oversees. All of these commodities are in short supply in the harried and increasingly specialized Congress of today."[55] Another scholar notes: "Congressmen tend to see opportunities for greater rewards in the things they value, more from involvement in legislative and constituent-service than from participation in oversight activity."[56] Therefore, congressmen are on the make for the "quick fix" and they must be shown that an "issue will make them look good" before they will take it on. "Most issues of general policy oversight, however, involve long standing and fairly intractable problems, ones in which the risk of looking bad is high."[57]

Morris Ogul, who assessed the legislative oversight activities of Subcommittee Five, from 1965 until 1971, found not only these problems but several others as well. First, he discovered that the chairman of the subcommittee, Rep. Emanuel Celler (D - N.Y.) was also chair of the overall House Judiciary Committee. This meant that the chairman was literally strapped for time to have formal oversight hearings.

Secondly, because Chairman Celler did not like to be turned down for an appropriations request, he never got enough money for Subcommittee Five to conduct investigations. Ogul writes: "Celler did not request it (money). . . . because he anticipated that his request might not be honored. One member in particular said that he had to use his own money to visit southern communities to see how civil rights legislation was working out."[58]

Thirdly, civil rights oversight was controversial, and Rep. Celler "was not anxious for a clash with the Justice Department." Therefore, no oversight took place, until a rebellion on the committee forced a special ad hoc advisory committee in October 1966 and a threat by the House Rules Committee, in the same month, that it would take civil rights jurisdiction for itself. Then Rep. Celler created Subcommittee Five in November 1966 and held its first hearing in December of the same year. Few additional hearings were held and Celler transferred jurisdiction for civil rights oversight to Subcommittee Four in February 1971.[59]

Thus, over the years, only a very *modest* amount of civil rights oversight took place by the subcommittees of the House Judiciary Committee, and the most recent oversight hearing has had little impact on an administration determined to reduce enforcement regulations.[60] Thus, while congressional oversight can be an internal pressure force, internal problems on the committee and an unsympathetic presidential administration can cause this pressure to have no more impact than the mere issurance of hearings and reports. Like its counterparts, pressuring through congressional oversight is a limited device and technique.

The most recent example of congressional oversight of civil rights regulatory action came in March 25, 1986 when the Subcommittee on Civil and Constitutional Rights held a hearing on the GAO's audit of the U.S. Commission on Civil Rights. The second day of hearings took place on April 22, 1986. The chairman of the subcommittee, Congressman Don Edwards (D-Calif.) opened with the following remarks.

> The subcommittee has had, for a long time, oversight and authorization jurisdiction over the U.S. Commission on Civil Rights. In the last 2½ years since the Commission was reconstituted, this subcommittee has been concerned that the Commission's historic factfinding mission was no longer being carried out. The Commission has issued only one report, on comparable worth, during this time. Until this subcommittee held oversight hearings last fall, not a single State Advisory Committee report had been issued. No reports have been issued analyzing Federal civil rights enforcement, in a period when the Reagan administration's efforts have been under increasing attack.
>
> During this period, the subcommittee received numerous and disturbing reports about the activities of the Commission. In order to objectively investigate these allegations, and to examine whether the Commission is meeting its mandate as a factfinding agency, last summer I joined with three other chairs, Mr. Hawkins of the Committee on Education and Labor, Mrs. Schroeder of the Subcommittee on Civil Service, who also sits on this subcommittee, and Mr. Martinez of the Subcommittee on Employment Opportunities, in requesting the General Accounting Office to do a comprehensive audit of the Commis-

sion. Today, the GAO will share with us their findings to date. Their findings have already been leaked right and left to the press, so this is a little bit late this morning, but that seems to be a way of life around here.[61]

As the chairman noted, just prior to the hearing a copy of the GAO's audit was leaked to the press, in an attempt to embarass both the leaders of the commission and President Reagan, who appointed the Chairman.[62] The GAO audit report indicated that since the commission had been reconstituted under the chairmanship of Clarence Pendleton, several irregularities have occurred in hiring, expenditures of funds, acceptance of gifts, lobbying against the Civil Rights Restoration Acts of 1985, grants of noncompetitive contracts, the use and employment of friends, promotions of a conservative ideology, "missing records and inept management."[63]

In addition, during the hearing, the two liberal members of the commission, Commissioners Blandina Cardeness Ramirez and Mary Frances Berry, revealed that not only was the agency out of control but that there was missing money—some $225,000—that was not accounted for.[64] It was all these issues that the congressional oversight hearing sought to address.

However, immediately after the hearing started, congressional supporters of President Reagan, Chairman Pendleton, and other conservatives ideologues on the Committee began by attacking the report and the subcommittee for holding hearings. Later these same foes would attack Commissioner Berry and her joint statement. As they saw it, the commission was doing nothing wrong. Congressman F. James Sensenbrenner, Jr. (R-Wis.), who led the opposition to the hearing and the report, made the following comments.

> *Mr. Sensenbrenner.* Thank you, Mr. Chairman. Once again I must state that I am very disturbed about the witch hunt of the Civil Rights Commission that is being conducted by this subcommittee. It rather reminds me of the Red Queen in Alice in Wonderland, who said, "Verdict first, trial afterwards."
> There is no doubt that the GAO audit has been recklessly wielded against the Commission by its political adversaries who oppose its policies. One need only look at this sample list of procedural irregularities in the way this audit was requested and conducted.[65]

Although the entire hearing was beset with charges and countercharges, some very interesting facts came to light. For instance, Congressman John Conyers (D. - Mich.) in questions to attorney Morris Abrams, the vice chairman of the commission, revealed that Abrams recommended for employment on the commission, his son's college roommate, Matthew Cooper. Cooper was subsequently hired at a GS-7 grade and later wrote an article attacking the commission.

Abram also recommended for employment another one of his son's college friends, David Schwartz, who was also employed by the commission.[66]

The hearing also revealed that the commission hired as consultants several individuals who had taken either anti–civil rights stands or positions against affirmative action and quotas. Amongst these were Professors Nathan Glazer, Glenn Loury, Claudia Goldin, and Sidney Hooks; most of these individuals would write negative articles for the commission publication, *New Perspectives*.[67] For instance, Glazer, who was a hired consultant, gave an extensive interview to *New Perspective* in which he argued that affirmative action for blacks had to be resisted because other groups in the years ahead would want the same thing. Thus, it was a bad precedent to give it to blacks.[68] Equality for one group had to be denied because such a concept would have to be extended to others entering American society.

Finally, the transcripts of the hearing revealed that the testimonies of the chairman and vice chairman were almost verbatim in some of their comments and sources of support. In defending the actions of the commission during his term, Pendleton wrote: "I remain devoted to the original principles of the civil rights movement as outlined by Dr. Martin Luther King, with whom I stood; Roy Wilkins, whom I loved; and Hubert Humphrey, who was my stalwart ally." Then, the chairman turned to Thomas Sowell's remarks about the commission in his defense.[69]

Vice Chairman Abrams wrote: "I remain devoted to the original principles of the civil rights movement as outlined by Dr. Martin Luther King, Jr., Roy Wilkins and Hubert Humphrey." Then, Abrams used the same quote from Thomas Sowell to bolster his point.[70] Both men, in their defense of the commission, made nearly identical remarks and called upon the same black conservative economist as proof that the commission was doing its job.

In the final analysis, however, despite their findings, these hearings didn't generate enough support to have Pendleton removed from the chairmanship of the commission, nor did they succeed in getting enough congressional support to have the Civil Rights Restoration Act of 1985 (see Appendix E) pass *both* houses and become law.

The hearings did, on the other hand, generate some discussions about *defunding* the commission and some reports that the commission would be directed to cut its staff and operations. Based on these reports that its budget would be cut from 11.5 million to six million, the commission itself voted to slash its staff. Chairman Pendleton, "who shares many of Mr. Reagan's views on civil rights issues, sees both the House and Senate measures as efforts to force him to step down."[71]

Senator Frank R. Lautenberg, (D -N.J.) who was sponsoring the bill to reduce the commission budget, indicated that his action came from the GAO report that noted that "the Commission had failed to prepare reports Congress mandated."[72] Despite Senator Lautenberg's argument, the reality of the matter is that on July 17, 1986 the House of Representatives voted to terminate the operations of the Civil Rights Commission (H.R. 5161) on the basis of the criticism in the GAO report. However, the Senate Appropriations Committee in acting on H.R. 5161 reduced the Civil Rights Commission's appropriation but refused to terminate it. Therefore, a compromise was worked out. Instead of passing H.R. 5161, Congress passed a continuing resolution, H.J. Res. 738 which provided for maintaining the Commission with reduced funding but placing certain restrictions on the use of certain funds. These restrictions involved: (1) a limitation on hiring consultants, (2) limitation on compensation for commissioners and their special assistants, (3) limitation on funds for research contracts, (4) and a limitation on research contract funds. Finally, Congress earmarked specific funds for certain Commission operations. On October 18, 1986 President Reagan signed H.J. RE. 73873, (P.L. 99–500). Hence, *defunding became reduced funding*. Though an oversight committee might want strong and forceful action, the executive branch or Senate might not go along with it or might find ways to get around it.

Another source of oversight activity, has been the unending efforts of black Congressman Augustus Hawkins (D-Calif.), who chairs the House Committee on Education and Labor which oversees both the EEOC and the Department of Labor's Office of Federal Contract Compliance. Since President Reagan's appointment of a black conservative, the attorney Clarence Thomas, to head up the commission[74] in 1982, Congressman Hawkins and his Subcommittee on Employment Opportunities have been extremely active in conducting hearings, writing letters to the president, and issuing reports on the EEOC.

In a committee report, based on the investigation of civil rights enforcement by the EEOC, that was itself based on a study of selected district offices, Congressman Hawkin's committee found that the EEOC (1) had shifted enforcement policies only to "identified victims," and not to class action cases; (2) had a new enforcement policy as of September 11, 1984, which requires a higher standard of proof to establish reasonable causes; and (3) had new policy directives which have created confusion as what constitutes "full relief." Further, (4) the commission's acting general counsel has orally directed the commission's regional attorneys not to recommend the use of goals and time tables and not to intervene in cases which they were proposed as a remedy for discrimination, (5) that the greater emphasis put on rapid closure had come at the expense of the quality of the investigation. (6) that virtually no fact-finding conferences were being conducted by most district offices before they initiated settlement negotiations, and (7) there were several other negative administrative and personnel practices.

The report offered eight policy and seven administrative and personnel practices recommendations. The report closed by saying, "It is hoped that the findings . . . will be used . . . by the EEOC to improve the efficiency of the agency's operation as prescribed by the civil rights statutes under its mandate."[75] However, in OMB's regulatory program for the 1985-1986 year, the EEOC mentioned none of these oversight committee concerns, nor drafted any SRAs to deal with them.[76]

Congressman Hawkins' Subcommittee on Employment Opportunities held a hearing on the Department of Labor's Office of Federal Contract Compliance, and Congressman Hawkins made an opening statement which indicated that "First, actual enforcement personnel were only 45% of all OFCCP personnel. This suggests that the agency is managerially top heavy and that insufficient funds are being used to perform the most essential functions of the OFCCP program. Second, that procedures for enforcement prevent the actual enforcement in a complete, timely and economical way."[77] But once again the findings from the hearing didn't force any SRAs in the Department of Labor's regulatory program.[78]

Beyond merely holding hearings and issuing reports that make recommendations, Congressman Hawkins has been very active in testifying at other oversight hearings and in matters connected with issues of employment discrimination. For instance, when the U.S. Senate Committee on Labor and Human Resources convened on July 23, 1986, to act on President Reagan's renomination of attorney Clarence Thomas to head the commission for another four years, Congressman Hawkins sent his objections in written testimony to the chairman of the committee, Senator Orrin C. Hatch (R -Utah):

> I have three principal reservations concerning Mr. Thomas' proposed second five year term at the EEOC.
> 1) I am concerned about Mr. Thomas's policies relating to Equal Employment Opportunity Law, including the use of goals and timetables as a remedy for employment discrimination, and the use of statistics to prove discrimination;
> 2) I am troubled about the way in which Chairman Thomas has conducted the business and policy-making of the EEOC, in possible contravention of the administrative procedure act and the "government in the sunshine" act;
> 3) And lastly, I am concerned about recurring problems relating to the EEOC's administrative enforcement practices under his chairmanship.[79]

In addition to these comments, Congressman Hawkins asked that the aforementioned report be made part of the nomination hearing record, in part because the chairman and the commission had failed to act on them.[80]

Beside the testimony of Congressman Hawkins, there was that of Congressman Don Edwards, chairman of the Subcommittee on Civil and Constitutional Rights;[81] Congressman Charles Hayes (D-Ill.); and Congressman Matthew C. Martinez (D-Calif.), Chairman of the Subcommittee on Employment Opportunities. They were joined by the joint testimony of the Black Leadership Forum (consisting of the heads of fifteen major civil rights organizations) and some four women's organizations.[82] Finally, all of this too came to naught; beside a promise to Senator Ted Kennedy (D-Mass.) that he would start unholding the law, Chairman Thomas was reappointed. This occurred despite voluminous reports and hearings that his office had achieved little, if anything, during his first term.

Understanding that the efforts of his numerous oversight hearings, testimony, and investigative report hadn't corrected much in the regulatory behavior of EEOC, Congressman Hawkins wrote and sponsored legislation—H.R. 700, better known as the Civil Rights Restoration Act of 1985—and held joint hearings on the act to help its passage. Extensive hearings were held in Pennsylvania; Washington, DC; Georgia; Illinois; California; and New Mexico at which nearly every civil rights leader in the country was permitted to testify.[83] The bill, H.R. 700, was favorably voted out of the Committee on Education and Labor (29–2) and the Subcommittee on Civil and Constitutional Rights (5–3) and the full Committee on the Judiciary (21–12). It became "stalled because of a dispute over abortion."[84] Because the abortion problem was never resolved, even though the Congressional Black Caucus met with the Catholic Conference, the bill died once again—this time in the House. A similar bill in 1984 died in the Senate.[85] Finally, these vigorous oversight efforts and legislation to mandate improvements in the enforcement of Title VI and VII ended in failure. Thus, a new act was introduced in the 100th Congress. On January 28, 1988, the Senate by a vote of 75–14 passed the legislation and on March 3 the House passed the measure by a vote of 315–98. President Reagan, however, had indicated that he plans to veto the bill.

In perhaps one of the most profound commentaries on the passage of civil rights laws, Professor Gaye Hewitt has remarked:

> A combination of the ideas and interests of legislators, and the written and unwritten rules of Congressional procedures allow the minority to thwart the will of the majority in the enactment of Civil Rights legislation. Failure to achieve equal accommodation of the races politically, economically, or socially through appropriate legislation is a result of preconceived ideas of Negro inferiority working in and through individuals and institutions to further the interests of one group at the expense of another. . . .

Thus, Civil Rights legislation in the United States has not provided adequate protection for the civil and political rights of minority groups in accordance with the basic values of American society.[86] In the end, another bill might just mean more inadequate enforcement.

Besides Congressman Hawkins himself, his committee and subcommittee, and the subcommittee of Congressman Don Edwards, another committee that has been doing oversight investigation in the case of civil rights regulatory agencies under Title VI and Title VII, is the House Committee on Government Operations and several of its subcommittees. For instance, in one of its reports, the Subcommittee on Intergovernmental Relations and Human Resources found in its "investigation of Civil Rights Enforcement by the Office for Civil Rights at the Department of Education," numerous problems and inadequate enforcement of Title VI requirements. This report found the following problems and made some nine recommendations. They are:

FINDINGS

A. OCR and DOJ have failed to obtain complete enforcement remedies in cases where serious violations of law were found.

B. OCR ignored the internal findings of its quality assurance staff, and instead of acting on the Service's recommendations, disbanded it.

C. OCR will now rely on a good faith standard, rather than actual achievements, in measuring the success of desegregation plans, despite its internal findings that many systems of higher education have not eliminated the vestiges of illegal dual systems of education.

D. OCR cannot ensure that more than 300 cases settled by early complaint resolution were resolved according to Federal law and DOED regulations, and will not jeopardize future litigation involving violations of civil rights laws enacted by Congress.

E. OCR is studying methods to substitute technical assistance for compliance reviews, a switch that OCRs own Policy and Enforcement Service considers illegal.

F. Despite insufficient resources, OCR has not used all funds appropriated by Congress for the enforcement of Federal civil rights laws.

G. OCR has weakened its criteria for verifying compliance information submitted by recipients of Federal education funds.

RECOMMENDATIONS

A. OCR should develop guidelines for the use of its two methods of enforcement.

B. OCR should not rely solely on the good faith standard in measuring the success of desegregation plans.

C. OCR should develop guidelines for the resolution of discrimination complaints by early complaint resolution and pre-letter of finding negotiations.

D. OCR should develop guidelines ensuring that all settlements of cases where violations of laws are found actually correct the violations.

E. OCR should use the Magnet School Assistance program more effectively as a means to monitor school systems' compliance with Federal civil rights laws.[87]

In one of the most poignant findings of the report, it was shown that in Dillion County, South Carolina, OCR (Office of Civil Rights Compliances) simply let the country violate the law. In fact, "eight years after the initial violation of the law was found, OCR had finally begun enforcement proceedings, but only after prodding from the *Adams* court (decision) and the subcommittee."[88]

Despite this committee report and its recommendations about the vast problem that the Department of Education had in enforcing Title VI regulations, this same department did not acknowledge them in OMB's regulatory document, nor did it list any SRAs designed to deal with them. Neither did it indicate any regulations that would improve program accountability and management on these matters.[89] Thus another attempt at oversight was simply overlooked.

In the same year, the House Committee on Government Operations issued another oversight report. This report dealt with the EEOC and the National Endowment for the Humanities.

On January 15, 1984, Dr. William J. Bennett, Chairman of the National Endowment for the Humanities (NEH), wrote to Clarence Thomas, Chairman of the Equal Employment Opportunity Commission (EEOC), to announce that NEH no longer planned to comply with the Federal directive which requires all Federal agencies to annually submit hiring and promotion goals and timetables for its work forces.[90]

But once this occurred, the chairman of the EEOC took no action. The report stated the problem in this manner, "NEH, in refusing to set goals, is in violation of its statutory obligation to comply with EEOC's regulations. However, as EEOC Chairman Clarence Thomas noted in a Subcommittee hearing on this issue, EEOC has no power to compel agencies to comply with its directives."[91] The Committee report, however, noted that: "Thus, the EEOC appears to be within its authority in requiring that the affirmative plans of equal employment opportunity submitted to it by federal departments and agencies contain numerical employment goals for minorities and women."[92] And the report blamed the commission for a failure to act. Once again the oversight report had no impact. Nothing came of the report.

One final oversight effort which deals with Title VII matters inside the federal government should be even more revealing. In his opening statement at the hearing, on October 8, 1985 Congressman Barney Frank, (D-Mass.), Chairman of the Subcommittee on Employment and Housing of the Committee on Government Operations said:

> This is one of a series of hearings we have been having pursuant to our jurisdiction to engage in oversight of the Equal Employment Opportunity Commission. We have had several hearings dealing with the question of sex discrimination in employment. Today we are going to return to a topic we have touched on some, central to the functioning of the Equal Employment Opportunity Commission, and that is its jurisdiction over antidiscrimination complaints lodged by employees of the Federal Government itself.
>
> Obviously nothing can be more important than for the Federal Government itself to be efficient and fair in dealing with complaints of discrimination that are made by Federal employees against the Federal structure.
>
> If the Federal Government cannot itself abolish discrimination against its own employees, its ability to impose national policies of fairness is going to be severely hampered. And I think it ought to be absolutely insisted upon in every area of the Federal policy role that the Federal Government has to hold itself to the highest possible standard if it is going to have any effect whatsoever in dealing with the private sector.[93]

While Congressman Frank indicated that this hearing arose as a bipartisan effort, another possible reason could have been the increasing number of complaints coming to congresspersons because of President Reagan's effort to reduce the size of the federal government. Two public policy specialists write: "President Reagan's determination to reduce the size of the federal government and to control federal spending has resulted in an unprecedented preoccupation with reductions-in-force (RIFs) and other adverse job actions among federal employees."[94]

They go on to show in great detail and specificity how this Reagan project adversely impacted minorities in the federal sector. They concluded:

> In its first report on December 30, 1981, the task force indicated that between January and October 1981 'minorities were RIFed at 1½ times the rate of nonminorities, or, simply stated, for every 2 non-

minority employees RIFed, three minority employees were RIFed.' In addition, the task force indicated that four minority employees were affected by an adverse personnel action such as a downgrade or a lateral reassignment for every three non-minority employees. This represented the first substantial wave of reductions-in-force during the Reagan administration.

In its third-quarter fiscal year 1982 report, the task force indicated that within the quarter, minorities experienced 33.41 percent of the total reductions-in-force, although they are only 19.9 percent of the total federal work force. Minority women received a higher share of RIF related actions (10.5 percent) than minority men (14 percent). Minority women experienced 26.48 percent of the lateral reassignments, compared to 8.43 percent for minority men. However, minority men were the victims of more downgrades and discontinued service retirements (two actions more severe than lateral reassignments). Minority men experienced 18.8 percent of the down grades, compared to 12.9 percent for minority women. Similarly, 19.8 percent of the discontinued service retirements were minority men, while 9.38 percent were minority women.[95]

Complaints about this flowed into offices handling Title VII matters. Yet these complaints were not handled in a timely manner. Table 5.3 illustrates the number of complaints in 1983 and 1984 in each department or agency and the number of days it took to process the complaint. In 1983, it took a complaint from as little as a year to a full four years to be heard. By 1984, the range in terms of time still stood at nearly a year—but as long as five years in the Environmental Protection Agency.

Table 5.4 highlights the six slowest agencies in handling complaints. Thus, using the government-wide average, it shows that in 1984 it took nearly three times as long in the EPA and Justice to get a federal complaint heard. This data brings us once again to the issues raised in Chapter Two about combined offices and the cut back in staff. Although this data doesn't prove impact, in terms of structural arrangements and staff size, it does suggest a negative impact on regulatory effectiveness.

Moreover, this oversight data illustrates that not only did blacks lose their federal employment, but that the agency created to deal with such problems, literally took its time. Hence, blacks had little or no job protection afforded by the federal civil rights regulatory agencies. The civil rights regulatory agency was, as the hearings revealed, near disfunctional. And all that the hearings got from the chairman was a promise to improve the system and assurances that a practical program to do it was working.

Two reports and one hearing by the Committee on Government Operations

Table 5.3   Average Number of Days to Closure of EEO Complaints by Agency Decision FY 1983 and 1984

	FY 1984		FY 1983	
Agency or Department	Number of Complaints	Average Days	Number of Complaints	Average Days
Agency for International Development	5	1323	5	1511
Agriculture	52	858	68	914
Commerce	42	1198	32	1241
Defense	1079	543	1245	552
Air Force	319	588	404	616
Army	311	508	341	619
Defense Logistics Agency	91	483	57	369
Navy	314	562	386	474
Other Defense	44	452	57	411
Education	6	1311	12	1728
Energy	16	797	14	603
Environmental Protection Agency	29	1450	27	1376
Equal Employment Opportunity Commission	47	539	46	453
General Services Administration	42	615	19	676
Government Printing Office	9	669	7	547
Health & Human Services	182	674	280	608
Housing & Urban Development	21	676	42	907
Interior	143	884	27	646
Justice	87	1443	52	932
Labor	46	793	35	833
National Aeronautics and Space Administration	12	792	10	1054
Small Business Administration	75	479	136	503
State	28	970	5	616
Tennessee Valley Authority	75	479	136	503
Transportation	55	326	115	467
Treasury	181	988	80	936
United States Postal Service	2258	461	2033	372
Veterans Administration	222	956	102	1000

Source: U.S. Congress, House of Representatives, Subcommittee on Employment and Housing, *Processing EEO Complaints in the Federal Sector—Problems and Solutions.* Hearing Before Subcommittee on Government Operations, 99th Cong., 1st Session, October 8, 1985, pp. 137–138.

like their counterparts, found problems, made recommendations, and extracted *"promises."*

Despite energetic efforts of Congressmen Hawkins, Edwards, and others, oversight has had very little impact on the enforcement efforts of the new civil rights regulatory agencies in an era of a conservative Republican president and his conservative chairman and agency heads. Despite strenuous efforts to the contrary, conservative Republican efforts to curtail civil rights regulatory efforts have been successful.

Table 5.4   Agencies Slowest in Decisionmaking in FY 1984

	Average Days from Filing of Complaint to Agency Decision		
Agency	FY 1984	FY 1983	FY 1982
EPA	1,450	1,376	1,117
Justice	1,443	932	1,119
AID	1,323	1,511	NA
Education	1,311	1,728	745
Commerce	1,198	1,241	1,025
SBA	1,082	949	NA
Government-Wide Average	590	524	595

Source: U.S. Congress, House of Representatives, Subcommittee on Employment and Housing, *Processing EEO Complaints in the Federal Sector—Problems and Solutions.* Hearing Before Subcommittee on Government Operations, 99th Cong., 1st Session, October 8, 1985, p. 135.

Thus, in the earlier years, in contrast to what Professor Ogul found, much more oversight activity was undertaken—but somehow, Congressional committees conducting such oversight functions must find a way to make them work in a hostile political environment. If not, the results will be little different from a period, in which little formal oversight take place. In the final analysis, the Oversight Committees are simply inside pressure groups trying to influence the course of events and regulation efforts.

Overall, we have seen that an array of federal agencies and offices within the federal government itself can and do play a part in the civil rights enforcement process. They can support enforcement, regulatory politics, and implementation at both the national level—i.e., in the bureaucracies of agencies and departments having Title VI responsibilities—as well as on the local level, at least in twenty-six cities. Some parts of the federal establishment—the president, his staff, the Domestic Council, and OMB—have considerable power but have chosen not to use it in a direct fashion; other federal agencies—the FEBs, GAO, and the Commission on Civil Rights—have only persuasive power to effect the process. And one agency, the Commission on Civil Rights, because of its adroit use of these pressure tactics in its early years and the changing mood in the country has recently been forced to change its focus and agendas.

Occasionally, these agencies or some parts of them work in unison. The former Acting Chairman (1981-1982) of the EEOC, a Black Republican, who was not reappointed by Reagan, writes: "During the year that I was Acting Chairman of EEOC, *it was clear to me that some personnel in OMB, Justice, Labor and even in GAO had a mission more important than the reversal of affirmative action.* The objective of the foes of Title VII was to eliminate all class based relief." He continues: "OMB, Justice and certain recent staff appointees at EEOC have been quietly working to undermine the Employment Selection Guidelines and erode—by oratory— the *Griggs Doctrine.* One policy has been to attempt to reduce the record-keeping requirements so that neither the government or a private litigant can prove discrimination." Thus, from this insider's perspective, these agencies can not only work together but on several negative goals simultaneously.

Finally all of these inside agencies provide many access points for sundry organizations and individuals who seek to influence the civil rights enforcement process, and many have taken advantage of the numerous opportunities. When these governmental bodies are viewed as internal pressure groups rather than as enforcers of civil rights programs, a much clearer picture of the complex federal civil rights apparatus comes to light.

The External Pressure Groups

Pressure from outside of the federal government comes from two opposing directions. One group, which we shall label the pro-civil rights forces, are those individuals, organizations, and coalitions that work to advance the idea of equality before the law.[96] The second group, which we shall label the anti–civil rights forces, are the individuals, organizations, and coalitions that work to oppose, particularly for minority groups in this society, the advancement of basic rights guaranteed to everyone by the Constitution.

Among the coterie of pro–civil rights pressure groups is an organization called the Lawyers' Committee for Civil Rights under Law (LCCRUL). It is a lobbying organization formed in 1963 at the request of the president of the United States. LCCRUL maintains an office and staff in Washington so as to secure "total acceptance of the concept that all Americans are entitled to equal rights under the law and that lawyers carry out their responsibilities to help solve serious modern problems through processes of the Law." Under this mandate, the committee carries out legal work ranging from "legal representation of minority and women federal employees seeking the adoption of fair employment politics" to efforts against *apartheid* in South Africa.

In order to conduct its work nationwide, the committee maintains offices in Los Angeles, San Francisco, Denver, Chicago, Philadelphia, Boston, and Jackson, Mississippi. The director of the LCCRUL is black attorney and former dean of Howard's law school, Wiley A. Branton. The organization usually employs filing law suits as a tactic, but it also resorts to tactics of persuasion, when the approach is appropriate. In addition to filing numerous lawsuits, the committee—like the Civil Rights Commission—issues reports criticizing federal agencies that are not carrying out their civil rights mandate.[97] It writes innumerable letters to agency heads, the president, senators, representatives, and other individuals of influence to promote stronger enforcement of the country's equal rights laws.[98] It represents individuals and civil rights organizations in court, as it did for SCLC when Senator Jesse Helms (R-N.C.) tried to get the court to give him the sealed tapes of conversations the FBI had made of Dr. King through illegal surveillance, tapes he intended to use to kill the King holiday bill.[99] The LCCRUL testified before the Senate Judiciary Committee on presidential nominees in regard to their civil rights records,[100] and it evaluates new civil rights initiatives sponsored by the federal government.[101] LCCRUL's greatest successes by far have been in the courts. Two examples show the committee's success on both the local and the national level.

On May 2, 1983, Federal Judge W. Earl Butt, in the case of *Williams v. City of New Bern*, issued a consent judgment that committed the city of New Bern, North Carolina, to "provide basic municipal service improvements to its black residential neighborhoods." Thirty-five percent of New Bern (15,000 people) is black and most live in the Duffy-field area of the city, "an area of paved streets too narrow for curbs and gutters and an area frequently flooded due to the absence of a storm drainage system that would accommodate water collected from higher land in New Bern and spilled onto Duffy-field." In the suit the black plaintiffs charged racial discrimination in the lack of adequate storm drainage, fire protection, street lighting, maintenance of the black cemetery, street, and low-income housing. They charged that local authorities were being racially discriminatory in the expenditure of federal revenue-sharing funds.

The LCCRUL won the case, and Judge Butt determined that the city of New Bern would spend $520,000 to improve storm drainage in the black residential neighborhoods, provide them with a "maintenance schedule to upgrade street repair and cemeteries," and seek funds to construct and rehabilitate low-income housing. "Prior to the settlement, two full-time employees were hired by the City to maintain ditches and control weed growth within the black neighborhoods."[102] Here, the city responded to the pressure by hiring people.

On the national level, the Lawyer's Committee participated as *amicus curiae* in support of the federal government as it moved to recover misused and misspent funds given to states before 1978 under Title I of the Elementary and Secondary Education Act (ESEA) of 1965.

The LCCRUL had a twofold concern with this issue. "First, if states did not have to repay Title I funds misspent before 1978, it would lessen the Department of Education's present enforcement power, without which, states and localities may not be as vigilant in following program requirements especially since after Title I was amended in 1981, the specific audit provisions were removed." The committee's second concern was that "allowing states to escape liability for misusing Title I funds would penalize program beneficiaries twice."[103] The Supreme Court in *Bell v. New Jersey* on May 31, 1983, ruled unanimously in favor of the government and the committee's position. The committee saw the ruling as a major victory because Title I services went to "educationally deprived children in poor areas."

These two examples indicate that the committee has been active in a wide range of issues, pressuring the federal government and its agencies to carry out federal responsibility for equal rights under the law.

Another pressure group that is sometimes mistaken for the committee is the umbrella organization known as the Leadership Conference on Civil Rights. This organization is a coalition of national labor, civil rights, and civic organizations and associations formed to promote the rights of minorities and women. It, too, has an office in Washington, and it took to lobbying for the enforcement of civil rights laws as well as for the passage of newer ones. Unlike the LCCRUL, the Leadership Conference directs its energies toward monitoring and persuasion. The conference most often works by meeting with federal officials who have civil rights responsibilities and by writing letters and testifying before congressional committees to lobby for support of new and better civil rights legislation.[104] The real force and mover in the conference before his death was the late Clarence Mitchell. Singlehandedly, he made such a mark that many on Capitol Hill dubbed him the 101st Senator.

A major effort by the conference was to pressure OMB into assuming a more aggressive role in the civil rights area. In June 1973, when OMB had seemed to dismiss civil rights oversight and monitoring as one of its principal concerns, Harold C. Fleming, chairman of the conference's Federal Programs Task Force, met with the deputy director of OMB, Frederick V. Malek, who had been put in charge of the agency's civil rights enforcement responsibilities. The conference put forth its major concerns and the things it hoped that OMB would accomplish, but little resulted from the meeting except that the deputy director arranged for a continuing liaison between OMB and the conference. The initiative for these future meetings would rest with the deputy director.

Another meeting was not held until nearly two years later, in May 1975. At this meeting the conference put forth once again its concerns about: (1) the small number of OMB staff members having civil rights responsibilities; (2) the need to collect in a systematic fashion racial and ethnic data; (3) the need of the agency to monitor the support of civil rights programs; and (4) OMB's lack of a position on revenue sharing and the coordinating performance of the Justice Department in the area of Title VI. The new deputy director listened but did not schedule any subsequent meetings.[105] Moreover, shortly after the meeting OMB moved responsibilities for civil rights to another division and left the director's spot vacant for one and a half years.

By 1985 OMB, in its special analysis section of the budget prepared to reveal the level of federal government civil rights activity, indicated that it agreed with the Supreme Court ruling in *Firefighters v. Stotts* and *Palmore v. Sidoti* that affirmative action and goals and quotas were "dead" programs and that the government and OMB would no longer move to enforce these civil rights concepts or the programs designed to support them.[106] In addition, the OMB report indicated that the government was moving toward a policy of voluntary compliance and of shifting civil rights responsibilities to the states.[107]

In addition to the Leadership Conference on Civil Rights, other organizations are involved in exerting pressure on the federal government. For years the NAACP has been lobbying the federal government to protect the civil rights of racial minorities, and although many of its early victories came in the courts and not in the halls of the executive and legislative branches of government, it has continued to lobby congress and the presidency in recent years. In fact, lately it has increased its testifying and lobbying activities on behalf of new initiatives and the better utilization of current enforcement machinery. When the federal government has failed to live up to its mandate, the NAACP has continued to bring cases into court to force the government to live up to its charge.

However, recent internal conflict between the NAACP and the NAACP Legal Defense Fund has slowed the organization's efforts, both the legal moves and its lobbying. In May 1982, the NAACP sued the NAACP Legal Defense and Educational Fund (LDF) over the use of its name; it sought to check the direction that the fund was taking in some civil rights cases.[108]

Essentially, the NAACP formed the LDF in 1939 "to provide a full-time staff to work in civil rights litigation and to allow contributors to make tax deductible contributions." It was a move in response to the Internal Revenue Service's refusal that year to grant to the NAACP tax-exempt status because of its lobbying activities. Thus, the LDF became the NAACP's litigating arm.[109] However, years later, "in the backlash from *Brown v. Board of Education*, Southern members of Congress prompted an Internal Revenue Service investigation of the NAACP-LDF relationship."[110] A majority of southern states began a wide variety of legal maneuvers to put the organization out of business in the South.[111]

To counteract this southern strategy Thurgood Marshall, who then headed the LDF, argued that the LDF should sever formal ties to the NAACP. The separation was eventually effected, with Marshall heading up the LDF.[112] Although the two organizations formally separated, they continued to work closely together until Marshall resigned to become first the solicitor general and then a justice of the Supreme Court. Marshall's hand-picked successor at the LDF, Jack Greenberg, eventually came into conflict with the NAACP's ambitious in-house counsel as they competed for cases. By now, each organization was beginning to pursue its own strategy and civil rights legal goals.

The friction came to a head with the case of *Adams v. Richardson*. The LDF sought to force the secretary of HEW (now Education) to carry out the government's objectives to enforce Title VI of the 1964 Civil Rights Act. This litigation, the NAACP felt, was not in the best interest of some of its constituents. Yet the LDF pursued it with zeal. Wasby explains:

> Proper treatment of the historically black colleges is one of the problems requiring most subtle attention from the NAACP because of its constituency: many Afro-American adults of all occupations and professions are graduates of such institutions and have emotional attachments to their alma maters so that they would not welcome the disappearance of those institutions, especially under external compulsion. Moreover, many Afro-Americans share the realistic view that the rapid-paced desegregation efforts in the South lead, apart from the merits of desegregation, to subordination of Afro-American faculty and administrators to white faculty and administrators. Thus when the *Adams* case was 'filed without notice or consultation with the NAACP or its board of Directors,' NAACP leaders felt that the organization had been put in 'the untenable position of appearing to foster the elimination of black colleges' (and they were noticeably 'put out' by the LDF's action. It is important to note that in this situation the NAACP, although committed to desegregation and willing to go as far as to displace a branch, such as the one in Atlanta, that diverged from that goal, found it necessary to adopt less than a mechanical position on desegregation.)[113]

The internal struggle between the NAACP and the LDF as well as a leadership struggle between Executive Director Benjamin Hooks and former Chairwoman of the Board Margaret Bush Wilson,[114] which Hooks eventually won, along with a struggle and competition for funds and a search for a new headquarters—left the organization able only to lobby, with some limited work by the NAACP in school desegration cases and the LDF working primarily in the area of Title VII employment discrimination cases.

On this point, Wasby writes: "There is a close relationship between mobilization of resources and mobilization of law: the need for resources constrains an organization's ability to engage in certain activities such as litigation (mobilization of law) and litigation successes—effective mobilization of law—increases resources available to the organization."[115] Thus, without solid resources to exert pressure legally, the executive director found himself testifying in Congress on March 7, 1985, in favor of the Civil Rights Restoration Act of 1985, which is designed to reverse the Supreme Court's 1984 Grove City College decision limiting coverage of the 1972 Civil Rights Act banning sex discrimination.[116]

Hooks also took the opportunity to tell the joint hearing of the House's Education and Labor Committee and a House subcommittee on constitutional rights that "some Pollyannas would have us believe that racial discrimination has been eliminated from the fabric of American society. . . . A look around the country will show that Jim Crow is alive and well in America, albeit in a slightly more subtle form."[117]

Thus, because of internal problems and dwindling resources, the NAACP has slowed its legal pressure tactics and switched in part to less costly ones like testifying and lobbying. But throughout its history and until recently, the organization relied on legal means to exert pressure on the government.[118]

New and more specialized black groups like the Congressional Black Caucus, the National Black Policemen Association, and sundry individuals and groups have emerged. They, too, seek to have the federal government maintain a meaningful civil rights enforcement position.

The Congressional Black Caucus, formed in 1971 and composed of all the black members of the House of Representatives,[119] has in recent years used its position inside the Congress, and particularly in the House, to try to influence presidential appointments and appointees by testifying before the Senate confirmation panel as to the background and commitment to civil rights of nominated individuals. For instance, when President Ford nominated a conservative white southerner, former congressman Ben Blackburn of Georgia, to head the Federal Home Loan Bank Board, black congressman Parren J. Mitchell went before the Senate Banking Committee and revealed that the former congressman had "long opposed legislation that would benefit poor and black people; and that he had voted against Title VIII of the Civil Rights Act of 1968, which guaranteed fair housing to everyone regardless of color, and against the extension of the Voting Rights Act of 1965." Blackburn's nomination was subsequently rejected by the Senate.

In another case, the chairman of the caucus, Congressman Charles B.

Rangel, sent a letter to the chairman of the Senate Foreign Relations Committee, John T. Sparkman (D-Ala.) and to Secretary of State Henry Kissinger noting that Nathaniel Davis, former U.S. ambassador to Chile, lacked sufficient knowledge of the problems confronting the African continent to become assistant secretary of state for African affairs. Kissinger rejected the caucus' opposition and gave Davis the post, asserting his prerogative as secretary of state to nominate and appoint whom he pleased.[120]

The caucus has also initiated hearings, pushed bills, and backed the Civil Rights Restoration Act of 1985. The caucus gave civil rights groups another important access point to the system as well as a group of friendly allies in the battle to get the system to enforce its civil rights obligations.

Before closing on the caucus, it must be said that it has been absent on some matters. For instance, the caucus could play an informal oversight role by holding joint hearings as it has done on other issues in the past.[121] Yet it has not done this, nor has it protested as much as it could have in regard to the black conservatives running the current civil rights regulatory agencies. For instance, when the chairman of the EEOC came up for renomination, the caucus filed no testimony for the record. Only Congressmen Hawkins and Hayes, who spoke for themselves, objected to Chairman Thomas' renomination. Yet many individual caucus members had denounced Thomas throughout his first term.

One could ask in retrospect, what good would it have done for the Black Caucus to get involved, given the track record of success of the other formal oversight agencies? The primary answer is that like other black civil rights organizations, the organization could at least have gone on the "record." It didn't.

If the caucus uses inside moves, the National Black Policemen Association has worked more from the perimeter, resorting primarily to legal tactics. When the LEAA would not force the Chicago police department to stop using Title VI funds in a discriminatory manner, and numerous visits and calls to Director Herbert Rice of LEAA's Office of Civil Rights Compliance availed nothing except talk and evasion, the black police association filed suit in 1975. The case, *National Black Police Association v. Velde* (Velde headed the agency), sought to require LEAA to carry out its constitutional and statutory civil rights obligations of not providing funds to discriminatory local police departments. The association sought damages against the federal officials for their refusal in the past to carry out these obligations.

The association lost the suit in 1976, but the internal ramifications following a national CBS News story on the case caused the agency to force Rice to resign early in 1976 as a sacrifice and reward to the association.[122] After Rice's resignation nothing happened; the office literally languished undirected until the Carter administration appointed a black.

But the Policemen Association did not stop with a token victory. It went to the Office of Revenue Sharing to close off funds, and it continued to pursue its case against Velde in the Court of Appeals. On June 30, 1983, the court said that the attorney general and other past Justice Department officials must stand trial for refusing to carry out civil rights duties in LEAA grants.[123] In this case the court set a new standard by noting that federal officials do not have absolute immunity and must carry out their duties and responsibilities under the law, in particular, Title VI, which requires them to terminate federal funding to racially discriminatory recipients—something they had not been doing. If this ruling is left standing by the Supreme Court, the pressure tactics of the Police Association may have significantly helped the civil rights forces by telling federal bureaucrats that they cannot be lax in enforcing the law of the land.

In addition to the specialized pressure groups, there are many individuals who are filing countersuits against the federal government to get it to enforce civil rights law. Shortly after Jesse Jackson campaigned for the presidency, black individuals in Waycross, Georgia, filed suit in federal court in Savannah to have the city fathers change the way they hold city elections. In 1984 no black had ever been elected to city office because of the discriminatory election process that persisted, despite the existence of the Voting Rights Act and the fact that the Justice Department was supposed to monitor elections to eliminate such violations. At about the same time black citizens of Effingham County, Georgia, took similar action. No black had ever been elected to any county office since the incorporation of the county in the 1700s. In fact, in the state of Georgia alone in 1985, fifteen such voting-rights suits brought by individuals were underway.[124]

Traditional civil rights organizations have been joined by umbrella groups, new black politicians, and specialized civil rights organizations along with a host of individuals at the local level to form the broader coalition that puts external pressure on government in behalf of civil rights. The methods of this loose coalition range from simple letter writing to filing complex legal suits. The greatest successes of this coalition have come in the courts. When legal efforts have run into reversals—as happened when the Supreme Court ruled in *Grove City College v. Bell* that the prohibition against sex discrimination in Title IX of the Education Amendment of 1972 covers *only* the particular program or activity receiving federal financial assistance, and not the institution as a whole—all of the groups have come together to work. These groups worked for new civil rights legislation in the 99th Congress through the enactment of the Civil Rights Restoration Bill because they felt that the *Bell* decision might be so narrowly interpreted by the conservative administration that it would limit the enforcement authority of Title VI of the Civil Rights Act of 1964; section 504 of the Rehabilitation Act of 1973, which protects the handicapped; and the Age Discrimination Act of 1975.

Although there are several bills on this issue, the lead legislation is H.R.

700 (Hawkins/S.432 Kennedy). Gus Hawkins is a black Democrat and member of the caucus from California. He is backed by the liberal senator from Massachusetts, Ted Kennedy. The fate of the legislation, as indicated earlier, was stalled in 1985 yet has been re-introduced in 1987 in the 100th Congress. What the actions and reactions of these external pressure groups suggest is: (1) when the complex and cumbersome civil rights enforcement machinery fails to work, the external groups will turn to the courts to force enforcement; (2) newer and different external pressure groups can and will enter the process; (3) they have more access points and new inside allies; and (4) when legal victory seems impossible, they will turn to the legislative process to achieve new and better laws.

Thus, overall, civil rights regulatory activity takes place under pressure from a myriad of inside and outside groups. The general result is a mixture of success and failure in enforcement. The results remain ambiguous and the struggle goes on. Anti–civil rights forces have attempted to capture part of the process and to instill in government bureaucracies their ideas and beliefs about enforcement. The work of this opposing coalition of forces in the process needs to be examined.

The Role of the Anti-Civil Rights Coalition

The most sustained opposition to civil rights has come from political forces based in the South. Political and social leaders of this region of the country have worked tirelessly to moderate or eliminate civil rights laws. Southern opposition is rooted in theories of white supremacy and cloaked in myths about black inferiority.

Over the years these political forces in the South have been able to attract allies, primarily conservatives who now have come to the position that too much governmental regulation curbs individual freedom and personal initiative. Because the laws advocating civil rights that came into effect in the 1960s put more governmental regulations into effect, many conservatives responded by joining in the battle with southerners against the full implementation and enforcement of these laws.

Into this mixture of racism and conservatism came the religious fundamentalists who saw many of the achievements won by women and minorities as being in conflict with God's law and thus immoral. They came to see many of the regulations emanating from the Civil Rights Act of 1964 as promoting untold evil and encouraging many new sins in society. Abortion, for instance, is an especially potent issue for fundamentalists. Thus, both directly and indirectly, they have fought against many of the new civil rights rules and regulations.

The Intellectual Foundation: Neo-Conservatism

The intellectual foundation for the attack on civil rights regulatory activity was constructed by a group of well-known scholars, writers, and academicians collectively known as "neo–conservatives." Ironically, what gave this group its credibility and a well–established place in the anti–civil rights movement was the fact that many of its members had been active participants in the civil rights movement. They had used their pens, wit, and positions of power in society to promote civil rights during the 1960s.[125]

However, by the late 1960s and early 1970s these individuals began to turn against the movement, claiming there were too many excesses and arguing that these excesses violated the Constitution and the intentions of the Founding Fathers. The movement, the neo–convervatives said, had elevated equality over liberty—and liberty was the "primary principle" of the Republic and its Revolutionary War.

In the preface to the Bicentennial issue of *The Public Interest*, the neo–conservatives editors, Irving Kristol and Nathan Glazer wrote, "We feel it to be a very special issue indeed . . . It certainly is special in size and also distinctive in its focus on issues of political philosophy, as against our usual focus on questions of social policy. This shift in focus would seem appropriate to the occasion."[126]

In the introduction to this issue, Daniel P. Moynihan elaborated on this shift in political philosophy. He wrote, "the guiding principle which illuminates the essays in this volume . . . is Liberty." He continues, "Liberty was the first principle of this Republic, . . . the animating principle of the Constitution no less than of the Declaration, . . . this which makes us what we are, be we conservative or liberal or, for that matter socialist. Plainly, any who espouse this principle too assertively may expect in time to have acquired a conservative air. . . . But this makes it no less the grandest and the most glorious idea man has ever had. To espouse it is virtue itself; to do so with a decent competence is all we have ever aspired to."[127] The drive to exalt liberty over all other principles was now clearly underway.

Such a bold switch in position caught many of the leaders of the civil rights movement off guard and quite unprepared for the turn of events and the ensuing conservative revolution.

Consider the words of one black Harvard academic as he called on these people to change their course.

> All of this, in turn, has fostered further development and cohesion in the neoconservative movement in recent years and has strengthened the new mood of government in public policy innovation. Deriving force and focus from Robert Nisbet's *The Twilight of Authority* and from the writings of Irving Kristol, James Q. Wilson, Nathan Glazer,

and Michael Novak, among others, this movement's message is clear, and clearly traditional in its major premises. The good life for Americans, it holds, is to be found in greater recourse to localism, voluntarism, and the restoration of old-fashioned values—familial, sexual, religious, economic, political, and (last but certainly not least) ethnic. In part as a reaction to the excesses that characterized social changes in the 1960s, the neoconservatives are more potent on the attack than in putting forth a positive vision of a better society. But they have been astonishingly successful in getting their message across, and the implications of their success do not bode well for the realization of racial integration.[128]

He continues:

Another and less sympathetic response by Negro leaders is warranted, however, in regard to the neoconservative white intellectuals and publicists whose current arguments regarding racial integration amount to adding insult to injury. These neoconservatives would have us believe that the American creed would have shed its white-only status quite of its own accord—without the pressure of the civil rights movement, the general cultural shifts of the 1960s, and the public policy initiatives of the Kennedy and Johnson administrations. The latter in particular come in for the loudest criticism from the neoconservatives. They condemn any role for government in racial integration beyond that of night watchman. Such transgression, they claim, can only produce bureaucratic excesses and profound distortions of the traditional American values of individual achievement—values that white ethnic groups like Jews, Irish, Slavs, and Italians presumably have assimilated. Nathan Glazer's book *Affirmative Discrimination* propounds this thesis; it is sharply critical of affirmative action in hiring policies for blacks, women, and Spanish-speaking citizens.[129]

Peter Steinfels, one of the most careful analysts of the "neoconservative" movement, has written:

Start with current issues. Neoconservatives, like most Americans, disapprove of the unequal treatment suffered by racial minorities, women, and poor. But they have given far more attention to criticizing current strategies for remedying those inequalities than they have to the inequalities themselves. They are strongly opposed to minority separatism, disruption as a means of dramatizing conditions and forcing action, and civil disobedience except in very extreme circumstances. They have been vocal critics of affirmative action and busing, and cool to community control, many poverty programs, campaign finance reform, and schemes to redistribute income through tax changes.[130]

He also says,

> Strategically installed in the marketplace of ideas, well connected with political, labor, and business leaders, the neoconservatives are clearly a group to be reckoned with. But it would be a serious underestimation to think of them as merely a successful lobby. The supposition that their influence will be both broad and lasting rests on several further facts.
>
> First, the questions the neoconservatives have addressed are fundamental ones and ones which do not promise to be resolved in the near future.[131]

And finally he concludes:

> The outstanding weaknesses of neoconservatism have already been amply suggested: its formulation of an outlook largely in negative terms; its lack of internal criticism; its unwillingness to direct attention to socioeconomic structures and to the existing economic powers; its exaggeration of the adversarial forces in society; its lack of serious respect for its adversaries. If neoconservatism is to construct a convincing defense of an outlook emphasizing a stoic rationality, public restraint, and the maintenance of an ethic of achievement and excellence, it will have to confront the extent to which such an ideal challenges contemporary capitalism. If it is to defend freedom in a richer sense than anti-communism and derived anti-statism, if it is to defend high culture and intellectural rigor, it will need to elaborate the enlarging and life-giving force of superior work and not merely issue self-satisfying strictures on the inferior or fashionable.[132]

But all of the pleading in the world did not sway neoconservatives; they had helped set into motion two revolutions—first, the civil rights revolution and now the conservative counter-revolution—and this was heady business. A small core group of people—the political and social elites, as they are called by some political scientists—was deciding the direction of American society and significantly influencing its social and political milieu. To have such power and be able to exercise it outside of the normal channels of government is not only intoxicating, but it legitimized what intellectual power is all about. A few men and women had come to believe they were truly superior intellectually to all their fellow citizens.[133]

This group was not and is not particularly committed to the downtrodden or to the right wing nearly as much as it is committed to promoting its own role and position and power in society. Whether it will be able to drop the conservative counter-revolution as easily as it did the civil rights revolution remains to be seen. Whatever the future brings, neo-conservatism still remains: through nationally known prestigious magazines, in books, on talk shows, and in high positions in and out of government. The neo-conservatives gave the anti–civil rights forces a means of coming together. They provided, it seems, an intellectual respectability for *strong opposition* to civil rights and civil rights enforcement.

As one neoconservative observer has attempted to show, the emphasis upon civil rights and its enforcement is simply one part of a larger process that is currently "disabling America." He writes:

> Many interest group advocates, law professors, activist lawyers, and publicists— what I call, collectively, the American rights industry—are no longer committed to the excruciating job of balancing individual claims against the claims of organized society. They are engaged in a different enterprise—creating new rights with unreflective enthusiasm. They have become separated from what are matters of constitutional law; some involve statutory law and administrative regulations (bureaucratic law). But even in these latter cases, the statutory or administrative initiatives are often justified and defended as advancing some general constitutional purpose or further safeguarding some constitutional right. Whether rights activists are operating in a court, within the staff of a congressional committee, or within an administrative agency, constitutional arguments and rhetoric are deployed in depth.[134]

He continues with this definition:

> Similarly, "disable" is not used with any overtones of wrecking or sabotage. But when costs are externally imposed on institutions—direct dollar costs, seclusion from public programs, cumbersome new procedures, substantial reductions in leadership authority, reduced discretion in recruitment and personnel decisions, and so on—the institutions will be less able to pursue excellence in performing their primary function, whether it be infantry combat, original work in medieval history, making widgets, or teaching children to read. They will be marginally disabled. In the same way, when popular majorities are forbidden to use the machinery of government in traditionally ac-

cepted ways to reinforce minimum standards of public behavior, these majorities are marginally disabled.[135]

And after tying the matter of civil rights to religious freedoms, the integration of public schools to curbs on police abuse and shabby and discriminatory hiring practices, he concludes that: "The rights industry needs to shrink, moderate, and ideologically detoxify itself in order to serve effectively as guardians of the open society rather than as its traducer."[136]

While the principle of "liberty" was being vigorously promoted, another group of these self-styled intellectuals went after the concepts of "affirmative action," "goals and quotas," and "preferential treatment" by labeling and defining them (though they had invented them in the first place) as a form of "reverse discrimination" and as being in violation of the Constitution of the United States.[137] In fact, these individuals wrote so negatively about these concepts that they eventually undercut any support for them in the top echelons of society. By 1985, as this research has demonstrated, the federal government had stopped enforcing such laws. It was a major victory for these groups, which then set into motion the next assault on governmental regulations.[138]

From the economic wing of neo-conservatism came arguments about how federal regulations were stifling the economy—slowing down economic progress and causing the United States to lose its position to the Japanese and other foreign competitors. The attack, coming when it did in the midst of a recession, caught on. Demands were made to measure such activity solely from the standpoint of cost-benefit analysis.[139] Deregulation, a term that had been drifting into American parlance and the economic sector without getting very far, came to the forefront.

Thus, with a redefinition of liberty, deregulation, and affirmative action as positive ends to be valued—slavery was once defined this way—conservatism began to be seen as the new American way. The complex and diverse civil rights enforcement machinery began to slow down. When elements of the conservative forces captured the White House under Ronald Reagan, this machinery nearly ceased to function. But now the old-line-liberals-turned conservative began to look racist, i.e., anti-nonwhite, and because favoring inequality taints the intellectual image (such persons are supposed to be fair, balanced, and unbiased), a shift began to take. Another group was needed to attack what had been rationalized as the regulatory extension of civil rights legislation. Who better than so-called conservative black intellectuals.[140]

Black Conservatism

Black conservatives have always existed in America, and each era in American history has helped to define these individuals' roles in espousing their conservative doctrine.[141] In the era of abolitionism, some conservative blacks sought to return to Africa. Many identified with the slave master and told of planned slave insurrections, rebellions, and escapes for freedom. In the Reconstruction era, many planned and joined "Back-to-Africa" movements, while others identified with and worked to support the southern Democrats who sought to redeem the southern governments from black Republicans and northerners. When this period closed with the era of disfranchisement, the greatest conservative spokesman of all times emerged—Booker T. Washington. He, along with others of this disposition, counseled the acceptance of and accommodation to segregation, to Jim Crow and discrimination. In fact, some blacks even came to defend segregation.[142]

By the 1960s, when the new civil rights revolution was underway, several black conservatives attacked the movement and Dr. Martin Luther King, Jr. as traitors and destroyers of the American dream and black progress.[143] They felt that black protest and agitation unnecessarily provoked whites, inflamed good race relations, and moved the pace of racial advancement too fast. And worst of all, they argued, black protest took the initiative for improvement of race relations out of the hands of whites and placed it in the hands of blacks. This, they argued, was a step in the wrong direction.

Prior to Reagan's first term, black conservatives were a small chorus of voices operating along the fringes of black politics and the black community. Within the black community black conservatives were ridiculed and held up for derision, occasionally by the black press. Booker Washington was a limited exception. All of that would change with Reagan's coming to office.

During Reagan's first term two forces were operating to counteract the legislative and regulatory advances of the civil rights movement. First, the conservative movement reconstituted itself and a major effort was undertaken to find, cultivate, and promote these lonely and diverse black conservative voices. John Saloma put it thus: "The Conservatives and the Republican Party, as part of their effort to form a new political majority, have solicited the support of racial and ethnic minority groups. Their largest and to date most successful achievement has been the building of a distinctly conservative black political movement."[144] He continues,

> The black population has always included cultural and religious conservatives. The network has simply identified them—as it has conservative intellectuals generally, funded them, and effectively promoted their ideas, which are supported by a minority within the black community. . . .
> The basic ideas of black conservatism, as articulated by intellectuals like Sowell and economist Walter Williams, are limited government, free-market enterprise, and individual self-reliance. They view

black dependence on federal programs, government, and grants from white liberal philanthropy as frustrating self-development and independent black leadership. Government-enforced minimum-wage standards, they claim, have increased black teenage unemployment. Government assistance and affirmative-action programs have stigmatized the majority of blacks, who would prefer to make it on their own. Instead, they believe the capitalist free-enterprise system offers blacks the best opportunities for advancement.[145]

Once selected blacks were brought in and made a part of the new conservative movement, they were given funds, access to leading white conservative magazines, publishers, and television and radio shows to promote their philosophies. Suddenly, they were everywhere. Overnight, they were challenging the black civil rights leaders. Then came the second force.

The Reagan administration appointed several of these blacks to top governmental positions. Samuel Pierce went to HUD, Clarence Pendleton was named chairman of the Civil Rights Commission, and Clarence Thomas was similarly named to head EEOC. These were all positions formerly held by blacks, and usually blacks of a liberal orientation. From these positions of power and high visibility, black conservatives began an attack on governmental regulations, social programs, civil rights, and the traditional black leadership. Thus, when black conservative "outsiders" like Thomas Sowell and Walter Williams combined with these appointed "insiders," it appeared to many black leaders in the civil rights movement that the bottom had fallen out. In fact, some black civil rights veterans like Charles Evers, Hosea Williams, Ralph David Abernathy, and others even came out and embraced Reagonomics and the Reagan administration. Conservative ideas and programs, they argued, should be the new thrust and concern in the black community. Although some blacks were won over, the struggle between the two groups has yet to play itself out. This promotion of black conservative spokesmen to the forefront of conservatism is similar to the promotion of Booker T. Washington by the white conservatives nearly a century ago—with the only difference being that then it was just one leader, whereas now it is a large group of leaders. And the same problem that faced Washington faces this new wave of leaders: they lack a strong grassroots base.

Washington, through the use of his Tuskegee machine, tried to build such a base using political patronage, dispensing favors, and wielding absolute power. But in the end, such a jerry-built system came apart at the seams. His support vanished nearly as quickly as he did, because he made the mistake of building his support from the top down. The reality was that he could not have built it any other way. The current black conservative movement will face this very same problem, and just possibly the same fate.

There is another similarity to the Washington era. The problems unleashed by the conservatve movement will affect the black community in ways that are not always to the advantage of the conservative black leaders. For instance, as these authors of social retrenchment increase the misery index in the black community, black conservatives will have greater difficulty in building a grassroots base—to say nothing of the violence unleased in the community by racism that goes unchecked. (Conservative interpretation, of course, says that "racism" means something else.) Those promoting themselves as spokespersons for the black community will have very little verbal ammunition as they try to sell their doctrine in the impacted community. But for now, these leaders are riding the crest and their inevitable dilemma seems very distant.

Having carefully selected and cultivated black intellectuals, entrepreneurs, economists, and leftover black Republicans, the neoconservatives stepped back and let their black conservative surrogates become the apologists in the black community for this new movement. The black economist Thomas Sowell took the lead and assaulted affirmative action and its goals, quotas, and timetables and eventually the concept of civil rights itself. Another black economist, Walter Williams, moved broadside to attack such governmental regulations as the minimum wage, such things as foodstamps, the idea of full employment, and social programs for the needy. He even urged support for South Africa. Williams ultimately argued that governmental programs hinder rather than help blacks.[146] With Sowell on the point and Williams on the flank, Ann Wortham, a black academic, reanalyzed the concept of black equality in America from a psycho-philosophical perspective and declared that it was not only negative and selfish, but in opposition to real equality.[147]

Although these blacks were moving in separate directions across the civil rights front, the self-styled entrepreneur J. A. Parker provided a forum for all of them to come together in his conservative quarterly, *The Lincoln Review*.[148] From this journal these and sundry other black conservatives presented a unified frontal assault on the efforts to effectively enforce civil rights regulations.

Such a well-organized, well-funded and promoted thrust not only caught black leaders of the civil rights movement unprepared, it also provided for the first time a fairly clear and rather articulate black dimension to the anti–civil rights coalition. These blacks spokespersons were joined by several black Reagan appointees—particularly, Clarence Pendleton of the Civil Rights Commission, who took the battle much further by labeling black civil rights leaders as the new racists. He was persuaded to stop further efforts to define civil rights leaders as the new racists.[149]

Overall, then, the anti–civil rights coalition, with the support of the Reagan administration, was able to capture a part of the complex civil rights enforcement machinery and to spur a new national debate on whether such enforcement should continue or whether, instead, civil rights enforcement should be radically modified or even eliminated.

Thus, by the beginning of Reagan's second term there was a full-fledged struggle going on between the pro–civil rights forces and their opponents, who were led by black surrogates strongly supported by white political conservatives and neo-conservative intellectuals.

In the context of this struggle, the federal government's enforcement of civil rights laws is perhaps understandably inconsistent: not enough to please the proponents and too much to please the opponents. The grave possibility is that effective enforcement might continued to be paralyzed by this inconsistency.

The Impact of Pressure Politics on Civil Rights Regulatory Enforcement Efforts

At the outset in this chapter, it was noted that the traditional theoretical perspectives that informed and undergirded pressure group politics in American government was of little use and value in explicating the black political experience. And as the numerous examples and assessment of pressure group politics in the civil rights regulatory area have shown, it is of little descriptive, explanatory and predictive value in this area. Hence, when one seeks to assess what impact the existence of these inside and external pressure groups have had on the enforcement of civil rights regulatory efforts, it is best once again to look to a new technique and new ideas.[150]

Perhaps the best way to conceptualize then the impact of the interplay between these two groups, the insiders and the outsiders, in the civil rights regulatory process is to understand that the gains and losses suffered in the legislative battles is not necessarily permanent and that the same battles can be fought in the regulatory process between friends and foes once again.

It has been well stated:

> The administrative process is, in this sense, an extension of the legislative arena, where those defeated in the lawmaking process can redirect their attention to influencing implementation. If the legislative coalition that was strong enough to pass a law does not continue to support the agency in charge of implementation, it may turn out on later examination that effects of law were different from those envisioned for it. It is not uncommon for those who failed to "carry the day" in the legislative struggle to recover some of their losses by applying pressure on administrative agencies, thus altering the nature of the program the majority thought it was adopting. Sometimes ad-

ministrators are willing allies in this effort, sometimes not. Either way, the outcome is the same: *substantive modification* of programs (or policies).[151]

Therefore, the logic and argument about the *substantive modification* of programs and policies can easily be extended to understand that the efforts and focus of some of the sundry pressure groups (both insiders and outsiders) have been to achieve *substantive modification* in civil rights regulatory enforcements as well. In short, such groups can achieve single or dual modifications in the regulatory process.

And in looking at the impact of Reagan's regulatory revolution, one observer has written: "Apart from budget reductions, the Reagan administration relied on two other means to control regulatory expansion: a rather single-minded pattern of appointments and a new system for prescreening agency rules at the Office of Mangement and Budget. Neither required as much cooperation from Congress and in this sense facilitated more central control."[152] The anti–civil rights forces provided the public opinion support and atmosphere for the administration to make these changes with a seemingly strong basis of support in the country. Although there is some question about whether these changes will last, the point is clear that the Reagan administration altered the enforcement of civil rights laws and that it lasted at least for his two terms. Finally, any basic understanding of the American political process, reveals that political majorities can come and go and with them certain levels of commitment and support.

Therefore, from a qualitative assessment, pressure group activity at least in the two Reagan terms, had the overall impact of reducing the federal government commitment to civil rights regulatory enforcement.[153]

6. THE CIVIL RIGHTS REGULATORY PROCESS: PROBLEMS AND PROSPECTS

A dualism has heretofore characterized the study of civil rights in this country. Most observers of this persistent problem in American society have focused upon particular presidents and their efforts to get civil rights laws enacted by Congress. There are studies of Roosevelt,[1] Truman,[2] Eisenhower,[3] Kennedy,[4] Johnson,[5] and several presidents collectively.[6] Some of these works make heroes out of particular presidents and try to establish their places in history because of what they did in the area of civil rights. But as the Commission on Civil Rights and others have noted, these works have focused more on these presidents as originators of civil rights legislation and less on how the legislation was enforced once it was passed. In fact, if many of the presidents' civil rights enforcement efforts were factored into these volumes, reevaluation of some of the men would have to follow. For as the Civil Rights Commission has noted: "When Presidential leadership is lacking, civil rights enforcement suffers."[7] For the time being this approach to the study of civil rights persists, and studies in the same mold continue to pour forth. The reason for this is that "most domestic programs give out funds or services to state, local, or private groups. This makes it physically impossible or politically unfeasible for the president to keep up supervision. Evaluation—seeing whether programs really work—is a bureaucratic stepchild. It is rarely done and even more rarely heeded," by presidents.[8]

176

Moreover, "following through on programs is unglamorous and politically risky. Presidents are rarely inclined or have the time to pursue it. That is why political history (and scholars) usually focuses on how presidents influence the passage of legislation; it rarely mentions whether the legislation made any difference."[9] This is why most presidents act as if their duties end once a legislative proposal is passed into law.

A second area of current academic research literature focuses on public policy analysis, particularly one aspect of public policy—implementation.[10] Under the rubric of implementation, studies of civil rights laws and how they are put into force have been coming forth at a very rapid rate. But because so many of these studies were case studies—of one agency at one moment in time—the proliferation of findings became so unwieldy that little knowledge and insights could be gained—nothing on which to build a solid, systematic, comprehensive body of knowledge.[11]

Seeing this case-study approach procedure as a hindrance in theory-building, one scholar, Charles Bullock, has developed from his comprehensive analysis of the literature a set of common variables (some ten in all) that would permit each case study to have some similarities and a common framework. Such a technique would permit findings to be additive and solve the problem of confusing and multifaceted case studies that fail to produce a coherent body of knowledge. At this point, it is difficult to say if the Bullock model of common variables will be accepted and used by other students of civil rights policy analysis in particular and public policy in general. But beyond the problem of a useful research model, there is a problem with the implementation concept itself.

As a concept, "implementation" begins with the assumption that the bureaucracy readily accepts its congressional and executive mandates and as soon as possible puts them into practice. As previous chapters have shown, this is certainly not the case in the area of black civil rights. Second, a focus on implementation overlooks a very important phase in the policy process, *that phase between the passage of the law and its implementation*. First of all the bureaucracy has to be created and mobilized to handle the new law, and only after the federal government itself gears up to carry out the law can implementation take place and then be evaluated. But to analyze implementation before analyzing *how the government itself geared up to implement* the law can lead to some rather curious findings.

Finally, implementation moves the analysts of public policy away from the entire policy process and forces them to study the end of the process as being the crucial element in the process. The entire process then is seen from the end, not the beginning or the middle, and policy proposals for reforms are generated in a backward fashion.

Therefore, seeing blacks and civil rights policy from these two narrow perspectives leaves much to be desired and a great deal undone. By studying only the president's role and the manner of implementation, one cannot view the whole picture in a longitudinal way.

Civil Rights Regulatory Procedures: A Theory

The first period of American history when federal civil rights regulatory and enforcement policy was put into practice was during the era of Reconstruction. In that period the Justice Department was given the responsibility of enforcing civil rights laws, but the department failed miserably in carrying out its bureaucratic responsibilities and congressional authority (Table 6.1). William

Table 6.1   Criminal Prosecutions under Enforcement Acts, 1870–1877, by Section and by Year

	South	Border	North	National
Total Convictions	1,143	38	65	1,246
Total Dismissals	2,241	601	99	2,941
Total Actions	3,384	639	164	4,187
Average Rate of Conviction	34%	6%	40%	30%

Sections are identified as follows: South (Alabama, Arkansas, Florida, Georgia, Louisiana, Mississipppi, North Carolina, South Carolina, Texas, Virginia); border states (Delaware, Kentucky, Maryland, Missouri, Tennessee, West Virginia); North (remaining states of the Union) which were listed in the reports of the attorney general under enforcement actions as: California, Connecticut, Indiana, Kansas, Michigan, New Jersey, New York, Ohio, Pennsylvania, Rhode Island, and Idaho Territory. House Executive Documents, 41st Cong., 3rd Sess., No. 90; 43rd Cong., 1st Sess., No. 6; 2nd Sess., No. 20; 45th Cong., 2nd Sess., No. 7; and Senate Executive Documents, 42nd Cong., 34th Sess., No. 32.
Source: William Gillette, *Retreat From Reconstruction 1869–1879* (Baton Rouge: Louisiana State University Press, 1979), p. 43.

Gillette writes: "The record of federal election enforcement was pitiable indeed; the few minor successes in South Carolina in 1872, in North Carolina in 1871 and 1873, and in Mississippi in 1872 and 1873, were limited both in length of time and in effect and subsequently turmoil *became* as endemic as in those places where little or no enforcement had been attempted." Gillette's research revealed that between 1870 and 1877 the mean rate of conviction for depriving a person of his right to vote in federal elections was thirty-four percent in the South, six percent in the Border states and forty percent in the North. The national mean was thirty percent. "Out of 4,187 enforcement cases in the entire country, only 1,246 resulted in convictions."[12] This was just the tip of the iceberg during this period of widespread political disorder, for as Gillette adds, "there were but two convictions under the enforcement acts in chaotic Louisiana, a mere ten in Alabama, four in Georgia, one in Texas and none in Arkansas. Indeed, there was scarcely any federal enforcement at all except in three southern states and that only between 1871 and 1873."[13]

Figure 6.1 permits one to compare over time the percentage of convictions in the South, the Border states, the North, and in the whole nation from 1870 to 1877. In the South enforcement peaked in the 1872 presidential election year, in the North and Border states in the 1870 congressional election year, and on the national level in 1870 and 1872. "Consequently, political violence flourished unabated and electoral fraud was commonplace, sophisticated and highly successful. . . . Indeed, political violence and disturbances were so persistent, so widespread and so formidable as to constitute civil disobedience and guerrilla warfare."[14] In fact, it is clear that long before the judicial decisions of 1876 that circumscribed the federal election enforcement laws, such enforcement had collapsed—by 1874 or well before in most of the country. In its first effort to enforce civil rights laws—in this instance, the protection of voting rights for blacks—the federal government had advanced "brave talk but timid action." One scholar summarized the federal regulatory and enforcement apparatus in that era:

> . . . the federal program to prosecute and punish perpetrators of force and fraud in southern elections had not accomplished much that was substantial or enduring. With election enforcement often characterized by pious platitudes and undercut by penny-pinching; governed by episodic expedients and often overseen by mediocre administrators; lacking central control and local coordination; plagued by delay and timidity and undermined by premature suspension and pardoning; beset by an unwieldy, inefficient court system and ravaged by an understaffed, underfinanced prosecution—moreover, with the magnitude of the enforcement problem being greater than the scope of the federal remedy, with unenforceable law being abandoned in the face of unyielding opposition, and with state statutes legalizing noncompliance and federal courts often rationalizing local practice—the law of enforcement was no law at all.[15]

The parallels between the federal regulatory and enforcement effort then and that which has been described in this research are striking and instructive. In both eras there was much to be desired and much more to be done.

In the reconstruction era, the federal government eventually abandoned its enforcement effort altogether and through a political deal returned the "racial problem" to the states for their solutions. Put another way, the federal government got out of the civil rights regulatory business. Slack enforcement gave

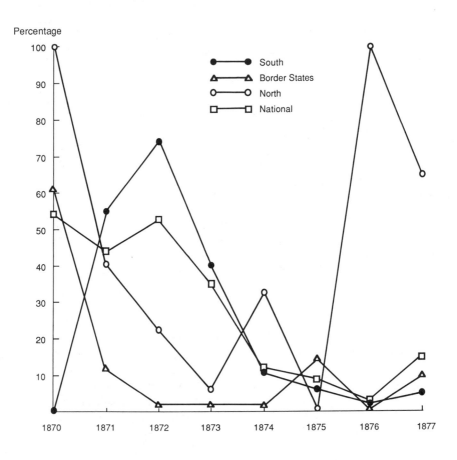

Figure 6.1
Convictions in the South, the Border States, the North,
and on the National Level: 1870–1877

way to no enforcement at all. On the state level, several black spokespersons, particularly the conservatives and apologists for segregation, assisted the white leaders of the Democratic party in eliminating equal rights for blacks in southern society and made the Republican abandonment of civil rights regulatory efforts more palatable. This coupled with the great silence of black Republican leaders—who stood by and waited for the Republican party to act—sealed their doom and that of the black electorate.[16] These sad events set up the legacy for the second period of governmental regulatory policies on civil rights.

This second era, which began in the 30s, 40s, and 50s and reached its peak with the 1964 and 1965 Civil Rights Acts, was led recently by the late Dr. Martin Luther King, Jr. Events of this period of time have been referred to and collectively described as the civil rights movement. How that movement worked to bring the federal government back into the business of civil rights regulation can be seen in Figure 6.2. There were three phases to the new movement. Phase one lasted from 1955 to 1961; it saw the struggle played out mostly between the movement and southern whites. In this phase, the federal government played the role of a neutral observer, for the most part. In this period most of the federal government's actions were little more than to act as mediator—intervening only to keep the peace and to get people to talk with each other. All during the Montgomery bus boycott, the early sit-in efforts, the freedom rides, and the Albany demonstrations, the federal government watched from the sidelines.

However, in the second phase of the movement, 1963–1968, King and his chief strategists decided to create so much tension, conflict, and struggle between blacks and whites through nonviolent marches, demonstrations, and protests that the federal government would be forced to step away from the sidelines and take sides with the movement and against those who used violence and fraud to deny individuals their basic human rights as promised in the Constitution and elaborated in the Declaration of Independence. Of this plan, one scholar writes:

> The aim of this strategy . . . is to demonstrate that segregation can no longer be enforced in the south except by constant police repression. An immediate objective is to force negotiation that will bring some changes in racial practices. Always in the thinking of the demonstrators is the desire to embarrass our national leaders, to assail the national conscience—and, if possible, to bring on federal intervention, to force the hand of the man in the White House, so that the slow pace of action on civil rights would be stepped up.[17]

King himself wrote that, "non-violent direct action seeks to create such a crisis and foster such a tension that a community which has constantly refused to negotiate is forced to confront the issue" and "non-violent action . . . is . . .

Figure 6.2
The Three Phases of the Government Involvement
in the Civil Rights Movement in the South

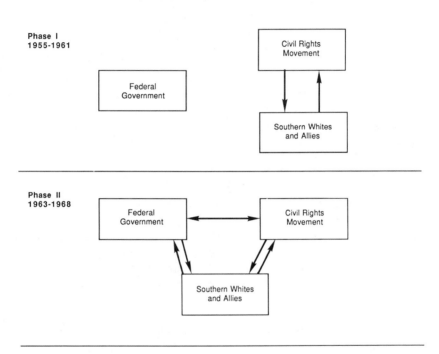

Phase I
1955-1961

Civil Rights Movement

Federal Government

Southern Whites and Allies

Phase II
1963-1968

Federal Government

Civil Rights Movement

Southern Whites and Allies

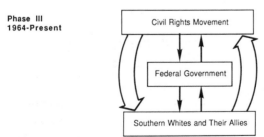

Phase III
1964-Present

Civil Rights Movement

Federal Government

Southern Whites and Their Allies

the way to supplement—not—replace the process of change through legal recourse."[18]

This was not exactly what the federal government wanted, and prior to the Birmingham demonstrations the government had watched from the sidelines. But it was clearly the Birmingham demonstrations and subsequent events that forced a reluctant government to take sides.[19] Once it took sides, it was not only operating against a large segment of its population but against several southern states as well. For a democratic nation, this could not continue without charges that it was a police state, using police repression and causing serious regional conflict. Hence, the stage was set for phase three—which went into effect shortly after the 1964 Civil Rights Act created the new civil rights regulatory agencies.

In this phase, the federal government moved to quickly defuse the situation and lower the conflict and the tensions. It did this by trying at the same time to move back to a neutral position, that is, by shifting sides away from blacks and the civil rights movement to a middle ground—a position that would allow it to get input from both sides and would let the government appear as friendly and as sympathetic to both sides as possible.[20] This shift, when it came, would ensure that the government would wave, waffle, and be flexible. Moreover, by being in charge to a large extent of the speed with which civil rights changes could take place, the government's own position could blunt the shock and pace of civil rights advances. Thus, by institutionalizing the movement, the government deradicalized it and lowered its revolutionary zeal. Now, the movement had to operate both through the government—i.e., demand better and more vigorous enforcement and/or new laws and try to get the government back to its side—while simultaneously trying to combat racism, discrimination, and the continuing legacy of slavery and segregation. This is a twofold task, now much greater and far more difficult because the federal government wants to remain neutral which to a large extent it can do because its civil rights enforcement apparatus is in part a crisis management program.[21]

It is a crisis management program because it operates as a buffer to both sides of the racial conflict. Southern whites and their allies and supporters can now, as did black civil rights leaders years ago, go to the different components of the civil rights enforcement apparatus and try to effect a change in regulatory policy and impact. They can contend that blacks are pushing too hard; that civil rights regulations are unfair, unreasonable, and too difficult to accept and live with; and now they can claim that these regulations and rules are un-American and unconstitutional. In addition, during his first term, Reagan showed that these groups and ideological organizations can even capture a part, if not all, of the civil rights enforcement machinery. Take, for instance, the contradictory actions of President Reagan in his first term in office in regard to civil rights. On one hand, he signed into law a bill giving the nation a national holiday for a black civil rights leader. Then, on the other hand he worked to dismantle or reorganize the Civil Rights Commission along conservative ideological lines. And in this effort he strongly attacked goals, quotas, and affirmative action as being unconstitutional and un-American. In one action he pleased blacks and the civil rights movement and angered the anti–civil rights forces. In the next action he pleased the anti–civil rights forces and angered blacks and the civil rights movement. Both sides got a little bit, and the government was able to continue to look like a neutral observer. There are no clear winners and no clear losers, as there seemed to be in the early phases of the movement.

The governmental pressure groups can operate on behalf of the civil rights movement and then again can operate, as the Reagan administration has shown, in opposition to the movement and in support of the anti–civil rights coalition. The inside group can operate, as it is presently doing, in a split fashion—with part of the apparatus working to support the movement while the other part is working to oppose it.

There is a final option. The internal governmental pressure groups can do nothing—waiting for a crisis to act—and simply continue in a rather slow, cumbersome, and unyielding fashion with a mix of reactions.

The problem lies in the nature of government itself. No government can long exist in a turbulent world of continuous revolution. Nor can the government permit continual tensions and crises to run rampant in society. So as a simple matter of self-preservation government has to moderate the pace of change and blunt the impact of shock and disruption and the unknown—the future. There is, of course, a cost involved in this, and that is that government itself becomes the focus of criticism. Those favoring a position blame the government and those opposing a position blame government. In America, the critics of the federal bureaucracy and Congress are legion, but because of the complexities and size of modern government—in this case, the vast civil rights enforcement bureaucracy—the entity simply absorbs the criticism and continues apace.

Thus, the two players, the opposing pressure groups in the civil rights area, can now contend with each other as much as they want, and with the federal civil rights enforcement apparatus operating as referee and player, the struggle is set to play until the two sides literally exhaust themselves and move on to another issue—which will certainly be some time in the distant future.

The Concept of "Deregulation" in Civil Rights Politics

Long before the neo-conservatives and the Reagan administration brought the concept of deregulation to Washington, the Department of Housing and Urban Development has started to delegate several of its fair housing cases to state and local governments for resolution and civil rights enforcement.[22] In fact, by June

15, 1983, HUD had determined that thirty states—listed in Table 6.2—had fair housing laws that provide rights and remedies "substantially equivalent" to those provided by Title VIII of the Civil Rights Act of 1968.[23] Such a designation entitled these states to have referred to their fair housing agencies certain housing discrimination complaints.[24]

Table 6.2   The States with Housing Laws Equivalent to Title VIII of the Civil Rights Acts of 1968

States		
Alaska	New Jersey	Wisconsin
California	Maine	New Mexico
Colorado	Maryland	New York
Connecticut	Massachusetts	Oregon
Delaware	Michigan	Pennsylvania
Illinois	Minnesota	Rhode Island
Indiana	Montana	South Dakota
Iowa	Nebraska	Virginia
Kansas	Nevada	Washington
Kentucky	New Hampshire	West Virginia

Source: Federal Register, (July 15, 1983).

The Reagan administration liked the procedures put into place by HUD because it shifted responsibilities to state and local governments. Thus, OMB during the Reagan administration was provoked to write: "During 1984, HUD continued its aggressive efforts to expand the involvement of the private sector and state and local governments in assuring fair housing. Through direct grants and technical assistance, HUD helped state and local agencies develop procedures, train staff, and complete other tasks necessary to develop the capacity to process fair housing complaints."[25]

OMB went on to praise the HUD procedure and suggest it as a model for other federal civil rights agencies. Their tables showed clearly how more and more power was delegated to state and local agencies by HUD. As can be seen in Table 6.3, HUD by 1984 delegated more than two-thirds of its complaints to state and local agencies for resolution. Gradually the civil rights responsibility under Title VIII has been shifted to the states.

By the end of Reagan's first term several other federal agencies began to move to imitate HUD, and the Department of Education had already signed several agreements with various states to begin to experiment with state enforcement of civil rights laws in education, especially vocational education.[26] In 1979 HEW had issued vocational education guidelines that required each state that administrated federal grants to school districts and area vocational-technical schools to devise and carry out a plan (Methods of Administration—MOA) to identify and eliminate unlawful discrimination.[27]

Table 6.3 Complaints Processed by Federal and State Governments: 1980–1984

Years	Federal Government		State	
1980	3,039	86%	410	14%
1981	4,209	60%	1,661	40%
1982	5,112	48%	2,679	52%
1983	4,551	40%	2,736	60%
1984	4,533	32%	3,062	68%

Source: Calculated and adapted from Office of Management and Budget, Special Analysis: 1986, p. J–24.

In 1983 officials at the Department of Education were claiming great success for this MOA process and were making suggestions that more areas of responsibility be delegated to the states. But the Lawyers' Committee—a civil rights external pressure group—immediately evaluated the MOA and found it to be completely ineffectual. Their report found that "some states" had made a "very good start" while "others have done little or nothing." And the report showed "a history of delayed, inept or missing initiatives by the federal agency to assist the states in carrying out their MOA's. Although most states had no experience in civil rights enforcement, the Department of Education has offered little training and assistance in either design or implementation phase—and when training was made available, it was too late to be of the greatest aid to the states."

Deregulation in the Reagan administration has come to mean the delegation of civil rights responsibilities to the states with as little guidance and assistance as possible and the reduction of some of the paper-work requirements that now go along with federal civil rights enforcement.[28]

There is the possibility that deregulation as defined during the Reagan administration might continue to grow. Whatever form it takes, deregulation helps the federal government maintain its neutral posture by allowing it to deflect its responsibilities to the states. And in the states there are potentials and liabilities that the various civil rights groups will surely illuminate in the days and years ahead.

Summary and Conclusions

In this second era of federal civil rights regulatory and enforcement activity, the machinery and procedures that have emerged have come to reflect our complex society. Moreover, because the government is not monolithic and the people who run it have some discretion in carrying out their duties and functions, the structure of the enforcement machinery is diverse, scattered, and fragmentary. And because governmental leaders constantly change, this hodge-podge of structures likewise constantly changes and shifts. Personnel and financial support have followed the same shifting patterns. Altogether, the constant shifting explains the inconsistent degrees of enforcement. Moreover, pressure groups which have varying degrees of influence and legal access have affected the vigor of government enforcement of civil rights law.

But more important is that the enforcement machinery is responsive to contending forces, and some segments of the enforcement apparatus have been captured by the anti–civil rights forces. The struggle goes on and the end is nowhere in sight. Given the creativity of the black leaders of the sixties, the potential is there to once again create a period of ideals and promise that will force the government to take sides and win a swift and possibly a permanent victory. But political victories can be compromised away, and new forces may shift the government to their side. In the meantime, the government will constantly struggle to gain neutral ground.

The final question before concluding is a simple one. What did the institutionalization of the civil rights revolution and movement really mean in this democratic soceity? Put otherwise, what are the outcomes in a democracy when the federal government goes into the business of civil rights?

In America, institutionalization of the civil rights movement means that the federal government itself can now affect the pace, mood, and the tenor of the movement. First of all, institutionalization meant the defusing of the revolutionary fervor and the emotionalism of the movement. This, in turn, means the defusing of some of the concerns and priorities of the movement. For as we have seen in earlier chapters, the protection and the promotion of civil rights by the federal government can be affected by the structuring of bureaucratic units, the staffing, financing, and commitments of presidential leadership. These forces can slow or speed up the pace, they can modify the mood of protection and promotion by retrenching or vigorously supporting the law of the land. And in regard to the tenor and tempo, procedures and techniques designed to enhance and enlarge civil rights can be made to appear as being anti-American, unconstitutional, and reverse discrimination.

In this democratic society, institutionalization of the civil rights movement has meant that civil rights is now treated as a "special interest" of minorities, just like the special interests of farmers, labor unions, women, consumers, peace groups, space enthusiasts, war mongers, etc. Thus, the budget for the protection and enhancement of civil rights must now compete with that of the farmers, NASA, the environmentalists, labor unions, and business as if these private interests are the same thing as guaranteed constitutional rights. They are not and never have been.

For instance, while civil rights is supposed to be a fundamental constitutional guarantee, treating it as any other or no more than the "special concerns" of a racial minority means that it can be given more or less protection depending upon what party is in power. Partisan support for this "special interest" literally depends upon political and electoral majorities. As these majorities change from one election to another, then so can the protection and enhancement of civil rights. This is identical to increasing or decreasing the military budget, price support for farmers, and space appropriations. Yet civil rights is not a material or a commodity but a quality of human existence in democratic society. A "special interest" designation does not make the distinction.

Institutionalization of the civil rights movement has meant not only a transformation but *open access*. By treating civil rights as just another special interest, the federal government has now permitted equal and *open access* to it by all sectors of this democratic society. Not only can anti–civil rights groups access the federal civil rights bureaucracy, but other groups as well who may not have anything against civil rights but just might be fiscal conservatives, state's righters, defense supporters, etc. These groups can become allies and engage in log rolling to limit the budgets and regulatory powers of the pro–civil rights forces, because they feel that the funds can be better used in their areas or that the regulations are too restrictive on profits. In a word *open access* means that anti–civil rights groups can now get more and newer allies. Thus, the protection and enhancement of civil rights in this *open access* area can become a very complex issue with innumerable strands, instead of a simple racial matter requiring a meaningful solution.

And because of *open access*, pro–civil rights leaders and supporters who can also access the federal bureaucracy find themselves fighting foes that come with different arguments and an array of technical, legal, and economic procedures and devices to halt the exercise of a guaranteed constitutional right. In this new type of struggle, the battle simply cannot be waged solely by arguments of moral suasion or protest demonstrations, but requires effective lobbying, legal expertise, powerful public relations, the adroit use of money, and electioneering. Both the battlefield and the nature of the conflict have changed under the special interest device of *open access*.

Ultimately, open access means that each side has a right to a fair hearing, fair play, and objective treatment. Thus, white supremacists, just plain ole racists, superpatriots, and others can now get equal time and equal hearing and—possibly—an equal chance for impact and influence as would those who believe in the equality of man, human brotherhood, and a pluralistic society. Victory goes not to the "moral" side but to the astute player in the political universe of the federal civil rights bureaucracy.

Finally, institutionalization means a continuous struggle. In the words of Reinhold Neibhur, the search for justice in a system of competing interests is a difficult and endless one—because such a system cannot completely dispense justice. Thus, the best that can be hoped for is compromised justice and, in the case of civil rights, it is "compromised compliance." The American political system and process is built on and survives due to compromises. In American politics, compromise is the name of the game and protection and enhancement of civil rights in this system of competing interests will always be compromised as long as it is treated as a special interest. In addition, it is inherent in the very nature of the system that each competing interest must be willing to compromise; each interest, as David Truman has shown in his work *The Governmental Process*, serves as a countervailing check and balance on every other interest.

For example, during both terms of the Reagan administration, individuals and groups that were opposed to civil rights selected members out of the black community to speak out against civil rights, and these black spokespersons argued that civil rights were not needed. What better way to check or counter another interest than to have spokespersons from that very community to deny that they need it or to assert that it is not achieving anything.

In fact, this game was so well played by the competing interests and the use of black spokespersons that black civil rights leaders lost significant ground in terms of public support, and in terms of strong regulatory enforcement of civil rights. The struggle to regain some of their power and influence is still under way and will continue as these competing interests vie with each other. In the end, compromise compliance and compromise justice will always motivate action and reaction, particularly in a democratic society. Therefore, institutionalization of the civil rights revolution and movement was not only not enough but it may beget exactly what it has hoped to moderate, a continuous struggle in the political arena for justice and the civil rights of racial minorities.

APPENDIX A
FEDERAL DATA:
A RESEARCH NOTE

In order to assess the role and function of federal agencies in general and the civil rights regulatory agencies in particular, the researcher must rely on the statistics that are produced by these agencies as they perform their day-to-day functions. The facts are gathered in the form of "numerical quantities like counts, measurements, averages, ratios and so forth."[1] These are reported to the general public and other branches of government as a basis for making decisions, designing public policy, or as proof that something has been accomplished and that the mandate for the office is being carried out.

William Kruskal writes: "The Constitution of the United States of America provided in its first article that the federal government shall collect statistics, a decennial census . . . (and) in . . . years since the first census, . . . the federal statistical system has grown persistently."[2]

He continues: "From a relatively few economic and demographic indexes, the variety of federal statistics (in the numerical sense) is now enormous: in economics from budget studies to national income accounts; in demography from fertility studies to detail small-area age distributions; . . . and in nearly every other area of national concern, numerical statistics are generated in new profusion and variety."[3] When the civil rights regulatory agencies started to collect racial and ethnic data, they were doing nothing new. The collection of federal statistics is deeply rooted in tradition, and in the very nature of the American political system itself.

Although several people and federal agencies in the Reagan administration have questioned the appropriateness of the federal government's collecting racial and ethnic statistics,[4] theirs is not a point of genuine concern. The real question is the matter of quality. A primary task, argues Kruskal, *"confront(ing) those who produce federal statistics: to improve the quality of these statistics in the decade ahead. This is the single most urgent need facing the federal statistical system."*[5] Since the "need to improve the quality of federal data cuts across nearly every field of applied statistics," then, the "urgency of knowing and improving the accuracy of these statistics has become great."[6]

This is a critical problem in the area of civil rights statistics. At least two weaknesses stand out. Every user of federal statistics who wants to be honest and fair should make readers aware of these two problems.

The first problem is that of collection and standardization. OMB, which has the authority in this area, has never used it, and under the Paperwork Reduction Act of 1980, OMB stopped certain agencies like HUD and the Veterans Administration from collecting racial and ethnic data altogether.[7] In addition, during Reagan's first term OMB abolished its statistical branch and informed the various state governments that unless there was a specific "federal" need, the government would no longer collect statistics that were useful to the states, even if these did assist them in carrying out their civil rights functions.[8]

In fact, OMB's action was so alarming that in 1982 and 1983, both the House and the Senate held hearings on OMB's action and its dissolution of the statistical policy branch.[9] In the House the chairman of the Committee on Government Operations wrote in his opening statement: "The Statistical Policy Branch of OMB has been abolished through a reorganization of the Office of Information and Regulatory Affairs. For the first time in 40 years, the nation is without a chief statistician and a distinct governmental unit with the primary responsibility of overseeing Federal Government Statistics and statistical policy."[10] He then concluded that Congress would take appropriate action to see to it that the government would have an "adequate and reliable statistical system."

However, while this struggle between the legislative and executive branches continued in the area of civil rights data, little that is adequate and reliable was assembled over the twenty-year period from 1964 to 1985. And as I have made the reader aware time and again throughout this study, some agencies for years did not collect such statistics because there was no policy from OMB and no pressure to do so.

In addition, those agencies that did collect such data did not report it uniformly for longer than three years. For instance, in its statistical yearbook HUD did not present the same data in comparable form for any length of time. The same problem mars the Department of Agriculture's *Annual Equal Oppor-*

tunity Handbook. As a consequence, it is extremely difficult to conduct a longitudinal study.

If one tries to avoid this problem by asking each agency to send copies of their A-11 reports—i.e., their civil rights reports—one discovers that these reports are either sketchy or incomplete. Worse still, a check of these reports against the civil rights data in the Federal Budget reveals discrepancies. OMB, which receives all of the A-11 reports does not present them in its Civil Rights Analysis section in a consistent and systematic fashion, and OMB reports do not always correspond with what the agencies send out.

If one tries to fill in gaps with telephone calls to the agencies, one can get only "estimates"—educated guesses and calculated responses. And the problem has gotten only worse in the politically charged atmosphere of the Reagan administration. In short, civil rights data is simply not available.

This study has relied primarily upon the data presented in OMB budget analyses and upon that made available in the reports contained in the Department of Justice's *Title VI Forum* (renamed under Reagan the *Civil Rights Forum*). These are the best data sources for this time series analysis. To help the reader understand the problem, in each chapter I have reminded the reader that the data has some limitations.

Previous studies usually have not done this, but instead have presented their analysis as if the data base was fully acceptable—thereby rendering each case study suspect.

The second problem—which is connected to the problem of scattered and uneven statistics—is that in the future, no data at all will be collected. At the Senate hearing on OMB's actions, a member of the Civil Rights Commission and the Joint Center for Political Studies (a black political think-tank) told the Senate Committee on Governmental Affairs how important it was to collect black and minority data.[11] Haven Tipps of the Commission on Civil Rights states: "The statistical products from census data are used to give the Nation an assessment of the progress or lack of progress that has been made towards such goals as equality of opportunity and equality in education, increased employment, and housing. Minorities and women should have a meaningful voice in the development of statistical procedures and social indicators that influence our definition of problems and suggest political options."[12] But despite the criticisms and suggestions made by blacks and other individuals, OMB is still refusing to approve the collection of racial and ethnic data in certain cabinet-level departments, and Congress has not at this writing passed a law to make them do so. This coming gap in the data may never be regained, and policy based upon estimates may end up being worse than policy based upon partial data.[13]

Those who want to analyze federal civil rights data must beware: the scattered and uneven data of today may be succeeded by no data at all in the case of some agencies. The researcher must maintain healthy skepticism before attempting a rigorous statistical manipulation of government facts and figures. Much depends on where data has come from and how it was obtained. Earlier analysts have overlooked some of these data problems on their way to making rather bold conclusions. As the reader can tell, I have tried to form and state my conclusions cautiously because of the unevenness of the data.

One final thought: maybe, just maybe, government does not really want the public to know what type of job it is doing. But no one can say with any certainty, either pro or con, how well the job is being done.

APPENDIX B
SAMPLE LETTERS
OF COMPLIANCE

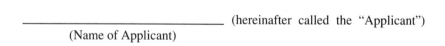 (hereinafter called the "Applicant")
(Name of Applicant)

HEREBY AGREES THAT it will comply with title VI of the Civil Rights Act of
1964 (P.L. 88–352) and all requirements imposed by or pursuant to the Regulation of the Department of Health, Education, and Welfare (45 CFR Part 80) issued pursuant to that title, to the end that, in accordance with title VI of that Act
and the Regulation, no person in the United States shall, on the ground of race,
color, or national origin, be excluded from participation in, be denied the benefits of, or be otherwise subjected to discrimination under any program or activity for which the Applicant receives Federal financial assistance from the Department; and HEREBY gives assurance that it will immediately take any measures necessary to effectuate this agreement.

195

If any real property or structure thereon is provided or improved with the aid of Federal financial assistance extended to the Applicant by the Department, this assurance shall obligate the Applicant, or in the case of any transfer of such property, and transferee, for the period during which the real property or structure is used for a purpose for which the Federal financial assistance is extended or for another purpose involving the provision of similar services or benefits. If any personal property is so provided, this assurance shall obligate the Applicant for the period during which it retains ownership or possession of the property. In all other cases, this assurance shall obligate the Applicant for the period during which the Federal financial assistance is extended to it by the Department.

THIS ASSURANCE is given in consideration of and for the purpose of obtaining any and all Federal grants, loans, contracts, property, discounts or other Federal financial assistance extended after such date on account of applications for Federal financial assistance which were approved before such date. The Applicant recognizes and agrees that such Federal financial assistance will be extended in reliance on the representations and agreements made in this assurance, and that the United States shall have the right to seek judicial enforcement of this assurance. This assurance is binding on the Applicant, its successors, transferees, and assignees, and the person or persons whose signatures appear below are authorized to sign this assurance on behalf of the Applicant.

Dated _____   _____
                                                        (Applicant)

                       By _____
                                          (President, Chairman of Board, or
_____   comparable authorized official)

(Applicant's mailing address)

U.S. DEPARTMENT OF THE INTERIOR
ASSURANCE OF COMPLIANCE
(TITLE VI, CIVIL RIGHTS ACT OF 1964)

_____ (hereinafter called "Applicant-Recipient")
(Name of Applicant-Recipient)

HEREBY AGREES THAT IT will comply with Title VI of the Civil Rights Act of 1964 9P.L. 88–352) and all requirements imposed by or pursuant to the Department of the Interior Regulation (43 CFR 17) issued pursuant to that title, to the end that, in accordance with Title VI of the Act and the Regulation, no person in the United States shall, on the ground of race, color, or national origin be excluded from participation in, be denied the benefits of, or be otherwise subjected to discrimination under any program or activity for which the Applicant-Recipient receives financial assistance from _____

Bureau or Office

and Hereby Gives Assurance That It will immediately take any measures to effectuate this agreement.

If any real property or structure thereon is provided or improved with the aid of Federal financial assistance extended to the Applicant-Recipient by _____ . This assurance obligates the

Bureau or Office

Applicant-Recipient, or in the case of any transfer of such property, any transferee for the period during which the real property or structure is used for a purpose involving the provision of similar services or benefits. If any personal property is so provided, this assurance obligates the Applicant-Recipient for the period during which it retains ownership or possession of the property. In all other cases, this assurance obligates the Applicant-Recipient for the period during which the Federal financial assistance is extended to it by _____ .

Bureau or Office

THIS ASSURANCE is given in consideration of and for the purpose of obtaining any and all Federal grants loans, contracts, property discounts or other Federal financial assistance extended after the date hereof to the Applicant-Recipient by the bureau or office, including installment payments after such date on account to arrangements for Federal financial assistance which were approved before such date. The Applicant-Recipient recognizes and agrees that such Federal financial assistance will be extended in reliance on the representation and agreements made in this assurance, and that the United States shall reserve the right to seek judiciary enforcement of this assurance. This assurance is binding on the Applicant-Recipient, its successors, transferees, and assignees, and the person or persons whose signature appear below are authorized to sign this assurance on behalf of the Applicant-Recipient.

_____   _____

DATED   APPLICANT-RECIPIENT

By _____

(President, Chairman of Board or
Comparable Authorized Official)

_____

APPLICANT-RECIPIENT'S MAILING ADDRESS

APPENDIX C
AN EXAMPLE OF THE
LETTER SENT TO *ALL*
CABINET DEPARTMENTS

October 23, 1981

Mr. Clarence Thomas
Director: Office of Civil Rights Compliance
Department of Education
Washington, D.C.

Dear Director Thomas:

I am currently preparing a comprehensive study of the Office of Civil Rights Compliance created by Title VI of the 1964 Civil Rights Act and need the following information from your particular department on how your office has carried out this mandate. The study is being supported by the Rockefeller Foundation and the areas in which I need to collect data are:

1. The most recent organization chart of your agency;
2. The line and staff sizes over the years since your inception;

3. If possible a copy of your budgets with the pertinent categories since the inception of your office;
4. Number of complaints coming to your office each year;
5. The number of complaint resolutions for your office each year;
6. The number of administrative actions, i.e., fund terminations, hearing, etc.;
7. Copies of your OMB reports dealing with management by objectives;
8. All internal and external departmental orders with Title VI implications;
9. Codes of Federal Regulations (CFRs) that address Title VI requirements;
10. Circulars, assurances and/or guidelines relating to the implementations of Title VI Program requirements; and
11. Copies and/or summaries of Title VI Compliance findings, mediations and litigations.

If I need to pay for any xeroxing, just let me know. Thanks for your help and cooperation in this matter.

Sincerely,

Hanes Walton, Jr.
Fuller E. Callaway Professor of
Political Science

APPENDIX D
COPY OF THE LETTER SENT
FROM THE WHITE HOUSE
TO AUTHOR

THE WHITE HOUSE
WASHINGTON

July 28, 1980

Dear Professor Walton:

Louis Martin asked me to send you a list of Offices of Civil Rights within the Federal Government. I have discovered, as you did before me, that no such comprehensive list exists and therefore, I am attempting to prepare one. I will send you a copy when I have completed the list.

Sincerely,

Robert A. Malson
Assistant Director
Domestic Policy Staff

Mr. Hanes Walton, Jr.
Fuller E. Callaway Professor
of Political Science
Savannah State College
Savannah, Georgia 31404

Appendix E
Copy of the Civil
Rights Restoration
Act of 1985

Copy of the Civil Rights Restoration Act of 1985 which was introduced in both the 98th and 99th Congresses because of the Supreme Court's decision in *Grove City College v. Bell*, (1984). In the House Report on the bill, the Committee on Education and Labor put the purpose of the bills in this manner. "Its purpose is simple and straightforward, to restore and thereby reaffirm the broad scope of coverage in the interpretations and enforcement practices of the executive branch and judical decisions supporting that broad reading prior to the Supreme Court's decision in *Grove City College v. Bell*." Although the bill passed the House in 1984, because it was not supported by the Reagan administration, it did not pass the Senate. In 1985, it became stalled in the House.

Also attached to the bill, is a list of the various sponsors and cosponsors of the bill and when they decided to support and sponsor it.

However, before looking at the 1985 bill that died with the ending of the 99th Congress, it should be mentioned that shortly after the 100th Congress started, Senate Edward Kennedy, introduced bill S.557, "The Civil Rights Restoration Act of 1987", and five days later Representative Augustus Hawkins, introduced a companion measure in the House. As mentioned earlier, the Civil Rights Restoration Act was passed by wide margin by both Houses of Congress in early 1988 but President Reagan has threatened to veto the legislation.

UNION CALENDAR NO. 583
H.R. 700
[REPORT NO. 99-963, PARTS I AND II]

To restore the broad scope of coverage and to clarify the application of Title IX of the Education Amendments of 1972, section 504 of the Rehabilitation Act of 1973, the Age Discrimination Act of 1975, and title VI of the Civil Rights Act of 1964

IN THE HOUSE OF REPRESENTATIVES

JANUARY 24, 1985

Mr. HAWKINS (for himself, Mr. EDWARDS of California, Mr. FISH, Mr. JEFFORDS, Mr. RODINO, Mr. CONYERS, Mrs. SCHROEDER, Mr. MILLER of California, Mr. TAUKE, Mrs. BURTON of California, Mr. FRANK, Mr. ACKERMAN, Mr. BOUCHER, Mr. FEIGHAN, Mr. KASTEN-MEIER, Mr. SCHUMER, Mr. CROCKETT, Mr. MARTINEZ, Mr. WIL-LIAMS, Mr. KILDEE, Mr. CLAY, Mr. OWENS, Mr. HAYES. Mrs. SCHNEIDER, Ms. SNOWE, Mr. ADDABBO, Mr. SAVAGE, Mr. DYM-ALLY, Mr. FRENZEL, Mr. MORRISON of Connecticut, Mrs. KENNELLY, Mr. COELHO, Mr. WHEAT, Mr. SCHEUER, Mr. LELAND, Mr. RICHARDSON, Mr. MINETA, Mr. VENTO, Mr. MOODY, Mrs. JOHNSON, Mr. TORRES, Mr. DE LUGO, Mr. GARCIA, Mr. ROYBAL, Mr. BUSTAMANTE, Mrs. COLLINS, Mr. DELLUMS, Mr. GRAY of Pennsylvania, Mr. MITCHELL, Mr. STOKES, Ms. OAKAR, Ms. KAP-TUR, Ms. MIKULSKI, Mr. FAUNTROY, Mrs. BOXER, Mr. TOWNS, Mr. CARPER, Mr. McKERNAN, Mr. FUSTER, Mr. ANDREWS, Mr. CONTE, and Mr. DIXON) introduced the following bill; which was referred jointly to the Committees on Education and Labor and the Judiciary

FEBRUARY 13, 1985

Additional sponsors: Mr. AUCOIN, Mr. ASPIN, Mr. BARNES, Mr. BATES, Mr. BEDELL, Mr. BERMAN, Mr. BIAGGI, Mr. BOLAND, Mr. BONIOR of Michigan, Mr. BOSCO, Mr. BROWN of California, Mr. COUGHLIN,

Mr. COYNE, Mr. DORGAN of North Dakota, Mr. DURBIN, Mr. DWYER of New Jersey, Mr. EDGAR, Mr. FASCELL, Mr. FORD of Tennessee, Mr. FOWLER, Mr. GEJDENSON, Mr. GEPHARDT, Mr. GILMAN, Mr. GLICKMAN, Mr. GREEN, Mr. GRADISON, Mr. GUARINI, Mr. HORTON, Mr. HOWARD, Mr. HOYER, Mr. HUGHES, Mr. JACOBS, Mr. KOLTER, Mr. LANTOS, Mr. LEACH of Iowa, Mr. LEHMAN of Florida, Mr. LEVIN of Michigan, Mr. LOWRY of Washington, Mr. McKINNEY, Mr. MARKEY, Mrs. MARTIN of Illinois, Mr. MOAKLEY, Mr. MRAZEK, Mr. NOWAK, Mr. OLIN, Mr. PANETTA, Mr. PEASE, Mr. PEPPER: Mr. PICKLE, Mr. RAHALL, Mr. ROE, Mr. ROSE, Mr. ROWLAND of Connecticut, Mr. SABO, Mr. ST GERMAIN, Mr. SEIBERLING, Mr. SIKORSKI, Mr. SMITH of Florida, Mrs. SMITH of Nebraska, Mr. STARK, Mr. STUDDS, Mr. SWIFT, Mr. SYNAR, Mr. TORRICELLI, Mr. TRAXLER, Mr. UDALL, Mr. VISCLOSKY, Mr. VOLKMER, Mr. WALGREN, Mr. WAXMAN, Mr. WEAVER, Mr. WEISS, and Mr. WOLFE

FEBRUARY 28, 1985

Additional sponsors: Mr. BLAZ, Mr. BOEHLERT, Mr. BRYANT, Mr. DASCHLE, Mr. DAVIS, Mr. EARLE, Mr. ECKART of Ohio, Mr. EVANS of Iowa, Mr. FAZIO, Mr. FROST, Mr. FORD of Michigan, Mr. FOGLIETTA, Mr. HAMILTON, Mr. HEFTEL of Hawaii, Mr. KLECZKA, Mr. LEVIN of California, Mr. LUDINE, Mr. MATSUI, Mr. MILLER of Washington, Mr. OBERSTAR, Mr. RANGEL, Mr. REGULA, Mr. SOLARZ, Mr. WHITEHURST, Mr. WIRTH, Mr. WISE, Mr. WORTLEY, Mr. WHLIE, Mr. YATES, Mr. ATKINS, Mr. ZSCHAU, Mr. BONER of Tennessee, Mr. ANDERSON, Mr. KOSTMAYER, Mrs. LUKEN, and Mr. EVANS of Illinois

APRIL 4, 1985

Additional sponsors: Mr. AKAKA, Mr. BENNETT, Mrs. BOGGS, Mr. BONKER. Mr. BROOKS, Mr. CARR, Mr. COLEMAN of Texas, Mr. DICKS, Mr. DOWNEY of New York, Mr. DYSON, Mr. GONZALES, Mr. KANJORSKI, Mr. LEHMAN of California, Mr. McHUGH, Mr. MANTON, Mr. MARVROULES, Mr. MAZZOLI, Mr. SLATTERY, Mr. TRAFICANT, and Mr. WYDEN

SEPTEMBER 9, 1985

Additional sponsors: Mr. ANTHONY, Mr. BEILENSON, Mr. BORSKI, Mr. CHANDLER, Mr. DONNELLY, Mr. FLORIO, Mr. HAMMERSCHMIDT, Mr. McCURDY, Mr. WATKINS, Mr. REID, Mr. DOWDY of Mississippi, Mrs. LONG, Mr. McCLOSKEY, Mr. PENNY, and Mr. SMITH of Iowa deleted sponsor: Mr. BLAZ (added February 26, 1985; deleted May 23, 1985)

OCTOBER 3, 1986

Reported from the Committee on the Judiciary with an amendment, and ordered to be printed

OCTOBER 7, 1986

Reported from the Committee on Education and Labor with an amendment, committed to the Committee of the Whole House on the State of the Union and ordered to be printed

A BILL

To restore the broad scope of coverage and to clarify the application of title IX of the Education Amendments of 1972, section 504 of the Rehabilitation Act of 1973, the Age Discrimination Act of 1975, and title VI Of The Civil Rights Act of 1964.

1*   Be it enacted by the Senate and House of Repre-
2   sentatives of the United States of America in Congress
3   assembled,
4   **SECTION 1. SHORT TITLE.**
5   This Act may be cited as the "Civil Rights Res-
6   toration Act of 1985".
7   **SEC. FINDINGS OF CONGRESS.**
8   The Congress finds that—
9   (1) certain aspects of recent decisions
10   and opinions of the Supreme Court have
11   unduly narrowed or cast doubt upon the
12   broad application of title IX of the Education
13   Amendments of 1972, section 504 of the Reha-
14   bilitation Act of 1973, the Age Discrimination
15   Act of 1975, and title VI of the Civil Rights
16   Act of 1964; and
17   (2) legislative action is necessary to re-
18   store the prior consistent and long-standing
19   executive branch interpretation and broad,

1   institution-wide application of those laws as
2   previously administered.

3 **SEC. 3. EDUCATION AMENDMENTS AMENDMENT.**
4   Title IX of the Education Amendments of 1972
5   is amended by adding at the end of the following new
6   section:
7   "INTERPRETATION OF 'PROGRAM OR ACTIVITY'
8   "SEC. 908. For the purposes of this title, the
9   term 'program or activity' and the term 'program'
10   means all of the operations of—
11   "(1) (A) a department, agency, special
12   purpose district, or other instrumentality of a
13   State or of a local government; or
14   "B) the entity of such State or local
15   government that distributes such assistance and
16   each such department or agency (and each
17   other entity) to which the assistance is ex-
18   tended, in the case of assistance to a State or
19   local government;
20   "(2) (A) a college, university, or other
21   postsecondary institution, or a public system
22   of higher education; or
23   "(B) a local educational agency (as de-
24   fined in section 198(a) (10) of the Elementary
25   and Secondary Education Act of 1965),
26   system of vocational education, or other
27   school system;
28   "(3) (A) an entire corporation, partner-
29   ship, or other private organization, or an
30   entire sole proprietorship—
31   "(i) if assistance is extended to such
32   corporation, partnership, private organi-
33   zation, or sole proprietorship as a whole;
34   or
35   "(ii) which is principally engaged in
36   the business of providing education,
37   health care, housing, social services, or
38   parks and recreation; or
39   "(B) the entire plant or other compara-
40   ble, geographically separate facility to
41   which Federal financial assistance is

1   extended, in the case of any other corpora-
2   tion, partnership, private organization, or
3   sole proprietorship; or
4   "(4) any combination comprised of two
5   or more of the entities described in para-
6   graph (1), (2), or (3);
7 any part of which is extended Federal financial as-
8 sistance, except that such terms do not include
9 any operation of an entity which is controlled by a
10 religious organization if the application of section
11 901 to such operation would not be consistent with
12 the religious tenets of such organization.".
13 **SEC. 4. REHABILITATION ACT AMENDMENT.**
14   Section 504 of the Rehabilitation Act of 1973
15 is amended—
16   (1) by inserting "(a)" after "SEC. 504.";
17   and
18   (2) by adding at the end the following
19   new subsections:
20   "(b) For the purposes of this section, the term
21   'program or activity' means all of the operations
22   of—
23   (1) (A) a department, agency, special
24   purchase district, or other instrumentality of a
25   State or of a local government; or
26   "(B) the entity of such State or local gov-
27   ernment that distributes such assistance and
28   each such department or agency (and each
29   other entity) to which the assistance is ex-
30   tended, in the case of assistance to a State or
31   local government;
32   "(2) (A) a college, university, or other
33   postsecondary institution, or a public system
34   of higher education; or
35   "(B) a local educational agency (as de-
36   fined in section 198(a) (10) of the Elementary
37   and Secondary Education Act of 1965),
38   system of vocational education, or other
39   school system;
40   "(3) (A) an entire corporation, partner-
41   ship, or other private organization, or an
42   entire sole proprietorship—

"(i) if assistance is extended to such corporation, partnership, private organization, or sole proprietorship as a whole; or

"(ii) which is principally engaged in the business of providing education, health care, housing, social services, or parks and recreation; or

"(B) the entire plant or other comparable, geographically separate facility to which Federal financial assistance is extended, in the case of any other corporation, partnership, private organization, or sole proprietorship; or

"(4) any combination comprised of two or more of the entities described in paragraph (1), (2), or (3);

any part of which is extended Federal financial assistance.

"(c) Small providers are not required by subsection (a) to make significant structural alterations to their existing facilities for the purpose of assuring program accessibility, if alternative means of providing the services are available. The terms used in this subsection shall be construed with reference to the regulations existing on the date of the enactment of this subsection.".

SEC. 5. AGE DISCRIMINATION ACT AMENDMENT.

Section 309 of the Age Discrimination Act of 1975 is amended—

(1) by striking out "and" at the end of paragraph (2)'

(2) by striking out the period at the end of paragraph (3) and inserting "; and" in lieu thereof; and

(3) by inserting after paragraph (3) the Following new paragraph:

"(4) the term 'program or activity' means all of the operations of—

"(a) (i) a department, agency, special purpose district, or other instrumentality of a State or of a local government; or

1   "(ii) the entity of such State or local
2   government that distributes such assist-
3   ance and each such department or
4   agency (and each other entity) to which
5   the assistance is extended, in the case of
6   assistance to a State or local government;
7   "(B) (i) a college, university, or other
8   system of higher education; or
9   "(ii) a local educational agency (as
10   defined in section 198 (a) (10), of the Ele-
11   mentary and Secondary Education Act of
12   1965), system of vocational education, or
13   other school system;
14   "(C) (i) an entire corporation, part-
15   nership, or other private organization, or
16   an entire sole proprietorship—
17   "(I) if assistance is extended to
18   such corporation, partnership, pri-
19   vate organization, or sole proprietor-
20   ship as a whole; or
21   "(II) which is principally en-
22   gaged in the business of providing
23   education, health care, housing,
24   social services, or parks and recrea-
25   tions; or
26   "(ii) the entire plant or other compa-
27   rable, geographically separate facility to
28   which Federal financial assistance is ex-
29   tended, in the case of any other corpora-
30   tion, partnership, private organization, or
31   sole proprietorship; or
32   "(D) any combination comprised of
33   two or more of the entities described in
34   subparagraph (A), (B), or (C);
35   any part of which is extended Federal finan-
36   cial assistance.".
37   **SEC. 6. CIVIL RIGHTS ACT AMENDMENT.**
38   Title VI of the Civil Rights Act of 1964 is
39   amended by adding at the end the following new
40   section:
41   "SEC. 606. For the purposes of this title, the
42   term 'program or activity' and the term 'program'

mean all of the operations of—

  "(1) (A) a department, agency, special
purpose district, or other instrumentality of a
State or of a local government; or

  "(B) the entity of such State or local government that distributes such assistance and
each such department or agency (and each
other entity) to which the assistance is extended, in the case of assistance to a State or
local government;

  "(2) (A) a college, university, or other
postsecondary institution, or a public system
of higher education; or

  "(B) a local educational agency (as defined in section 198(a) (10) of the Elementary
and Secondary Education Act of 1965),
system of vocational education, or other
school system;

  "(3) (A) an entire corporation, partnership, or other private organization, or an
entire sole proprietorship—

    "(i) if assistance is extended to such
corporation, partnership, private organization, or sole proprietorship as a whole;
or

    "(ii) which is principally engaged in
the business of providing education,
health care, housing, social services, or
parks and recreation; or

  "(B) the entire plant or other comparable, geographically separate facility to which
Federal financial assistance is extended, in
the case of any other corporation, partnership, private organization, or sole proprietorship; or

  "(4) any combination comprised of two
or more of the entities described in paragraph (1), (2), or (3);

any part of which is extended Federal financial
assistance.".

SEC. 7. RULE OF CONSTRUCTION.

  Nothing in the amendments made by this Act

1   shall be construed to extend the application of the
2   Acts so amended to ultimate beneficiaries of Fed-
3   eral financial assistance excluded from coverage
4   before the enactment of this Act.
5   **SEC. 8. DISCLAIMER WITH RESPECT TO ABORTION.**
6   The amendments made by this Act are not in-
7   tended to convey either the approval or disapprov-
8   al of Congress concerning the validity or appropri-
9   ateness of regulations issued under title IX of the
10   Education Amendments of 1972 concerning health
11   care insurance or services, or both, for employees
12   and students with regard to abortion.

---

*The column numbers here are representative of the number placed on bills for use in mark-up sessions. Such numbers are to serve as specific locators when words, phrases, and entire sentences are to be modified and altered.

NOTES

PREFACE

[1]See, Paul Burstein, *Discrimination, Jobs, and Politics: The Struggle for Equal Opportunity in the United States since the New Deal* (Chicago: University of Chicago Press, 1985); Benjamin W. Wolkinson, *Blacks, Unions and the EEOC* (Massachusetts: Lexington Books, 1973); David Rosenbloom, *Federal Equal Employment Opportunity: Politics and Public Personnel Administration* (New York: Praeger Publishers, 1977) and his, *Federal Service and the Constitution: The Development of the Public Employment Relationship* (Ithaca: Cornell University Press, 1971); Alfred W. Blumrosen, *Black Employment and the Law* (New Brunswick: Rutgers University Press, 1971); R. Lynn Rittenoure, *Black Employment in the South: The Case of the Federal Government* (Austin: Bureau of Business Research. Study No. 4, 1976); William B. Gould, *Black Workers in White Unions: Job Discrimination in the United States* (Ithaca: Cornell University Press, 1977). For an early work on FEPC, see, Herbert Hill, *Black Labor and the American Legal System: Race, Work and the Law* (Washington, D.C.: Bureau of National Affairs, 1977). See also: Floyd Weatherspoon, *Equal Employment Opportunities Affirmative Action: A Sourcebook* (New York: Garland Publishers, 1984). Additional insights can be had by seeing, Frances R. Cousens, *Public Civil Rights Agencies and Fair Employment* (New York: Praeger, 1969) and EEOC, *Legislative History of Titles VII and XI of Civil Rights Act of 1964* (Washington, D.C.: Government Printing Office, N.D.)

[2]Augustus J. Jones, Jr. *The Law, Bureaucracy and Politics: The Implementations of Title VI of the Civil Rights Act of 1964* (Washington, D.C.: University Press of America, 1982) and Charles S. Bullock, III and Charles M. Lamb, (eds.) *Implementation of Civil Rights Policy* (Monterey: Brooks/Cole Publishing Company, 1984). For two outstanding works that look at the implementation of the Voting Rights Act, see:

Lorn Foster (ed.) *The Voting Rights Act: Consequences and Implications* (New York: Praeger Publishers, 1985) and Howard Ball, et. al. *Compromised Compliance* (Westport: Greenwood Press, 1982).

[3]For insights into those problems see Lenneal J. Henderson, "Administrative Advocacy and Black Urban Administrator," *Annals of the American Academy of Political and Social Science* Vol. 439 (September 1978), pp. 68-70, and his, *Administrative Advocacy: Black Administrators in Urban Bureaucracy* (Palo Alto, Calif: R & E Research Associates, 1979); and Mylon Winn, "Black Public Administrators and Opposing Expectations" in Mitchell F. Rice and Woodrow Jones, Jr., *Contemporary Public Policy Perspectives and Black Americans: Issues in an Era of Retrenchment* (Westport: Greenwood Press, 1984), pp. 187-196.

[4]For another one of his innovative works see, Tobe Johnson, *Metropolitan Government: A Black Analytical Perspective* (Washington, D.C.: Joint Center for Political Studies, 1972).

[5]See Joseph D. Cooper, *The Act of Decision-Making* (Garden City, New York: Doubleday and Company, 1961)

[6]For more of his insight, see, Samuel Dubois Cook, "Democracy and Tyranny in America: The Radical Paradox of the Bicentennial and Blacks in the American Political System." *Journal of Politics* Vol. 38 (August 1976) pp. 276–294.

[7]Thomas C. Holt, "Introduction: Whither Now and Why?" in Darlene Clark Hine, (ed.), *The State of Afro-American History: Past, Present and Future* (Baton Rouge: Louisiana State University Press, 1986) pp. 1–10.

[8]John Hope Franklin, "On the Evolution of Scholarship in Afro-American History," in Hine, pp. 13–22.

CHAPTER 1

[1]On W. T. Walker, see Lerone Bennett, *What Manner of Man*, 1st ed. (Chicago: Johnson Publishing Company, 1964); on Rustin, see his "From Protest to Politics: The Future of the Civil Rights Movement" in his book *Down the Line: The Collected Writings of Bayard Rustin* (Chicago: Quadrangle Books, 1979), pp. 111–112.

[2]For some of the recent works on the movement see, Charles W. Eagles (ed.) *The Civil Rights Movement in America* (Jackson: University Press of Mississippi, 1986); Aldon Morris, *Origins of the Civil Rights Movement* (New York: Free Press, 1984). This is an exceptional work and must be read by any student of the movement. And see, Clayborne Carson, "The King Within Us All," *Focus* (January 1987), pp. 6-7 for a reinterpretation of King's leadership role. See also, Rhoda Goldstein Blumberg, *Civil Rights: The 1960's Freedom Struggle* (Boston: Twayne Publishing, 1984).

[3]Pendleton Herring, *The Politics of Democracy* (New York: W. W. Norton, 1965), p. 184.

[4]See Ingel P. Bell, *Core and the Strategy of Nonviolence* (New York: Random House, 1968).

[5]Martin Luther King, Jr., *Where Do We Go From Here: Chaos or Community?* (New York: Harper and Row, 1967), pp. 1–23.

[6]Charles and Barbara Whalen, *The Longest Debate: A Legislative History of the 1964 Civil Rights Act* (Cabin John: Sevens Locks Press, 1984).

[7]Ibid., pp. 124–148.

[8]On the point of a non-democratic society, see Manning Marable, *Black American Politics: From the Washington Marches to Jesse Jackson* (London: Verso, 1985).

[9]Robert Allen, *Reluctant Reformers: Racism and Social Reform Movements in the United States* (Washington: Howard University Press, 1974).

[10]On this point see Robert Tucker, "The Deradicalization of Marxist Movements," *American Political Science Review* Vol. LXI, No. 2 (June 1967) pp. 346–348.

[11]Ibid., p. 348.

[12]Arthur Schlesinger, *A Thousand Days* (New York: Houghton Mifflin, 1965), pp. 976–977.

[13]These two documents can be seen in Rayford W. Logan and Michael R. Winston, *The Negro in the United States*, Vol. 2 (New York: Van Nostrand Reinhold Company, 1971), pp. 157–162. (Titles VI and VII are in Appendix One).

[14]See Louis Kohlmeier, *The Regulators: Watch Dog Agencies and the Public Interest* (New York: Harper and Row, 1969); and James Q. Wilson, ed., *The Politics of Regulation* (New York: Basic Books, 1980).

[15]Whalen, p. 231.

[16]Ibid., p. 126.

[17] Robert K. Carr, *Federal Protection of Civil Rights: Quest for a Sword* (Ithaca: Cornell University Press, 1947), p. 24.

[18]*Ibid.*

[19]*Ibid.*, footnote 35.

[20]*Ibid.*, p. 25. footnote 37.

[21]For a fascinating part of the story as it focuses upon blacks, see Patrick S. Washington, *A Question of Sedition: The Federal Government's Investigation of the Black Press During World War II* (New York: Oxford University Press, 1986).

[22]Carr, p. 29.

[23]*Ibid.*, pp. 31, 33.

[24]*Ibid.*, p. 5.

[25]*Ibid.*, p. 39.

[26]*Ibid.*, p. 58.

[27]*Ibid.*, p. 124.

[28]Milton R. Konvitz and Theodore Leskes, *A Century of Civil Rights* (New York: Columbia University Press, 1961), p. 194; and Alton Hornsby, Jr., *The Black Alamanac*, Rev. (New York: Barron's Educational Series, 1973) pp. 67–68.

[29]Konvitz, p. 195.

[30]*Ibid.*

[31]For studies of the FEPC, see Louis C. Ruchames, *The Social Politics of FEPC* (Chapel Hill: University of North Carolina Press, 1948); Louis Ruchames, *Race, Jobs and Politics* (New York: Columbia University Press, 1953); Herbert Garfinkel, *When Negroes March* (New York: Free Press, 1959).

[32]Robert Birsbane, Jr., *The Black Vanguard* (Valley Forge: Judson Press, 1970), p. 168.

[33]Konvitz & Leskes , p. 196.

[34]Executive Order 10590, 20 *Federal Register* 409 (1955); and Ruth P. Morgan, *The President and Civil Rights* (New York: St. Martin's Press, 1970), pp. 53–54.

[35]Executive Order 10590.

[36]Morgan, pp. 54–55.

[37]For an evaluation of the EEOC, see U.S. Commission on Civil Rights, *The Federal Civil Rights Enforcement Effort - 1977: To Eliminate Employment Discrimination: A Sequel* (Washington, D.C.: Government Printing Office, 1977), pp. 176–243.

[38]*Ibid.*, p. 329.

[39]Konvitz and Leskes, p. 197.

[40]*Ibid.*, p. 199.

[41]*Ibid.*, p. 220 and Duane Lockard, *Toward Equal Opportunity: A Study of State and Local Antidiscrimination Laws* (New York: Macmillan Company, 1968), pp. 21–24.

[42]Herbert Hill, "Twenty Years of State Fair Employment Practice Commission: A Critical Analysis with Recommendations," *Buffalo Law Review* 14 (1964) p. 23.

[43]Paul Norgen and Samuel E. Hill, *Toward Fair Employment* (New York: Columbia University Press, 1964), p. 115.

[44]*Ibid.* and Lockard, p. 101.

[45]*Ibid.*

[46]Bernard Schwartz, ed., *Statutory History of the United States: Civil Rights Part II* (New York: Chelsea House, 1970), p. 839.

[47]*Ibid.*

[48]*Ibid.*

[49]*Ibid.*, p. 949; see also Committee on the Judiciary House of Representatives, *Civil Rights Acts of 1957, 1960, 1964, 1968, and Voting Rights Act of 1965* (Washington: U.S. Government Printing Office, 1971), p. 5.

[50]Schwartz, p. 935.

[51]*Ibid.*

[52]Foster Rhea Dulles, *The Civil Rights Commission: 1957-1965* (East Lansing: Michigan State University Press, 1968), p. 221; and Theodore M. Hesburgh, "Integer Vitae: Independence of the United States Commission on Civil Rights," *Notre Dame Lawyer*, (Spring 1971), pp. 445–460.

[53]*Ibid.*, p. 938.

[54]Ibid., p. 225.

[55]Donald S. Strong, *Negroes, Ballots and Judges: National Voting Rights Legislation in the Federal Courts* (Alabama: University of Alabama Press, 1968), p. 6; and Charles V. Hamilton, *The Bench and the Ballot: Southern Federal Judges and Black Voters* (New York: Oxford University Press, 1973).

[56]Schwartz, p. 1019.

[57]Committee on the Judiciary, p. 20.

[58]*Ibid.*

[59]Commission on Civil Rights, *The Federal Civil Rights Enforcement Effort— 1974, Volume VI to Extend Federal Financial Assistance* (Washington: Government Printing Office, 1975), pp. 8–9.

[60]*Ibid.*, p. 3.

[61]Duane Lockard, "Race Policy" in Fred I. Greenstien and Nelson Polsby (ed.) *Handbook of Political Science* Vol. 6 (Reading, MA: Addison-Wesley Publishing Company,1973), p. 287. For a similar but unique and innovative argument see Mack Jones, "The Voting Rights Act as an Intervention Strategy for Social Change: Symbolism or Substance," in Foster pp. 63–83. Jones sees both the law and the implementation of it as merely symbolic.

[62]Joseph Parker Witherspoon, *Administrative Implementation of Civil Rights* (Austin: University of Texas Press, 1968), p. 8.

[63]Wilson, p. xi.

[64]Jeremy Rabkin, "Office for Civil Rights," in Wilson, pp. 304 and 352.

[65]Commission on Civil Rights, *Federal Civil Rights Enforcement Effort—1974*, p. 3.

[66]*Ibid.*, p. 5.

[67]*Ibid.*, p. 6.

[68]*Ibid.*

[69]Gary Orfield, *The Reconstruction of Southern Education* (New York: Wiley, 1969), pp. 33–44.

[70]Whalen, p. 114.

[71]*Ibid.*, pp. 115–116, 117.

[72]*Ibid.*, pp. 166–167.

[73]Hanes Walton, Jr., *The Political Philosophy of Martin Luther King, Jr.* (Westport: Greenwood Press, 1971), p. 71; see also M. L. King, Jr., *Why We Can't Wait* (New York: Harper and Row, 1964). This is his work with the greatest number of policy proposals regarding blacks in America.

[74]David J. Garrow, *Bearing the Cross: Martin Luther King, Jr. and the Southern Christian Leadership Conference: A Personal Portrait* (New York: William Morrow and Company, 1986) p. 199.

[75]*Ibid.*, p. 269.

[76]Whalen, pp. 71–99.

[77]Garrow, p. 325.

[78]Rabkin, p. 309.

[79]*Ibid.*

[80]Orfield, pp. 33–44.

[81]Harrell R. Rodgers, Jr., and Charles S. Bullock, III *Coercion To Compliance* (Massachusetts: Lexington Books, 1976), p. 123.

[82]See Stephen L. Wasby, *The Impact of the United States Supreme Court: Some Perspectives* (Chicago: Dorsey Press, 1970).

[83]See Theodore L. Becker and M. M. Peeley, eds., *The Impact of Supreme Court Decisions: Empirical Studies* (New York: Oxford University Press, 1973).

[84]Frederick M. Wirt, *Politics of Southern Equality: Law and Social Change in a Mississippi County* (Chicago: Aldine, 1970).

[85]C. Bullock, III, and H. Rodgers, *Law and Social Change: Civil Rights Laws and Their Consequences* (New York: McGraw-Hill, 1972); their *Racial Equality in America* (Pacific Palisades: Goodyear, 1973); and *Racism and Inequality* (San Francisco: W. H. Freeman, 1975).

[86]Rodgers and Bullock, *Coercion to Compliance*, pp. 1–2.

[87]*Ibid.*, p. 10. In appendix F, "Compliance and Impact Literature: Selected Works," pp. 157–168, the authors provide the most comprehensive listing of the literature in print up through the early 1970s. The bibliography alone is worth the price of the book.

[88]*Ibid.*, p. 125.

[89]Wirt, p. 290.

[90]U.S. Congress, House Committee on Judiciary, *Title VI Enforcement in Medicare and Medicaid Programs, Hearing Before a Subcommittee of the Committee on the Judiciary*, 93rd Cong., 1st sess., 1973, pp. 1–184.

[91]Hanes Walton, Jr., *Invisible Politics: Black Political Behavior* (Albany: SUNY Press, 1985), pp. 1–14.

[92]Bullock and Lamb, "A Search for Variables Important in Polity Implementation," in Charles S. Bullock and Charles Lamb (ed.) *Implementation of Civil Rights Policy* (Monterey: Brooks/Cole Publishing Company, 1984), p. 5.

[93]See Augustus J. Jones, Jr., *Law, Bureaucracy and Politics: The Implementation of Title VI of the Civil Rights Act of 1964* (Washington: University Press of America, 1982), p. 245.

[94]Lester M. Salamon, "Rethinking Implementation," (Washington, D.C.: The Urban Institute, N.D.) p. 1. Professor Joe McCormick loaned me his file copy of this paper. I am deeply grateful that he brought this paper to my attention.

[95]*Ibid.*

[96]*Ibid.*, p. 2. And Peter Drucker, "The Sickness of Government," *The Public Interest* No. 14, (Winter 1969), pp. 3-23.

[97]Quoted from comments on an early draft of this research by Professor Joseph McCormick.

[98]Michael B. Preston, *The Politics of Bureaucratic Reform: The Case of the California State Employment Service* (Urbana: University of Illinois Press, 1985) p. xi.

[99]*Ibid.*, pp. 33–34.

[100]See Kenneth J. Meier, "The Impact of Regulatory Organization Structure: IRCs or DRAs," *Southern Review of Public Administration* Vol. 3 (March 1980) pp. 427–443.

[101]One astute observer of public bureaucracies has noted that these public organizations have imperialistic tendencies. Hence, it is possible that the DRAs would be dominated and controlled by their cabinet departments while the IRA would probably be more successful. See, Matthew Holden, Jr., "'Imperialism' in Bureaucracy," *American Political Science Review* Vol. 60 (December 1966) pp. 943–951.

[102]See William Willey, III and James C. Miller, III, "The New Social Regulations," *The Public Interest* No. 47 (Spring 1977).

[103]Salamon, p. 8.

[104]See Lester Salamon, "The Rise of Third Party Government," *Washington Post*, June 29, 1980.

[105]Salamon, *Rethinking Implementation*, p. 6.

[106]Burton Levy "Effects of Racism on the Racial Bureaucracy" *Public Administration Review*, (September/October 1972) p. 483; see also his "The Bureaucracy of Race: Enforcement of Civil Rights Laws and Its Impact on People, Process and Organization," *Journal of Black Studies*, (September 1971); see also Howard Knovitz, "Affirmative Action Official Quits Over Staff Cuts, Lack of Support," *Washington Post*, January 22, 1987, p. A10; see also Henderson, "Administration Advocacy . . .," p. 68–79.

[107]Rabkin, p. 352.

[108]Randall Ripley and Grace Franklin, *Bureaucracy and Policy Implementation* (Illinois: The Dorsey Press, 1982), pp. 77, 144.

[109]*Ibid.*, p. 198.

[110]*Ibid.*

[111]See Richard A. Pride and J. David Woodward, *The Burden of Busing: The Politics of Desegregation in Nashville, Tennessee* (Knoxville: University of Tennessee Press, 1985).

CHAPTER 2

[1]Garrow, p. 338–339.

[2]George J. Gordon, *Public Administration in America* 2nd ed. (New York: St. Martin's Press, 1982) p. 491. See also Kenneth J. Meier, "The Impact of Regulatory Organization Structure: IRCs or DRAs?" *Southern Review of Public Administration* Vol. 3 (March 1980), pp. 427–443.

[3]See Appendix A.

[4]Letter, Robert A. Malson, Assistant Director, Domestic Policy Staff, to Hanes Walton, Jr., July 28, 1980. See Appendix A.

[5]Commission on Civil Rights, *The Federal Civil Rights Enforcement Effort—*

1974, Volume VI to Extend Federal Financial Assistance (Washington: Government Printing Office, 1975).

[6]Letter, William J. Harris, Deputy Director, Office of Civil Rights, Department of Labor, to Hanes Walton, Jr. September 30, 1981. And Secretary of Labor, Secretary's Order 8–80, October 28, 1980, 4 pages; and Secretary's Order 2–81, June 1, 1981, 3 pages. Copies of these orders are in my personal files.

[7]The cabinet-level departments are: Agriculture, Commerce, Defense, Education, Energy, Health and Human Services, Housing and Urban Development, Interior, Justice, Labor, State, Transportation, and Treasury.

[8]See Joseph A. Califano, Jr., *Governing America* (New York: Simon & Schuster, 1981), pp. 212–270.

[9]Laurence E. Lynn, Jr., *Managing Public Policy* (Boston: Little, Brown and Company, 1987), pp. 103–190. See also Michael D. Reagan, *Regulation: The Politics of Policy* (Boston: Little, Brown and Company, 1987), Chapters 2 and 3.

[10]Lynn, pp. 239–268, for a set of case studies of the Reagan administration.

[11]Shelton finally left the position after 1985, giving him a total of sixteen years in the position.

[12]The ten federal regions are listed in the U.S. Governmental Manuals. There are no names for each region, they are simply referred to by Roman numerals.

[13]Interview with two regional Title VI heads, who for obvious reasons wanted their names withheld.

[14]Office of Management and Budget, *Special Analysis J. Civil Rights Activities: The Budget for Fiscal Year 1984* (Washington: Government Printing Office, 1984), p. J–15.

[15]*Ibid.*

[16]For the theoretical arguments on this point see, Lynn pp. 249–261; for an actual discussion of this matter by a former Title VI Agency head in HEW, see Leon E. Panetta and Peter Hall, *Bring Us Together: The Nixon Team and the Civil Rights Retreat* (Philadelphia: J. B. Lippincott, 1971), pp. 47–351. Congressman Panetta relates his resignation in protest of the secretary's actions, and that of a black woman, Ruby Martin, who not only preceded him as director of the Office of Civil Rights Compliance, but who resigned in protest and went out and led demonstrations against the agency. See pp. 81–82, 97, 103, 127, and 201.

However, after he resigned in protest, Panetta returned to Washington as a moderate Democratic congressman from California, joined with the OMB Director David Stockman and President Reagan, and cut the budget for these programs. Stockman reveals that Congressman Panetta became one of his main allies both in Congress and at several budget trimming sessions off Capital Hill. See David A. Stockman, *The Triumph of Politics: How the Reagan Revolution Failed* (New York: Harper and Row, 1986), pp. 171, 173, 205.

[17]This observation was based upon my visiting scholar year with the office.

CHAPTER 3

[1]See OMB, *Special Analysis J: Civil Rights Activity 1985* (Washington: D.C.: Government Printing Office, 1985) pp. J1–J32.

[2]There has never been any systematic and comprehensive treatment of the federal civil rights budget, nor is such an analysis available even in truncated form in the various books in political science on the politics of budgeting. The closest is a study of the budget for the Civil Rights Commission for its first twenty years, and this article is more than disturbing. This study analyzes the agency's requests and final appropriations by using two linear models and in these models checks for unemployment and media attention to civil rights issues. The article finds, predictably, that presidential increases in appropriations changes with "the levels of unemployment among blacks." Congress on the other hand increased their appropriation to the commissions when there were "substantial increases in the attention given by the media to civil rights issues . . ." Since no other explanatory variables were added to the model, no other explanations are offered about the budget for the commission. Nor do they deal with the fact that the budget for the commission remained in recent years at two percent of the entire civil rights budgets. See A. T. Cowart and F. D. Gilliam, Jr., "Budgeting in a Newly Established Agency: The First Twenty Years of the United States Civil Rights Commission," *Environment and Planning C: Government and Policy* Vol. 3, (1985) pp. 235–241.

[3]Lynn, p. 191.

[4]Gordon, pp. 383–384.

[5]For more on this distinction between minority assistance and civil rights enforcement see, OMB, *Special Analysis N: Federal Civil Rights Activities—1973* pp. 209–210.

[6]In 1980, HEW was dissolved into two new departments, which means, in effect, a net gain of one department. However, the newly created Energy Department brought the total number of cabinet level departments to a net gain of two.

[7]For a careful discussion of those pressures from the South see Leon E. Panetta and Peter Gall, *Bring Us Together: The Nixon Team and the Civil Rights Retreat* (Philadelphia: J.B. Lippincott, 1971) pp. 34–305.

[8]Data on IP are provided for from 1971 to 1974.

[9]The FSEEO monies are used by federal departments and agencies to maintain an affirmative program of equal employment opportunity in each department. This program addresses the needs of women and Spanish-speaking Americans as well as racial minorities.

The MSEEO monies are used by each of the military services to "guide, monitor, and evaluate all matters pertaining to equal opportunity and treatment of military personnel and their dependents and are responsible for and participate in race relations, councils, seminars and training."

The PSEEO Monies are dollars spent by the EEOC, the Justice Department and the Office of Federal Contract Compliance and 15 cooperating agencies to prohibit discrimination by either employers, unions or employment agencies in the private sector.

Finally the EEO monies are the dollars spent by HEW and the Justice Department to ensure equal educational opportunity in public schools for all categories on a nondiscriminatory basis and to assure that there is no discrimination against either faculty or administrators.

[10]Gordon, p. 384.

[11]*Ibid.*, p. 496.

[12]Panetta and Gall, p. 187.

[13]It is possible to analyze only a few of the departmental budgets because most of the departments did not have detailed budgets available. As one officer wrote to the author, civil rights enforcement programs are not a line item. Only those departments that could supply figures are used here.

[14]On this point see Augustus J. Jones., Jr., *Law, Bureaucracy and Politics: The Implementation of Title VI of the Civil Rights Act of 1964* (Washington: University Press of America, 1982).

[15]Aaron Wildavsky, *The Politics of the Budgetary Process* (Boston: Little, Brown, 1964).

[16]On this point see Gary C. Bryner, *Bureaucratic Discretion: Law and Policy in Federal Regulatory Agencies* (New York: Pergamon Books, 1987).

[17]Panetta and Gall, p. 131.

[18]Stockman, p. 101–102.

CHAPTER 4

[1]Jeffrey M. Berry, *Feeding Hungry People: Rulemaking in the Food Stamp Program* (New Brunswick: Rutgers University Press, 1984) p. 1.

[2]George J. Gordon, *Public Administration in America* 3rd ed. (New York: St. Martin's Press, 1986) p. 527.

[3]Berry, p. 5.

[4]*Ibid.*, pp. 5–6.

[5]Gordon, 3rd ed., p. 527.

[6]Berry, p. 6.

[7]Gordon, 3rd ed., p. 507.

[8]*Ibid.*

[9]*Ibid.*

[10]"Agency Regulations Implements Section 504 of Rehabilitation Act," *Civil Right Forum*, (Winter-Spring 1983), p. 2.

[11]Quoted in Augustus Jones, Jr., *Law, Bureaucracy and Politics: The Implementation of Title VI of the Civil Rights Act of 1964* (Washington: University Press of America, 1982), p. 77.

[12]Letter, William J. Harris, Deputy Director, Office of Civil Rights, U.S. Department of Labor, to Hanes Walton, Jr., September 30, 1981.

[13]Letter, James P. Hood, Freedom of Information Office, Civil Rights Division, U.S. Department of Agriculture, to Hanes Walton, Jr., December 30, 1981.

[14]Issuance of the yearbook by the Government Printing Office runs several years behind the date of release. See HUD, 1979 *Statistical Yearbook* (Washington: Government Printing Office, 1980).

[15]*Ibid.*, p. 43.

[16]The reasons that more complaints focus on Title VIII than on Title VI are (a) the length of time that it takes to conclude the investigation, (2) fewer blacks know of Title VI, and (3) compensation cannot be received for damages under Title VI but can be obtained under Title VIII. See Clarke Cable Ward, *An Analysis of Remedies Obtained Through Litigation of Fair Housing Cases: Title VIII and Civil Rights Act of 1964* (Washington: Department of Housing and Urban Development, n.d., on microfilm at Library of Congress (HHA.83.979).

[17]See Department of Agriculture, *Equal Opportunity Report, 1980* (Washington: Government Printing Office, 1981), p. 5.

[18]*Ibid.*, pp. 5–6.

[19]Department of Agriculture, *Equal Opportunity Report, 1978* (Washington: Government Printing Office, 1979), p. 12.

[20]A recent pioneering study on the Food Stamp Program doesn't even mention or treat Title VI realities. This is another example of conceptual and definitional ommissions, see Berry pp. 127–153.

[21]Jeffrey Berry, pp. 127–153 and the *Equal Opportunity Report 1980*, p. 28.

[22]Department of Defense, *Title VI Enforcement Effort and Related Matters - 1964–1980*, Vol. 1 (Washington: Department of Defense Civil Rights Assessment, June 1980), p. 8.

[23]Letter, Alfred R. Gordon to Hanes Walton, Jr., July 14, 1981, p. 1.

[24]The Departments of Commerce, Treasury, and State sent no data at all on compliance efforts.

[25]Letter, Wesley A. Plummer, Director of Civil Rights, to Hanes Walton, Jr., July 30, 1981, p. 5.

[26]Letter, William J. Harris to Hanes Walton, Jr., September 30, 1981, p. 1.

[27]Office of Management and Budget, *Special Analyses Civil Rights Activities*, 1984, p. J–13.

[28]*Ibid.*, p. J–15.

[29]Mary Francis Berry, "Civil Rights Enforcement in Higher Education," *Integreducation* 22 (January-June 1985), pp. 2–6.

[30]"Agency Enforcement Compared," *Title VI Forum*, (Fall 1979), p. 6.

[31]Mary Francis Berry, pp. 2–6.

[32]"Title VI - Fifteen Years Later," *Title VI Forum*, (Fall 1979), p. 6.

[33]*Ibid.*

[34]*Code of Federal Regulations* 42, pp. 401–415.

[35]*Code of Federal Regulations* 42, p. 403.

[36]"President Issues Title VI Directive to Agencies," *Title VI Forum*, (Fall 1977), pp. 1, 8.

[37]*Ibid.*

[38]*Ibid.*, p. 8.

[39]"Days Reorganized Civil Rights Division," *Title VI Forum*, (Spring-Summer 1979), p. 104.

[40]Gordon, 3rd ed., pp. 529, 524. See also George C. Eads, and Michael Fix (ed.) *The Reagan Regulatory Strategy: An Assessment* (Washington, D.C.: Urban Institute Press, 1984); and their *Relief or Reform: Reagan's Regulatory Dilemma* (Washington, D.C.: Urban Institute Press, 1984).

[41]Gordon, 3rd ed., pp. 529, 524.

[42]"A Reintroduction," *Civil Rights Forum*, (Fall 1982), p. 1.

[43]"Justice Department Revises Its Coordination Regulations," *Civil Rights Forum*, (Fall 1982), pp. 1, 3.

[44]"DOJ Will Not Issue Coordination Reg," *Civil Rights Forum*, (Winter, Spring 1983), p. 1.

[45]"Interview with the Assistant Attorney General," *Civil Rights Forum*, (Winter, Spring 1983), p. 1.

[46]*Ibid.*

[47]"Postscripts," *Civil Rights Forum*, (Winter 1984), p. 12.

[48]See Rodgers and Bullock, *Coercion to Compliance*, pp. 89–91.

[49]One lawyer has argued that in order to improve civil rights regulatory compliance in a period of a conservative president bent on reducing such compliance that third parties should step in and force the government to do its job. Arthur R. Block, "Enforcement Title VI Compliance Agreement by Third Party Beneficiaries *Harvard Civil Rights—Civil Liberties Law Review* vol. 18 [Winter, 1983], p. 1–52.

CHAPTER 5

[1]Jeffrey Berry, p. 11.

[2]*Ibid.*, pp. 11–12.

[3]Gordon, 3rd ed. pp. 68–69.

[4]On this point see Hugh Helco, "Issue Networks and the Executive Establishment," in Anthony King, (ed.), *The New American Political System* (Washington D.C.: American Enterprise Institute, 1978), pp. 87–124. For an entire book that is based on the "iron triangle"—political subsystem concept see Theodore J. Lowi, *The End of Liberalism*, 2nd ed. (New York: W. W. Norton, 1979).

[5]Walton, *Invisible Politics*, Chapter One.

[6]See Michael A. Rebell and Arthur R. Black, *Equality and Education: Federal Civil Rights Enforcement in the New York City School System* (Princeton: Princeton University Press, 1985); Richard A. Pride and J. David Woodward, *The Burden of Busing: The Politics of Desegregation in Nashville, Tennessee* (Knoxville: University of Tennessee Press, 1985); David V. Monti, *A Semblance of Justice: St. Louis School Desegregation and Order in Urban America* (Columbia: University of Missouri Press, 1985); Robert L. Green, (ed.) *Metropolitian Desegregation* (New York: Plenum Press, 1985) and Reginald Wilson, *Race and Equity in Higher Education* (Washington, D.C.: American Council on Education, 1982).

[7]Panetta and Gall, pp. 107–121.

[8]Thomas E. Cronin, *The State of the Presidency*, 2nd ed. (Boston: Little Brown & Company, 1980), pp. 154–161.

[9]Samuel C. Patterson, Roger H. Davidson and Randall B. Ripley, *A More Perfect Union*, 3rd ed. (Homewood: Dorsey Press, 1985), p. 229.

[10]*Ibid.*, p. 299.

[11]U.S. Commission of Civil Rights, *The Federal Civil Rights Enforcement Effort—1974*, Vol 7 (Washington, D.C.: Government Printing Office, 1977), p. 3.

[12]*Ibid.*

[13]*Ibid.*, p. 5.

[14]*Ibid.*, p. 6.

[15]See Appendix A.

[16]Walton, *Invisible Politics* pp. 264–265.

[17]Juan Williams, "Pendleton Says He'll Start Being the Silent Type," *Washington Post*, March 25, 1985, national weekly edition, p. 28. However, Pendleton didn't stop; see "At Odds Over Rights: Pendleton Accuses Lawmakers of Racism," *Washington Post*, September 30, 1985, p. A4.

[18]Commission on Civil Rights, p. 21. On the domestic council see John Kessel, *The Domestic Presidency* (Massachusetts: Duxbury Press, 1974).

[19]*Ibid.*, p. 81.

[20]*Ibid.*, p. 92.

[21]*Ibid.*, p. 101.

[22]"OMB Issues Paperwork Requirements," *Civil Rights Forum*, (September 1984), pp. 6, 8, 12. See also Juan Williams "Chairman of EEOC Tells Panel Statistics Misused to Prove Bias," *Washington Post*, December 15, 1984, p. A4.

[23]Juan Williams, p. A4.

[24]Commission on Civil Rights, p. 713.

[25]U.S. Senate, Committee on the Judiciary, *Report on the Administrative Procedure Act,* 79th Cong., 1st sess. (Committee Print 1945).

[26]50 *Federal Register* (No. 5, January 8, 1985), pp. 1036–1038.

[27]Memorandum to the Heads of Executive Departments and Agencies, "Development of Administrations and Agencies—Regulatory Program from President Ronald Reagan," January 4, 1985, in *Weekly Compilation of Presidential Documents* (Vol. 21, No. 1), pp. 13–14.

[28]*Ibid.*

[29]Cass Peterson, "OMB Regulation Power, Part II: Now Justice Says Agencies Can Ignore Reagan's Order," *Washington Post*, September 15, 1985, national weekly edition, p. 33.

[30]Office of Management and Budget, *Regulatory Program of the United States Government—April 1, 1985–March 31, 1986* (Washington, D.C.: Government Printing Office, 1985), p. vii.

[31]*Ibid.*, p. xi.

[32]*Ibid.*, p. 3.

[33]See, U.S. Congress, House Subcommittee on Employment and Housing, *Processing EEO Complaints in the Federal Sector—Problems and Solutions*, Hearings Before a Subcommittee of the Committee on Government Operations, 99th Cong., 1st sess. October 8, 1985 (Washington, D.C.: Government Printing Office, 1985); and U.S. Congress, House Subcommittee on Employment and Housing, *Processing EEOC Complaints in the Federal Sector—Problems and Solutions Part 2*, Hearings Before a Subcommittee of the Committee on Government Operations, 99th Cong., 2nd sess, June 17, 1985 (Washington: D.C., Government Printing Office, 1986).

[34]OMB, "Regulatory Program . . . ," p. 527.

[35]Commission of Civil Rights, *The Federal Civil Rights Enforcement Effort—1974* Vol. 11 (Washington, D.C.: Government Printing Office, 1977) p. 160.

[36]*Ibid.*, p. 165.

[37]*Ibid.*

[38]Jeffrey M. Elliot and Sheith R. Ali, *The Presidential Congressional Political Dictionary* (California: ABC-Clio, 1984) pp. 149–150.

[39]General Accounting Office, "Actions Taken by Federal Agencies to Implement Title VI of Civil Rights Act of 1964," press release, April 15, 1980, p. 3.

[40]*Ibid.*, p. 5.

[41]Eddie Fleming, "Anderson's Savannah Expose Called Lies," *Savannah Morning News*, Nov. 14, 1978, pp. 1A, 3; "Jack Anderson Defends His Column," *Ibid.*, p. 3A and for the article, see Jack Anderson, "Did Bell Influence Savannah Annexation," *Ibid.*, p. 4A.

Later, Jack Anderson made some corrections in his story: see Jack Anderson, "The Savannah Story: Corrections. Savannah Morning News, November 27, 1988, p. 4A. For more on this program see General Accounting Office, *Justice Can Further Improve Its Monitoring of Changes in State/Local Voting Laws* (Washington, D.C.: GAO/66d-84-9 Report, December 19, 1983).

[42]See Lawyer's Committee for Civil Rights Under Law, Report Nos. 46, 49, 50, 51. See also General Accounting Office, *Department of Justice Making Efforts to Improve Litigative Management Information System* (Washington, D.C.: GAO Report, 7–80).

[43]General Accounting Office, *A Compilation of Federal Laws and Executive Orders For Nondiscrimination and Equal Opportunity Program* (Washington, D.C.: GAO Report - GRD-78-138, 1978).

[44]U.S. Congress, Senate, Committee on the Judiciary, *Federal Civil Rights Laws: A Sourcebook* (Washington, D.C.: Government Printing Office, 1984).

[45]For more on the GAO's role as a protest group, see U.S. House, Hearing Before A Subcommittee for the Committee on Government Operation, *Constitutionality of GAO's Bid Protest Function*, 99 Cong., 1st sess. (Feb. 28 and March 7, 1985) pp. 544–549.

[46]U.S. Congress, House Committee on the Judiciary, *Title VI Enforcement in Medicare and Medicaid Programs: Hearings Before a Subcommittee of the Committee on the Judiciary,* 93rd Cong., 1st sess. 1973, pp. 1–285.

[47]*Ibid.*, p. 285.

[48]See Mitchell Rice and Woodrow Jones, Jr., "Public and Black Health Care: A Civil Rights Perspective in Mfanya Donald Tryman (ed.) *Institutional Racism and Black America: Challengers, Choices, Change* Volume 1 (Boston: Ginn Press, 1985) pp. 88–89; see also Kenneth Wing and Marilyn Rose, "Health Facilities and the Enforcement of Civil Rights," in Ruth Roemer and George McKoray (eds.) *Legal Aspects of Health Policy,* (Westport: Greenwood Press, 1980); Kenneth Wing "Title VI and Health Facilities: Forms without Substance," *Hastings Law Journal* (September 1978) pp. 137–190; M. Rice and W. Jones, "Black Health Inequities and the American Health Care System," *Health Policy and Education: An International Journal* (Fall 1982), pp. 195–214; and their, "Black Health Care in an Era of Retrenchment Politics" in Mitchell F. Rice and Woodrow Jones, Jr. (eds.) *Contemporary Public Policy Perspectives and Black Americans: Issues in an Era of Retrenchment Politics* (Westport: Greenwood Press, 1984), pp. 157–172.

[49]"Commission on Civil Rights," *Weekly Compilation of Presidential Documents,* 10 (November 7, 1983) p. 1521. For the best scholarly discussion and analysis of what happened when President Reagan reorganized the Civil Rights Commission, see—James C. Harvey, "Civil Rights, Blacks and the Reagan Administration," in Mfanya Donald Tryman, (ed.)—*Institutional Racism and Black America: Challenges, Choices, Change* Volume 1 (Lexington: Ginn Press, 1985), pp. 177–180.

[50]Carl T. Rowan, "Abolish the Civil Rights Commission," *Washington Post,* March 19, 1985, p. A–19.

[51]*Ibid.* For the response of another black columnists see William Raspberry, "Pendleton's Misjudgement," *Washington Post,* March 8, 1985, p. A–23.

[52]"The Pendleton Prose," *Washington Post* March 25, 1985, national weekly edition, p. 22. See also, Howard Kurtz, "Civil Rights, Chairman, Aide Boost Salaries," *Washington Post,* March 25, 1986, p. A–1.

[53]U.S. Commission on Civil Rights, *The Federal Civil Rights Enforcement Effort—1974,* vol. 7.

[54]Morris S. Ogul, *Congress Oversees the Bureaucracy: Studies in Legislative Supervision* (Pittsburgh: University of Pittsburgh Press, 1976), p. 11.

[55]Robert J. Art, "Congress and the Defense Budget: Enhancing Policy Oversight," *Political Science Quarterly,* 100 (Summer 1985), p. 240.

[56]Seymour Scher, "Conditions for Legislative Control," *Journal of Politics,* 25 (August 1983), p. 531.

[57]Art, p. 240.

[58]Ogul, p. 130.

[59]*Ibid.*, pp. 151–152.

[60]Loretta Tofari, "Education Department Acused of Laxness on Bias Laws: House Panel Calls Enforcement Inadequate," *Washington Post*, September 12, 1985, p. A–6.

[61]U.S. Congress, House of Representatives, Subcommittee on Civil and Constitutional Rights, *U.S. Commission on Civil Rights/GAO Audit,* Hearings Before a Subcommittee of the Committee on the Judiciary, 99th Cong., 2nd sess., March 25 and April 22, 1985, p. 1.

[62]Kurtz, "Civil Rights Chairman . . .", pp. A1 and A4; see also, Jacqueline Prescott and Eve Ferguson, "Chairman Clarence Pendleton, Jr.: A Wild Card on the Civil Rights Commission," *The Washington Post*, November 14, 1982, pp. H1 and H5.

[63]House, *U.S. Commission on Civil Rights/GAO Audit*, p. 157.

[64]*Ibid.*, pp. 252–263.

[65]*Ibid.*, pp. 157–158.

[66]*Ibid.*, pp. 279–281.

[67]*Ibid.*, pp. 175 and 402.

[68]"An Interview with Nathan Glazer, "*New Perspectives* (Fall 1985), pp. 27–30. For other negative articles, even by staffers, see the entire issue.

[69]House, *U.S. Commission on Civil Rights/GAO Audit*, p. 167.

[70]*Ibid.*, p. 177.

[71]"U.S. Civil Rights Commission Votes to Slash Its Staff," *The New York Times*, September 28, 1986, p. 4E.

[72]*Ibid.*

[73]U.S. Congress, House of Representatives, Subcommittee on the Departments of Commerce, Justice and State, The Judiciary and Related Agencies, *Department of Commerce, Justice, and State, The Judiciary, and Related Agencies Appropriations for 1987*, Hearing Before a Subcommittee of the Committee on Appropriations, 99th Cong., 2nd sess. (February 24, 1986), pp. 536–551.

[74]For a lengthy interview with Chairman Clarence Thomas that is quite perceptive and revealing see, Jeffrey Elliot, *Black Voices in American Politics* (New York: Harcourt, Brace Jovanovich, 1986) pp. 147–166. For an attack on the agency and its efforts prior to the Thomas era, published in the Civil Rights Commission's own magazine by one of its own in-house staff members, see Phil Lyons, "An Agency with a Mind of Its Own: The EEOC's Guidelines on Employment Testing," *New Perspectives* (Fall 1985), pp. 20–26.

[75]U.S. Congress, House of Representatives, Committee on Education and Labor, *A Report on the Investigation of Civil Rights Enforcement by the Equal Employment*

Opportunity Commission Serial No. 99–0 (Washington, D.C.: Government Printing Office, 1986), p. 2.

[76]OMB, *"Regulatory Program . . ."*, pp. 523–528.

[77]U.S. Congress, House of Representatives, Subcommittee on Employment Opportunities, *Oversight Review of the Department of Labor's Office of Federal Contract Compliance Programs and Affirmative Action Programs,* Hearings Before a Subcommittee of the Committee on Education and Labor, 99th Cong. 1st sess., (September 18, 1985), p. 211.

[78]OMB, *"Regulatory Programs . . ."*, pp. 233–261.

[79]U.S. Congress, Senate Committee on Labor and Human Resources, *Nomination of Clarence Thomas, of Missouri, to be Chairman of the Equal Employment Opportunity Commission Hearings*, Before Committee on Labor and Human Resources, 99th Cong., 2nd sess. (July 23, 1986), p. 61.

[80]*Ibid.*, For an earlier hearing see, U.S. Congress, House of Representatives, Subcommittee on Employment Opportunities, *Oversight Hearings on the EEOC's Enforcement Policies,* Hearings, Before a Subcommittee of the Committee on Education and Labor, 98th Cong., 2nd session, 1984.

[81]Congress, *Nomination of Clarence Thomas*, pp. 84–110.

[82]*Ibid.*

[83]U.S. Congress, House of Representatives, Committee on Education and Labor and the Subcommittee on Civil and Constitutional Rights, *Civil Rights Restoration Act of 1985,* Joint Hearings Before Committee on Education and Labor and Subcommittee of the Committee on the Judiciary - March 4-25, 1985, pp. 1–1329.

[84]"Grove City Civil Rights Measure Stalled," *Congressional Quarterly Almanac* Volume XLI, 99th Cong., 1st sess., 1985 (Congressional Quarterly, 1986), pp. 230–232.

[85]*Ibid.*

[86]Gaye H. Hewitt, "An Evaluation of Civil Rights Legislation with Special Emphasis on the 1968 Civil Rights Act," (East Texas State College, M.A. Thesis, August, 1968), pp. iv–v.

[87]U.S. Congress, House of Representatives, Committee on Government Operations, *Investigation of Civil Rights Enforcement by the Office for Civil Rights at the Department of Education,* Report by Committee on Government Operations (Washington, D.C.: Government Printing Office, 1985), pp. 1–36.

[88]*Ibid.*, p. 8.

[89]OMB, *"Regulatory Programs . . . "*, p. 53.

[90]U.S. Congress, House of Representatives Committee on Government Operation,

National Endowment for the Humanities and the Equal Employment Opportunity Commission, Report, Committee on Government Operations (Washington, D.C.: Government Printing Office, 1985), p. 1.

[91]*Ibid.*, p. 2.

[92]*Ibid.*, p. 3.

[93]U.S. Congress, House of Representatives, Subcommittee on Employment and Housing, *Processing EEO Complaints in the Federal Sector - Problem and Solutions,* Hearing, Before a Subcommittee of the Committee on Government Operations, 99th Cong., 1st session, (October 8, 1985), p. 1. For a recent study by a private group see Washington Council of Lawyers, *On The Federal EEO Administrative Process,* (June 25, 1987). The average in 1985 was 630 days an increase of 40 days in one year.

[94]Lenneal J. Henderson, Jr. and Michael B. Preston, "Black Public Employment and Public Interest Theory," in Mitchell Rice and Woodrow Jones, Jr., (eds.) *Contemporary Public Policy Perspectives and Black Americans* (Westport, CT: Greenwood Press, 1984) p. 40.

[95]*Ibid.*, p. 42. See also, *Impact of 1981 RIF's on Minorities and Women and Updated RIF Projections for Fiscal Year 1982* (Washington, D.C.: Government Printing Office, 1983) and Federal Government Service Task Force, *Reduction in Force Survey, Third Quarter, Fiscal 1982* (Washington, D.C.: Government Printing Office, 1983).

[96]On the use and origin of this term, see Hanes Walton, Jr., *Black Politics* (Philadelphia: J.B. Lippincott, 1972), pp. 174–178.

[97]See "Lawyers's Committee to Participate in CRC," *Committee Report No. 53,* (July 1984), p. 1.

[98]*Ibid.*

[99]"Judiciary Refuse to Open for Jesse Helms' View Illegally Obtained Tapes of Dr. Martin Luther King, Jr.'s Conversations," *Committee Report No. 51,* (January 1984), p. 1.

[100]"Lawyers' Committee Testifies on Meese Nomination; 89 Trustees Endorse Statement Attacking Civil Rights Record of Reagan Administration," *Committee Report No. 52,* (May 1984), p. 4.

[101]"Experiment with State Enforcement of Federal Civil Rights Laws in Education Found Flawed," *Committee Report, No. 52,* (May 1984), pp. 6–11.

[102]"Black Neighborhoods in New Bern, North Carolina to Get Municipal Service Improvements," *Committee Report No. 49,* (April 1983), p. 2.

[103]"OE's Authority to Recoup Misspent Title I Funds Affirmed," *Committee Report No. 50,* (September 1983), pp. 5–11.

[104]For a look at the unending efforts of letter writing and presentations of the

Conference, researchers and academicians should see their file of papers and collections at the National Archives.

[105]Commission on Civil Rights, p. 87.

[106]See "OMB Special Analysis J: Civil Rights Activities," *Special Analysis: Budget of the United States Government Fiscal Year: 1986* (Washington, D.C.: Government Printing Office, 1985), pp. J–1–J–4.

[107]*Ibid.*, pp. J-18–J-29.

[108]For the best and perhaps most succinct scholarly analysis of this conflict, see Stephen L. Wasby, "The NAACP and the NAACP Legal Defense Fund: Preliminary Observations on Conflict Between Allies" (Paper presented at National Conference of Black Political Scientists Meeting, April 1984, Washington, D.C.). For a recent update on the Adams Case, see "Adams States: a Status Report," *Black Issues in Higher Education*, Vol. 3., (March 1, 1987) pp. 6–7.

[109]Wasby, p. 17.

[110]*Ibid.*

[111]Aldon Morris, *Origins of the Civil Rights Movement* (New York: Free Press, 1984), pp. 31–37.

[112]Wasby, pp. 18–20.

[113]*Ibid.*, p. 39. See also Keith B. Richburg, "U.S. Seeks End to Lengthy Civil Rights Case," *Washington Post*, March 8, 1985, p. A–21.

[114]Wasby, pp. 23–24.

[115]*Ibid.*, p. 9.

[116]Bill Peterson, "Reynolds Opposes Bill to Counter Bias Ruling," *Washington Post*, March 8, 1985, p. A-2.

[117]*Ibid.*

[118]Walton, *Black Politics* pp. 147–153.

[119]Marquerite Ross Barnett, "The Congressional Black Caucus: Illusions and Realities of Power," in Michael Preston, Lenneal Henderson, and Paul Puryear (eds.), The New Black Politics (New York: Longman, 1982), pp. 55–70.

[120]Jake Miller, *The Black Presence in American Foreign Affairs* (Washington, D.C.: University of America, 1978), pp. 141–142. See also "Confirmations," *Department of State Bulletin*, March 31, 1975, p. 427.

[121]On such a hearing see, U.S. Congress, House of Representatives, Congressional Black Caucus—Brain Trust on Aging and the Select Committee on Aging, *The Black Elderly in Poverty*, Hearing Before Congressional Black Caucus Brain Trust and Select Committee on Aging, 99th Cong., 1st sess. (September 27, 1985), pp. 1–64.

[122]The author during this time was a National Association of Public Administration Fellow serving in the office as a visiting scholar and special assistant to Rice. He was present at Rice's tearful reading of his resignation letter to the staff.

[123]"Attorney General and other Past Justice Department Officials Must Stand Trial in Suit Alleging Their Refusal to Carry Out Civil Rights Duties Re LEAA Grants," *Committee Report No. 50*, (September 1983), pp. 4, 10.

[124]For more on this, see Chandler Davidson, (ed.), *Minority Vote Dilution* (Washington, D.C.: Howard University Press, 1985).

[125]Peter Steinfels, *The New Conservatives: The Men Who are Changing America's Politics* (New York: Simon & Schuster, 1979).

[126]Editors, "Preface," *The Public Interest, No. 41*, (Fall 1975), p. 3.

[127]Daniel P. Moynihan, "Introduction: The American Experiment," *The Public Interest, No. 41*, (Fall 1975), p. 8.

[128]Martin Kilson, "Whither Integration," *The American Scholar* Vol. 45 (Summer 1976), p. 366.

[129]*Ibid.*, p. 371.

[130]Steinfels, p. 50.

[131]*Ibid.*, p. 12.

[132]*Ibid.*, p. 294.

[133]*Ibid.*, pp. 273–294.

[134]Richard E. Morgan, *Disabling America: The "Rights" Industry In Our Time* (New York: Basic Books, 1984), p. 3.

[135]*Ibid.*, p. 7.

[136]*Ibid.*, p. 214. For an opposing viewpoint especially from women, see "Full Steam Ahead: The Women's Movement Toward 2000," *Graduate Women* (January 1986), pp. 1, 6. In fact, the entire issue is devoted to women's concerns and their movement.

[137]See Nathan Glazer, *Affirmative Discrimination: Ethnic Inequality and Public Policy* (New York: Basic Books, 1975).

[138]Ellen Paul and Philip Russo, Jr., "Regulation Policy: The Visible Hand" in Ellen Paul and Philip Russo, Jr. (eds.), *Public Policy* (Chatham: Chatham House, 1982), p. 99.

[139]Steven Kolman, "Regulations That Work," in Paul and Russo, pp. 214–225.

[140]John Saloma, *Ominous Politics: The New Conservative Labyrinth* (New York: Hill & Wang, 1984), pp. 130–137.

[141]Hanes Walton, Jr., "Blacks and Conservative Political Movements," *Quarterly*

Review of Higher Education Among Negroes No. 37 (October 1969) p. 177–183.

[142]*Ibid.*

[143]*Ibid.*

[144]Saloma, p. 130.

[145]*Ibid.*, pp. 131, 132.

[146]See Walter E. Williams, *The State Against Blacks* (New York: New Press, 1982).

[147]See Anne Wortham, *The Other Side of Racism: A Philosophical Study of Black Race Consciousness* (Columbus: Ohio State University Press, 1981).

[148]Editor, "The Role of the Black Journalist," *Lincoln Review*, (Summer, 1984): 3–5, and the entire issue.

[149]Juan Williams, "Pendleton Says He'll Start Being the Silent Type," p. 28 and see Walton, *Invisible Politics*, Chapter 9.

[150]For some new attempts to measure the impact of the political processes on the regulatory enforcement efforts, see—Richard Barke and Alan Stone, "Political Parties and Regulation" in Benjamin Ginsberg and Alan Stone, (ed.), *Do Elections Matter?* (New York: M.E. Sharpe, 1986), pp. 35–51 and Jeremy Rabkin, "The Reagan Revolution Meets the Regulatory Labyrinth, in Ibid., pp. 221–239.

[151]Gordon, *Public Administration in America*, 2nd ed., p. 460.

[152]Rabkin, "The Reagan Revolution . . .," pp. 228–250.

[153]For more on how the Reagan Republicans decided to employ black conservatives in reducing the overall effectiveness of the civil rights regulatory agencies, see the comments and writings of a black Republican, J. Clay Smith, Jr. See his "Keep Your Eyes on E.E.O.C." (Speech delivered before the NAACP's Emergency Summit Meeting on Friday, May 17, 1985). Smith, who served on the EEOC from 1978–1981 and as Chairman, 1981–1982, reveals that in December, 1980, Reagan approved black conservative Jay A. Parker as the Republican Transition Team Captain for EEOC and he was aided by others such as Clarence Thomas and William Keyes. Thomas is the current Chairman.

For a black Republican critique of these black conservatives, see J. Clay Smith, Jr., "A Black Lawyer's Response to the Fairmont Papers," *Howard Law Journal* volume 26 (1983), pp. 195-225.

The earlier comments and quote from Smith is from the Speech, p. 5–6. He furnished the author with a copy of the Speech, the article and a very revealing Events Fact Sheet for his tenure as EEOC Acting Chair.

CHAPTER 6

[1]John B. Kirby, *Black American in the Roosevelt Era* (Knoxville: University of Tennessee Press, 1980).

[2]W. C. Berman, *The Politics of Civil Rights in the Truman Administration* (Columbus: Ohio State University Press, 1970). Donald McCoy and Richard Ruetten, *Quest and Response: Minority Rights and the Truman Administration* (Lawrence: University of Kansas Press, 1973).

[3]J. Anderson, *Eisenhower, Brownell, and the Congress* (University: University of Alabama Press, 1964); and Richard F. Burk, *The Eisenhower Administration and Black Civil Rights* (Knoxville: University of Tennessee Press, 1985).

[4]J. C. Harvey, *Black Civil Rights During the Kennedy Administration* (Jackson: University and College Press of Mississippi, 1971).

[5]J. C. Harvey, *Black Civil Rights During the Johnson Administration* (Jackson: University and College Press of Mississippi, 1973).

[6]Allan Wolk, *The Presidency and Black Civil Rights: Eisenhower to Nixon* (East Brunswick: Fairleigh Dickenson University Press, 1971).

[7]U.S. Commission on Civil Rights, *The Federal Civil Rights Enforcement Effort—1974.*

[8]Samuel C. Patterson, Roger H. Davidson, and Randall Ripley, *A More Perfect Union*, 3rd ed. (Chicago: Dorsey Press, 1985) p. 298.

[9]*Ibid.*

[10]See James E. Anderson, *Public Policy-Making*, 3rd ed. (New York: Holt, Rinehart and Winston, 1984), pp. 44–149.

[11]In Bullock and Lamb, (1984) "The Implementation of Civil Rights Policy," pp. 2–17.

[12]William Gillette, *Retreat From Reconstruction, 1869–1879* (Baton Rouge: Louisiana State University Press, 1979), p. 42.

[13]*Ibid.* For a detailed look at federal enforcement in the border states, see his "Anatomy of a Failure: Federal Enforcement of the Right to Vote in the Border States During Reconstruction," in Richard Curry (ed.), *Radicalism, Racism, and Party Realignment* (Baltimore: John Hopkins Press, 1969), pp. 265–304. The table is on p. 298.

[14]Gillette, pp. 42–43, 45.

[15]*Ibid.*, p. 54.

[16]Hanes Walton, Jr., "Black Politics in the Centennial Year: 1876," *National Scene Magazine Supplement—New York Amsterdam News*, (July-August, 1977), pp. 3–10.

[17]Samuel Lubell, *White and Black: Test of a Nation* (New York: Harper & Row, 1964), pp. 103–104.

[18]King, Why We . . ., pp. 105, 27.

[19]See Louis Lomax, *The Negro Revolt* (New York: Harper & Row, 1963).

[20]On the role of this government as a neutral observer and blacks trying to change that role in the political process, see Walton, *Black Politics*, pp. 1–2.

[21]One scholar has argued that it is inherent in American society and government to remain neutral. Charles Hamilton, "Political Access, Minority Participation, and the Normalcy," in Leslie Dunbar (ed.), *Minority Report* (New York: Pantheon, 1984), pp. 1–25.

[22]Committee on the Judiciary, *Federal Civil Rights Laws: A Sourcebook* (Washington, D.C.: Government Printing Office, 1984), pp. 142–143.

[23]*Ibid.*

[24]*Federal Register*, July 15, 1983.

[25]See Office of Management and Budget, *Special Analysis: Civil Rights Activities, 1986*, p. J-25.

[26]The author requested from the Secretary of Education copies of these agreements and a list of the various states, but the department refused to answer my correspondence. See Robert Pear, "U.S. Would Let States' Officials Monitor Rights," *New York Times*, September 30, 1984, p. 113.

[27]"Experiment with State Enforcement of Federal Civil Rights Laws in Education found Flawed," *Lawyers' Committee for Civil Rights Under Law Report, No. 52* (May 1984), pp. 6, 11.

[28]See "OMB Issues Paperwork Requirements," *Civil Rights Forum*, (Spring 1984), pp. 6, 8.

APPENDIX A

[1]William H. Kruskal, "Issues and Opportunities," in William B. Fairley and Frederick Mosteller (eds.) *Statistics and Public Policy* (Reading: Addison-Wesley, 1977), p. 4.

[2]*Ibid.*, p. 3.

[3]*Ibid.*, p. 6.

[4]Williams, "Chairman of . . .," p. A-4; and Ann Mariano, "OMB Doesn't Want Forms to Ask Race Questions," *Washington Post*, June 17, 1985, national weekly edition, p. 32.

[5]Kruskal, p. 15.

[6]*Ibid.*

[7]Mariano, p. 32.

[8]U.S. Congress, House, *Federal Government Statistics and Statistical Policy*,

Hearing Before the Committee on Government Operations, 97th Cong., 2nd sess. (June 3, 1982), pp. 222–223.

[9]*Ibid.*, p. 1.

[10]*Ibid.*, pp. 1-2.

[11]U.S. Congress, Senate, Committee on Governmental Affairs, *Federal Statistical and National Needs* (Washington, D.C.: Government Printing Office, 1984), pp. 80, 106.

[12]*Ibid.*, pp. 106–107. See also, U.S. Congress, House, Committee on Government Operations, *The Federal Statistical System, 1980 to 1985* (Washington, D.C.: Government Printing Office, 1984).

[13]See James T. Bonner, "Federal Statistical Coordination Today: A Disaster or Disgrace?" in *Federal Government Statistics and Statistical Policy*, pp. 365–401.

BIBLIOGRAPHY

BOOKS

Allen, Robert. *Reluctant Reformers: Racism and Social Reform Movements in the United States.* Washington, DC: Howard University Press, 1974.

Anderson, James E. *Eisenhower, Brownell, and the Congress.* University, AL: University of Alabama Press, 1964.

_____. *Public Policy-Making*, 3rd edition. New York: Holt, Rinehart and Winston, 1984.

Ball, Howard, et. al. *Compromised Compliance.* Westport, CT: Greenwood Press, 1982.

Barke, Richard and Stone, Alan, "Political Parties and Regulation," in Benjamin Ginsberg and Alan Stone (eds.) *Do Elections Matter?* New York: M. E. Sharpe, 1985.

Barnett, Marguerite Ross. "The Congressional Black Caucus: Illusions and Realities of Power." In *The New Black Politics* edited by Preston, Michael, Henderson, Lenneal, and Puryear, Paul. . New York: Longman, 1982.

Becker, Theodore L. and Peeley, M. M., eds. *The Impact of Supreme Court Decisions: Empirical Studies.* New York: Oxford University, 1973.

Bell, Ingel P. *Core and the Strategy of Nonviolence.* New York: Random House, 1968.

Bennett, Lerone. *What Manner of Man*, Chicago: Johnson Publishing Company, 1964.

Berman, W. C. *The Politics of Civil Rights in the Truman Administration.* Columbus: Ohio State University Press, 1970.

Berry, Jeffrey. *Feeding Hungry People: Rulemaking in the Food Stamp Program* New Brunswick, NJ: Rutgers University Press, 1984.

Blumrosen, Alfred W. *Black Employment and the Law* New Brunswick, NJ: Rutgers University Press, 1971.

Brisbane, Jr., Robert. *The Black Vanguard.* Valley Forge, PA: Judson Press, 1970.

239

Bullock, III, Charles S. and Lamb, Charles M. eds. *Implementation of Civil Rights Policy*. Monterey: Brooks/Cole Publishing Company, 1984.

Bullock, III, Charles and Rodgers, H. *Law and Social Change: Civil Rights Laws and their Consequence*. New York, NY: McGraw-Hill, 1972.

_____ . *Racial Equality in America*. Pacific Palisades, CA: Goodyear, 1973.

_____ . *Racism and Inequality*. San Francisco: W. H. Freeman, 1975.

Burk, Richard F. *The Eisenhower Administration and Black Civil Rights*. Knoxville: University of Tennessee Press, 1985.

Burkey, Richard M. *Racial Discrimination and Public Policy in the United States*. Lexington, KY: Heath-Lexington, 1971.

Burstein, Paul. *Discrimination, Jobs, and Politics: The Struggle for Equal Opportunity in the United States Since the New Deal* Chicago: University of Chicago Press, 1985.

Bryner, Gary C. *Bureaucratic Discretion: Law and Policy in Federal Regulatory Agencies*. New York: Pergamon Books, 1987.

Califano, Jr., Joseph A. *Governing America*. New York: Simon & Schuster, 1981.

Carr, Robert K. *Federal Protection of Civil Rights: Quest for a Sword* Ithaca: Cornell University Press, 1947.

Cooper, Joseph D. *The Act of Decision-Making*. Garden City, NY: Doubleday and Company, 1961.

Cousens, Frances, R. *Public Civil Rights Agencies and Fair Employment*. New York: Praeger, 1969.

Cronin, Thomas E. *The State of the Presidency*, 2nd ed. Boston: Little, Brown & Company, 1980.

Davidson, Chandler, ed. *Minority Vote Dilution*. Washington, DC: Howard University Press, 1985.

Dulles, Foster Rhea: *The Civil Rights Commission: 1957–1965*. East Lansing, MI: State Press, 1968.

Dye, Thomas R. *Policy Analysis*. University, AL: The University of Alabama Press, 1978.

_____ . *Understanding Public Policy*. Englewood Cliffs, NJ: Prentice-Hall, 1972.

Dye, Thomas and Zeigler, Harmon. *The Irony of Democracy*. Englewood Cliffs, NJ: Prentice-Hall, 1979.

Eagles, Charles, ed. *The Civil Rights Movement in America*. Jackson: University Press of Mississippi, 1986.

Eads, George C. and Fix, Michael, eds. *Relief or Reform: Reagan's Dilemma*. Washington, DC: Urban Institute Press, 1984.

_____ . *The Reagan Regulatory Strategy: An Assessment*. Washington, DC: Urban Institute Press, 1984.

Elliott, Jeffrey M. *Black Voices in American Politics*. New York: Harcourt, Brace Jovanovich, 1986.

Elliott, Jeffrey M. and Ali, Sheith R. *The Presidential-Congressional Political Directory*. Santa Barbara: ABC-Clio, 1984.

Fairley, William B. and Mosteller, Frederick, eds. *Statistics and Public Policy*. Reading, MA: Addison-Wesley, 1977.

Foster, Lorn ed. *The Voting Rights Act: Consequences and Implications.* New York: Praeger Publishers, 1985.

Garfinkel, Herbert. *When Negroes March.* New York: Free Press, 1959.

Garrow, David J. *Bearing the Cross: Martin Luther King, Jr. and the Southern Christian Leadership Conference: A Personal Portrait.* New York: William Morrow and Company, 1986.

Gillette, William. "Anatomy of a Failure: Federal Enforcement of Rights to Vote in the Border States During Reconstruction," In *Radicalism, Racism, and Party Realignment.* edited by Richard Curry. Baltimore, MD: Johns Hopkins Press, 1969.

————. *Retreat from Reconstruction, 1869–1879.* Baton Rouge: Louisiana State University Press, 1979.

Glazer, Nathan. *Affirmative Discrimination: Ethnic Inequality and Public Policy.* New York: Basic Books, 1975.

Goldstein, Rhoda. *Civil Rights: The 1960's Freedom Struggle.* Boston: Twayne Publishers, 1984.

Gordon, George J. *Public Administration in America.* 2nd ed. New York: St. Martin's Press, 1982.

————. *Public Administration in America.* 3rd ed. New York: St. Martin's Press, 1986.

Gould, William B. *Black Workers in White Unions: Job Discrimination in the United States.* Ithaca: Cornell University Press, 1977.

Green, Robert L., ed. *Metropolitan Desegregation.* New York: Plenum Press, 1985.

Hamilton, Charles. "Political Access, Minority Participation, and the New Normalcy." in *Minority Report* edited by Leslie Dunbar. New York: Pantheon Press, 1984.

Harvey, J. C. *Black Civil Rights During the Kennedy Administration.* Jackson: University and College Press of Mississippi, 1971.

————. *Black Civil Rights During the Johnson Administration.* Jackson, MS: University and College Press of Mississippi, 1973.

————. "Civil Rights, Blacks and the Reagan Administration: in Mfanya Donald Tryman (ed.) *Institutional Racism and Black America.* Lexington: Ginn Press, 1985.

Helco, Hugh. "Issue Networks and the Executive Establishment," In *The New American Political System.* Edited by Anthony King, Washington, DC: American Enterprise Institute, 1978.

Henderson, Jr., Lenneal J. *Administrative Advocacy: Black Administrators in Urban Bureaucracy.* Palo Alto, CA: R & E Research Associates, 1979.

Henderson, Jr., Lenneal J. and Preston, Michael B. "Black Public Employment and Public Interest Theory." In *Contemporary Public Policy Perspectives and Black Americans,* edited by Mitchell Rice and Woodrow Jones, Jr. Westport, CT: Greenwood Press, 1984.

Herring, Pendleton. *The Politics of Democracy.* New York: W. W. Norton, 1940.

Hill, Herbert. *Black Labor and the American Legal System: Race, Work and the Law.* Washington, DC: Bureau of National Affairs, 1977.

Holt, Thomas C. "Introduction: Whither Now and Why?" In *The State of Afro-American History: Past, Present and Future,* edited by Darlene Clark Hine. Baton Rouge: Louisiana State University Press, 1986.

Hornsby, Jr., Alton. *The Black Almanac*, revised edition. New York, NY: Barron's Educational Series, 1973.

Johnson, Tobe. *Metropolitan Government: A Black Analytical Perspective*. Washingion, DC: Joint Center for Political Studies, 1972.

Jones, Jr., Augustus J. *The Law, Bureaucracy and Politics: The Implementation of Title VI of the Civil Rights Act of 1964*. Washington, DC: University Press of America, 1982.

Kessel, John. *The Domestic Presidency*. Duxbury: Duxbury Press, 1974.

King, Jr., Martin Luther. *Where Do We Go from Here: Chaos or Community?* New York: Harper and Row, 1967.

———. *Why We Can't Wait*. New York: Harper and Row, 1968.

Kirby, John B. *Black Americans in the Roosevelt Era*. Knoxville: University of Tennessee Press, 1980.

Knovitz, Milton R. and Leskes, T. *A Century of Civil Rights*. New York: Columbia University Press, 1961.

Kohlmeir, Louis. *The Regulators: Watch Dog Agencies and the Public Interest*. New York: Harper and Row, 1969.

Lockard, Duane. "Race Policy." In *Handbook of Political Science* Vol. 6, edited by Fred I. Greenstein and Nelson Polsby. Reading, MA: Addison-Wesley Publishing Company, 1973.

———. *Toward Equal Opportunity: A Study of State and Local Antidiscrimination Laws*. New York: Macmillan Company, 1968.

Logan, Rayford W. and Winston, Michael R. *The Negro in the United States* Vol. 2. New York: Van Nostrand Reinhold Company, 1971.

Lomax, Louis. *The Negro Revolt*. New York: Harper and Row, 1983.

Lowi, Theodore J. *The End of Liberalism* 2nd ed. New York: W. W. Norton, 1979.

Lubell, Samuel. *White and Black: Test of a Nation*. New York: Harper and Row, 1964.

Lynn, Jr., Laurence. *Managing Public Policy*. Boston: Little Brown and Company, 1987.

Marable, Manning. *Black American Politics: From the Washington Marches to Jesse Jackson*. London: Verso, 1985.

Miller, Jake. *The Black Presence in American Foreign Affairs*. Washington, DC: University of America, 1978.

Monti, David. *A Semblance of Justice: St. Louis School Desegregation and Order in Urban America*. Columbia: University of Missouri Press, 1985.

Morgan, Richard E. *Disabling America: The Rights Industry in Our Time*. New York: Basic Books, 1984.

Morgan, Ruth P. *The President and Civil Rights*. New York: St. Martin's Press, 1970.

Morris, Aldon. *Origin of the Civil Rights Movement*. New York: Free Press, 1984.

Norgen, Paul and Hill, Samuel E. *Toward Fair Employment*. New York: Columbia University Press, 1964.

Ogul, Morris S. *Congress Oversees the Bureaucracy: Studies in Legislative Supervision*. Pittsburgh: University of Pittsburgh Press. 1976.

Orfield, Gary. *The Reconstruction of Southern Education*. New York: John Wiley, 1969.

Panetta, Leon E. and Gall, Peter. *Bring Us Together: The Nixon Team and the Civil Rights Retreat*. Philadelphia: J. B. Lippincott, 1971.

Patterson, Samuel C., Davidson, Roger H. and Ripley, Randall B. *A More Perfect Union*. 3rd edition. Homewood, IL: Dorsey Press, 1985.

Paul, Ellen and Russo, Jr., Phillip, eds. *Public Policy*. Chatham, NF: Chatham, 1982.

Preston, Miahael B. *The Politics of Bureaucratic Reform: The Case of the California State Employment Service*. Urbana: University of Illinois Press, 1985.

Pride, Richard A. and Woodward, J. David, *The Burden of Busing: The Politics of Desegregation in Nashville, Tennessee*. Knoxville: University of Tennessee Press, 1985.

Rabkin, Jeremy. *"Office for Civil Rights."* In J. Q. Wilson, *The Politics of Regulation*. New York: Basic Books, 1980.

_____ . The Reagan Revolution Meets the Regulatory Labyrinth," in Benjamin Ginsberg (ed.) *Do Elections Matter?* New York: M. E. Sharpe, 1986.

Reagan, Michael D. *Regulation: The Politics of Policy*. Boston: Little, Brown and Company, 1987.

Rebell, Michael A. and Black, Arthur B. . *Equality and Education: Federal Civil Rights Enforcement in the New York City School System*. Princeton: Princeton University Press, 1985.

Rice, Mitchell and Jones, Jr., Woodrow. "Public Policy and Black Health Care: A Civil Rights Perspective." In *Institutional Racism and Black America: Challengers, Choices, Change* Vol. 1. edited by Mfanya Donald Tryman. Lexington: Ginn Press, 1985.

Ripley, Randell and Franklin, Grace.*Bureaucracy and Policy Implementation*. Homewood: The Dorsey Press, 1986.

Rittenhoure, R. Lynn. *Black Employment in the South: The Case of the Federal Government*. Austin: Bureau of Business Research, Study No. 4, 1976.

Rosenbloom, David. *Federal Equal Employment Opportunity: Politics and Public Personnel Administration*. New York: Praeger Publishers, 1977.

_____ . *Federal Service and the Constitution: The Development of the Public Employment Relationship*. Ithaca: Cornell University Press, 1971.

Ruchames, Louis C. *The Social Politics of FEPC*. Chapel Hill: University of North Carolina Press, 1948.

_____ . *Race, Jobs and Politics*. New York: Columbia University Press, 1953.

Rustin, Bayard. "From Protest to Politics: The Future of the Civil Rights Movement." In *Down the Line: The Collected Writings of Bayard Rustin*. Chicago: Quadrangle Books, 1971.

Saloma, John. *Ominous Politics: The New Conservative Labyrinth*. New York: Hill & Wang, 1984.

Schlesinger, Arthur. *A Thousand Days*. New York: Houghton Mifflin, 1965.

Schwartz, Bernard, ed. *Statutory History of United States: Civil Rights Part II*. New York: Chelsea House, 1970.

Steinfels, Peter. *The New Conservatives: The Men Who Are Changing America's Politics*. New York: Simon & Schuster, 1979.

Stockman, David. *The Triumph of Politics: How the Reagan Revolution Failed*. New York: Harper and Row, 1986.

Strong, Donald S. *Negroes, Ballots and Judges: National Voting Rights Legislation in the Federal Courts*. University, AL: University of Alabama Press, 1968.

Walton, Jr., Hanes. *Black Politics: A Theoretical and Structural Analysis*. Philadelphia: J. B. Lippincott, 1972.

_____. *Invisible Politics: Black Political Behavior*. Albany, NY: SUNY Press, 1985.

Washington, Patrick S. *A Question of Sedition: The Federal Government's Investigation of the Black Press During World War II*. New York: Oxford University Press, 1986.

Weatherspoon, Floyd. *Equal Employment Opportunities and Affirmative Action: A Sourcebook*. New York: Garland Publishers, 1984.

Wasby, Stephen L. *The Impact of the United States Supreme Court: Some Perspectives*. Chicago: Dorsey Press, 1970.

Whalen, Charles and Barbara. *The Longest Debate: A Legislative History of the 1964 Civil Rights Act*. Cabin John, MD: Sevens Locks Press, 1985.

Wildavsky, Aaron. *The Politics of the Budgeting Process*. Boston: Little, Brown and Company, 1964.

Williams, Walter E. *The State Against Blacks*. New York: New Press, 1982.

Wilson, James Q., ed. *The Politics of Regulation*. New York Basic Books, 1980.

Wilson, Reginald. *Race and Equity in Higher Education*. Washington, DC: American Council on Education, 1982.

Wing, Kenneth and Rose, Marilyn. "Health Facilities and the Enforcement of Civil Rights," In *Legal Aspects of Health Policy* edited by Ruth Roemer and George McKoray. Westport, CT: Greenwood Press, 1980.

Winn, Mylon. "Black Public Administrators and Opposing Expectations." In *Contemporary Public Policy Perspectives and Black Americans: Issues in an Era of Retrenchment* edited by Mitchell F. Rice and Woodrow Jones, Jr. Westport, CT: Greenwood Press, 1984.

Wirt, Frederick M. *Politics of Southern Equality: Law and Social Change in a Mississippi County*. Chicago: Aldine, 1970.

Witherspoon, Joseph Parker. *Administrative Implementation of Civil Rights*. Austin: University of Texas Press, 1968.

Wolk, Allan. *The Presidency and Black Civil Rights: Eisenhower to Nixon*. East Brunswick, NJ: Fairleigh Dickenson University Press, 1971.

Wolkinson, Benjamin W. *Blacks, Unions and the EEOC*. Lexington: Lexington Books, 1973.

Wotham, Anne. *The Other Side of Racism: A Philosophical Study of Black Race Consciousness*. Columbus: Ohio State University Press, 1981.

ARTICLES

"A Reintroduction." *Civil Rights Forum* (Fall 1982). p. 1.

"Adam States: A Status Report." *Black Issues in Higher Education* Vol. 3, (March 1, 1987). p. 6–7.

"Agency Enforcement Compared." *Title VI Forum* (Fall 1979). p. 1, 3–13.

"Agency Regulations Implementing Section 504 of Rehabilitation Act." *Civil Rights Forum* (Winter-Spring 1983). pp. 2–3.

"An Interview with Nathan Glazer." *New Perspectives* (Fall 1985). p. 27–30.

Anderson, Jack. "Did Bell Influence Savannah Annexation?" *Savannah Morning News*, November 14, 1978. p. 4A

Art, Robert J. "Congress and the Defense Budget: Enhancing Oversight." *Political Science Quarterly* 100 (Summer 1985). p. 238–245.

Berry, Mary Francis. "Civil Rights Enforcement in Higher Education." *Integreducation* 22 (January-June 1985). pp. 2–6.

Block, Arthur R. "Enforcement of Title VI Compliance Agreements by Third Party Beneficiaries," *Harvard Civil Rights-Civil Liberties Law Review* (Winter, 1983), p. 1–52.

Carson, Clayborne. "The King Within Us all." *Focus* (January 1987). p. 6–7.

Cook, Samuel Dubois. "Democracy and Tyranny in America: The Radical Paradox of the Bicentennial and Blacks in the American Political System." *Journal of Politics* Vol. 38 (August 1976). pp. 276–294.

Cowart, A. T. and Gilliam, Jr., F. D. "Budgeting in a Newly Established Agency: The First Twenty Years of the United States Civil Rights Commission." *Environment and Planning C: Government and Policy* Vol. 3, (1985). p. 235–241.

"Days Reorganizes Civil Rights Division." *Title VI Forum* (Spring-Summer 1979). p. 1, 4.

"DOJ Will Not Issue Coordination Reg." *Civil Rights Forum* (Winter-Spring 1983). p. 9.

Drucker, Peter. "The Sickness of Government," *The Public Interest* No. 14, (Winter 1969). p. 3–23.

Fleming, Eddie. "Anderson's Savannah Expose Called Lies." *Savannah Morning News*, November 14, 1978. pp. 1A, 3.

"Full Steam Ahead: The Women's Movement Toward 2000." *Graduate Woman* (January 1986). p. 1, 6.

Henderson, Lenneal J. "Administrative Advocacy and Black Urban Administrator," *Annals of the American Academy of Political and Social Science* Vol. 430 (September 1978). p. 65–70.

Hesburgh, Theodore M. "Integer Vitae: Independence of the United States Commission on Civil Rights." *Notre Dame Lawyer* (Spring 1971). p. 445–460.

Hill, Herbert. "Twenty Years of State Fair Employment Practice Commissions: A Critical Analysis with Recommendations." *Buffalo Law Review* 14 (1964). p. 23–40.

Holden, Jr., Matthew. "'Imperialism' in Bureaucracy." *American Political Science Review* Vol. 50 (December 1966). pp. 943–951.

"Interview with the Assistant Attorney General." *Civil Rights Forum* (Winter-Spring 1983). p. 1, 3.

"Jack Anderson Defends His Column." *Savannah Morning News*, November 14, 1978. p. 3A.

"Justice Department Revises Its Coordination Regulations." *Civil Rights Forum* (Fall 1982), p. 1, 3.

Kilson, Martin. "Whiter Integration." *The American Scholar* (Summer 1976). p. 330–338.

Kurtz, Howard. "Civil Rights Chairman, Aide Boost Salaries." *Washington Post*, March 25, 1986. p. A1, A4.

Knovitz, Howard. "Affirmative Action Official Quits Over Staff Cuts, Lack of Support." *Washington Post*, January 22, 1987. p. A10.

Levy, Burton. "Effects of Racism on the Racial Bureaucracy." *Public Administration Review* (September/October 1972). p. 479-486.

———. "Bureaucracy of Race: Enforcement of Civil Rights Laws and Its Impact on People, Process and Organization." *Journal of Black Studies* (September 1971).

Lyons, Phil. "An Agency with a Mind of Its Own: The EEOC's Guidelines on Employment Testing." *New Prespectives* (Fall 1985). p. 20–25.

Mariano, Ann. "OMB Doesn't Want Forms to Ask Race Questions." *Washington Post*, June 17, 1985. p. 32.

Meier, Kenneth J. "The Impact of Regulatory Organization Structure: IRCs or DRAs." *Southern Review of Public Administration* Vol. 3 (March 1980). p. 427–443.

"OMB Issues Paperwork Requirements." *Civil Rights Forum* (Spring 1984). p. 6, 8.

Pear, Robert. "U.S. Would Let States' Officials Monitor Rights." *New York Times*, September 30, 1984. p. 113.

Peterson, Bill. "Reynolds Opposes Bill to Counter Bias Ruling." *Washington Post*, March 8, 1985.

Peterson, Cass. "OMB Regulation Power, Part II: Now Justice Says Agencies Can Ignore Reagan's Order." *Washington Post*, September 15, 1985. p. 33.

"Preface." *The Public Interest* 41 (Fall 1975). p. 3.

Prescott, Jacqueline and Ferguson, Eve. "Chairman Clarence Pendleton, Jr., A 'Wild Card' on Civil Rights Commission." *Washington Post*, November 1, 1982. p. H1, H5.

"President Issues Title VI Directive to Agencies." *Title VI Forum* (Fall 1977). p. 1, 8.

Raspberry, William. "Pendleton's Misjudgement." *Washington Post*, March 8, 1985. p. A-23.

Rice, M. and Jones, W. "Black Health Inequities and the American Health Care System." *Health Policy and Education: An International Journal* (Fall 1982). pp. 195–214.

Richburg, Keith B. "U.S. Seeks End to Lengthy Civil Rights Case." *Washington Post*, March 8, 1985. p. A-21.

Rowan, Carl T. "Abolish the Civil Rights Commission." *Washington Post*, March 19, 1985. p. A-19.

Salamon, Lester. "The Rise of Third Party Government." *Washington Post*, June 29, 1980.

Scher, Seymour. "Conditions for Legislative Control." *Journal of Politics* 25 (August 1963). p. 526–551.

Smith, J. Clay, "A Black Lawyer's Response To The Fairmont Papers," *Howard Law Journal* 26 (1983), p. 195–225.

"The Pendleton Prose." *Washington Post*, March 25, 1985. p. 22.

"The Role of the Black Journalist." *Lincoln Review* (Summer 1984). p. 3–5.

"Title VI - Fifteen Years Later." *Title VI Forum* (Fall 1979), p. 1,3.

Tofari, Loretta. "Education Department Accused of Laxness on Bias Laws: House Panel Calls Enforcement Inadequate." *Washington Post* September 12, 1985. p. A-6.

Tucker, Robert. "The Deradicalization of Marxist Movements." *American Political Science Review* 61 no. 2 (June 1967). pp. 346–348.

"U.S. Civil Rights Commission Votes to Slash Its Staff," *The New York Times*, September 28, 1986. p. 40.

Walton, Jr., Hanes. "Black Politics in the Centennial Year: 1876." *National Scene Magazine Supplement—New York Amsterdam News* (July-August 1977). p. 3–10.

_____ . "Blacks and Conservative Political Movements." *Quarterly Review of Higher Education Among Negroes* 37 (October 1969). p. 177–183.

Williams, Juan. "At Odds Over Rights: Pendleton Accuses Lawmakers of Racism." *Washington Post*, September 30, 1985. p. A4.

_____ . "Chairman of EEOC Tells Panel Statistics Misused to Prove Bias." *Washington Post*, December 15, 1984. p. A4.

_____ . "Pendleton Says He'll Start Being the Silent Type." *Washington Post*, March 25, 1985. p. 28.

Wing, Kenneth. "Title VI and Health Facilities: Forms Without Substance." *Hastings Law Journal* (September 1978). pp. 137–190

GOVERNMENT PUBLICATIONS

"Commission on Civil Rights." *Weekly Compilation of Presidential Documents*, 19 November 7, 1983.

"Confirmations." *Department of State Bulletin*, March 31, 1975.

Department of Housing and Urban Development. *Statistical Yearbook*. 1979. Washington, DC: U.S. Government Printing Office, 1980.

"Development of Administrations and Agencies—Regulatory Planning Process from President Ronald Reagan." *Weekly Compilation of Presidential Documents*, 21 January 4, 1985.

Equal Employment Opportunity Commission, *Legislative History of Titles VII and XI Of Civil Rights Act of 1964* Washington, D,C,: Government Printing Office, N.D.

Federal Government Service Task Force, *Reduction in Force Survey, Third Quarter, Fiscal 1982*. Washington, DC: Government Printing Office, 1983.

"Grove City Civil Rights Measure Stalled." *Congressional Quarterly Almanac* Volume 41, 99th Cong., 1st sess., 1985. *Congressional Quarterly*, 1986.

Impact of 1981 RIFS on Minorities and Women and Updated RIF Projections for Fiscal Year 1982. Washington, DC: Government Printing Office, 1985.

"OMB Special Analysis J: Civil Rights Activities," *Special Analysis: Budget of the United States Government Fiscal Year: 1986*. Washington, DC: Government Printing Office, 1985.

U.S. Congress, House of Representatives. Committee on Education and Labor. *A Report on the Investigation of Civil Rights Enforcement by the Equal Employment Opportunity Commission*, Serial No. 99–0. Washington, DC: Government Printing Office, 1986.

_____ . Committee on Education and Labor and the Subcommittee on Civil and Constitutional Rights, *Civil Rights Restoration Act or 1985*, Joint Hearings Before Committee on Education and Labor and Subcommittee of the Committee on the Judiciary - March 25, 1985.

————— . Committee on Government Operations. *The Federal Statistical System, 1980 to 1985*. Washington, DC: Government Printing Office, 1984.

————— . Committee on Government Operations, *Investigation of Civil Rights Enforcement by the Office for Civil Rights at the Department of Education*, Report by Committee on Government Operations. Washington, DC: Government Printing Office, 1985.

————— . Congressional Black Caucus—Brain Trust on Age and the Select Committee on Aging. *The Black Elderly in Poverty*. Hearing Before, Congressional Black Caucus Brain Trust and Select Committee on Aging, 99th Cong., 1st sess., September 27, 1985.

————— . Committee on Government Operations. *National Endowment for the Humanities and the Equal Employment Opportunity Commission*. Report, Committee on Government Operations. Washington, DC: Government Printing Office, 1985.

————— . Subcommittee on Civil and Constitutional Rights. *U.S. Commission on Civil Rights/GAO Audit*, Hearings Before a Subcommittee of the Committee on the Judiciary, 99th Cong., 2nd sess., March 25 and April 22, 1985.

————— . Subcommittee on Employment and Housing. *Processing EEO Complaints in the Federal Sector—Problems Solutions*. Hearing, Before a Subcommittee of the Committee on Government Operations, 99th Cong., 1st sess., October 8, 1985.

————— . Subcommittee on Employment and Housing. *Processing EEOC Complaints in the Federal Sector—Problems and Solutions Part 2*. Hearings before a Subcommittee of the Committee on Government Operations, 99th Cong., 2nd sess., June 17, 1985. Washington, DC: Government Printing Office, 1986.

————— . Subcommittee on Employment Opportunities. *Oversight Hearings on the EEOC's Enforcement Policies*. Hearings Before a Subcommittee of the Committee on Education and Labor, 98th Cong., sess., 1984.

————— . Subcommittee on Employment Opportunities. *Oversight Review of the Department of Labor's Office of Federal Contract Compliance Programs and Affirmative Action Programs*. Hearings Before a Subcommittee of the Committee on Education and Labor, 99th Cong. 1st sess., September 18, 1985.

————— . Subcommittee on the Departments of Commerce, Justice and State, the Judiciary and Related Agencies. *Department of Commerce, Justice, and State, the Judiciary, and Related Agencies Appropriations for 1987*. Hearing Before a Subcommittee of the Committee on Appropriations, 99th Cong., 2nd sess., February 24, 1986.

U.S. Congress, Senate Committee on Governmental Affairs, Senate. *Federal Statistical and National Needs*. Washington, DC: U.S. Government Printing Office, 1984.

U.S. Congress, Senate Committee on Labor and Human Resources. *Nomination, of Clarence Thomas, of Missouri, to be Chairman of the Equal Employment Opportunity Commission*. Hearings Before Committee on Labor and Human Resources, 99th Cong., 2nd sess., July 23, 1986.

U.S. Commission on Civil Rights. *The Federal Civil Rights Enforcement Effort—1974. Volume 6: To Extend Federal Financial Assistance*. Washington, DC: U.S. General Accounting Office, 1975.

————— . *The Federal Civil Rights Enforcement Effort—1977: To Eliminate Employ-*

ment Discrimination: A Sequel. Washington, DC: U.S. General Accounting Office, 1977.

U.S. Comptroller General. *Allegations that IRS Harassed Mississippi Civil Rights Activist Unsupported.* Washington, DC: U.S. General Accounting Office, 1978.

_____ . Department of Agriculture. *The FHA Recreation Loan Program.* Washington, DC: U.S. General Accounting Office, 1970.

_____ . *Review of the Department of Health Education and Welfare's Office for Civil Rights.* Washington, DC: U.S. General Accounting Office, 1977.

_____ . Report to the Committee on the Judiciary House of Representative. Department of Health, Education and Welfare. *Observation on the Implementation of Title VI of the Civil Rights Act of 1964 in the Hill-Burton Program for the Construction and Modernization of Health Facilities.* Washington, DC: U.S. General Accounting Office, 1972.

_____ . Report to the Congress. *Equal Employment Opportunity in State and Local Governments: Improving the Federal Role.* Washington, DC: U.S. General Accounting Office, 1980.

_____ . Report to the Congress. *Further Improvements Needed in EEOC Enforcement Activities.* Washington, DC: U.S. General Accounting Office, 1981.

_____ . Report to the Congress. *The Revenue Sharing Act's 1976 Amendments: Little Effect on Improving Administration and Enforcement of Nondiscrimination Provision.* Washington, DC: U.S. General Accounting Office, 1980.

_____ . Report to the House Committee on Judiciary. *Nondiscrimination Provision of the Revenue Sharing Act Should be Strengthened and Better Enforced.* Washington, DC: U.S. General Accounting Office, 1976.

_____ . Report to the Subcommittee on Employment, Poverty, and Migratory Labor and Public Welfare, Senate. *The Emergency Employment Act: Placing Participants in Nonsubsized Jobs and Revising Hiring and Requirements.* Washington, DC: U.S. General Accounting Office, 1974.

_____ . *Schools Closed Since 1969 As a Result of Actions to Promote Racial Balance.* Washington, DC: U.S. General Accounting Office, 1973.

_____ . *The Office for Civil Rights in the Department of Education and HHS Have Improved the Management of Their Civil Rights Enforcement Responsibilities.* Washington, DC: U.S. General Accounting Office, 1981.

_____ . *Voting Rights Act—Enforcement Needs Strengthening.* Washington, DC: U.S. General Accounting Office, 1978.

U.S. Department of Agriculture. *Equal Opportunity Report, 1980,* Washington, DC: U.S. General Accounting Office, 1981.

_____ . Department of Agriculture. *Equal Opportunity Report, 1978.* Washington, DC: U.S. Government Printing Office, 1979.

U.S. Department of Defense. *Title VI Enforcement Effort and Related Matters— 1964–1980,* Vol. 1. Washington, DC: Department of Defense Civil Rights Assessment, June 1980.

U.S. General Accounting Office. Committee on the Judiciary, House. *Civil Rights Acts of 1957, 1950, 1964, 1968 and Voting Rights Act of 1965.* Washington, DC: U.S. Government Printing Office, 1981.

_____ . Committee on the Judiciary, House. Department of Health, Education and Welfare. *Compliance with Antidiscrimination Provision of Civil Rights Act by Hospitals and other Facilities Under Medicare and Medicaid.* Washington, DC: U.S. General Accounting Office, 1972.

_____ . Committee on Judiciary, House. *Title VI Enforcement in Medicare and Medicaid Programs.* Hearing Before a Subcommittee of the Committee on the Judiciary. 93rd Cong. 1st sess. Washington, DC: U.S. General Accounting Office, 1973.

_____ . Committee on the Judiciary, Senate. *Report on the Administrative Procedure Act,* 79th Cong. 1st sess. Washington, DC: U.S. General Accounting Office, 1945.

_____ . *A compilation of Federal Laws and Executive Orders for Non-discrimination and Equal Opportunity Programs.* Washington, DC: U.S. General Accounting Office, 1978.

_____ . Department of Defense. *Status of Equal Opportunity in the Military Departments.* Washington, DC: U.S. General Accounting Office, 1973.

_____ . *Department of Justice Making Effort to Improve Litigative Management Information System.* Washington, DC: U.S. General Accounting Office, 1979.

_____ . Hearing Before A Subcommittee of the Committee on Government Operations, House. *Constitutionality of GAO's Bid Protest Function,* 99th Cong. 1st sess., February 28 and March 7, 1985.

_____ . *Justice Can Further Improve Its Monitoring of Changes in the State/Local Voting Laws.* Washington, DC: U.S. General Accounting Office, 1983.

_____ . Report to Congress. Committee on the Judiciary, Senate. *Federal Civil Rights Laws: A Sourcebook.* Washington, DC: U.S. General Accounting Office, 1984.

_____ . Report to the Congress, House. *Federal Government Statistics and Statistical Policy.* Hearing Before the Committee on Government Operations, 97th Cong. 2nd sess., June 3, 1982.

_____ . Report to the Honorable Gilespie V. Montgomery. *Justice's Processing of Mississippi's Proposed Voting Change.* Washington, DC: U.S. General Accounting Office, 1984.

_____ . Report to the House Committee on the Judiciary Subcommittee on Civil and Constitutional Rights. *Actions Taken by Federal Agencies to Implement Title VI of the Civil Rights Act of 1964.* Washington, DC: U.S. General Accounting Office, 1980.

_____ . Report to the Select Committee on Equal Educational Opportunity, Senate. *Weaknesses in School Districts' Implementation of the Emergency School Assistance Program.* Washington, DC: U.S. General Accounting Office, 1971.

_____ . Report to the Subcommittee on Civil and Constitutional Rights Committee on the Judiciary, House. *Operations of the United States Commission on Civil Rights.* Washington, DC: U.S. General Accounting Office, 1986.

_____ . *Uniform Guidelines on Employee Selection Procedures Should by Reviewed and Revised.* Washington, DC: U.S. General Accounting Office, 1982.

U.S. Government Printing Office. "Executive Order 10590." *Federal Register,* 20, Washington, DC: Government Printing Office, 1955.

_____ . *Federal Register*, 6, Washington, DC: Government Printing Office, 1941.

_____ . *Federal Register*, 18, Washington, DC: Government Printing Office, 1943.

_____ . *Federal Register*, 50 Washington, DC: Government Printing Office, 1985.

U.S. Office of Management and Budget. *OMB Special Analysis U: Civil Rights Activities: The Budget for Fiscal Year: 1984*. Washington, DC: U.S. General Accounting Office, 1984.

_____ . *OMB Special Analysis J: Civil Rights Activities: Special Analysis: Budget of the United States Government Fiscal Year: 1985*. Washington, DC: U.S. General Accounting Office, 1984.

_____ . *Regulatory Program of the United States Government—April 1, 1985 - March 31, 1986*. Washington, DC: Government Printing Office, 1985.

_____ . Report to the Chairman, Subcommittee on Manpower and Housing Committee on Government Operations, House. *Problems Persist in the EEO Complaint Processing System for Federal Employees.* Washington, DC: Government Printing Office, 1983.

U.S. Secretary of Labor. *Secretary's Order 8–808*, October 28, 1980.

U.S. Secretary of Labor. *Secretary's Order 2–81*, June 1, 1981.

Ward, Clarke Cable. *Analysis of Remedies Obtained Through Litigation of Fair Housing Cases: Title VIII and Civil Rights Act of 1964*. Washington, DC: Department of Housing and Urban Development.

OTHER REPORTS

"Attorney General and Other Past Justice Department Officials Must Stand Trial in Suit Alleging Their Refusal to Carry Out Civil Rights Duties Re LEAA Grants." *The Lawyer's Committee for Civil Rights Under Law* 50 (September 1983).

"Black Neighborhoods in New Bern, North Carolina to Get Municipal Service Improvements." *The Lawyers' Committee for Civil Rights Under Law* 49 (April 1983).

"Experiment with State Enforcement of Federal Civil Rights Laws in Education Found Flawed." *The Lawyers' Committee for Civil Rights Under Law* 52 (May 1984).

"Judiciary Refuse to Open for Jesse Helms' View Illegally Obtained Taped of Dr. Martin Luther King, Jr.'s Conversations." *The Lawyers' Committee for Civil Rights Under Law* 51 (January 1984).

"Lawyers' Committee Testifies on Meese Nomination: 89 Trustees Endorse Statement Attacking Civil Rights Record of Reagan Administration." *The Lawyers' Committee for Civil Rights Under Law* 52 (May 1984).

"Lawyers' Committee to Participate in CRC." *The Lawyers' Committee for Civil Rights Under Law* 53 (July 1984).

McCormick, Joseph P.; Minter, Vanessa Band; and Ellis, William W. *Develop a Methodology for the Evaluation of Civil Rights Programmatic Input on the Transit Industry*. Washington, DC: Center for Systems and Program Development, Inc., 1981.

OE's Authority to Recoup Misspent Title I Funds Affirmed." *The Lawyers' Committee for Civil Rights Under Law* 50 (September 1983).

Washington Council of Lawyers, *On The Federal EEO Administrative Process* (June 25, 1987).

LETTERS TO AUTHOR

Gordon, Alfred R., July 14, 1981.

Harris, William J., Deputy Director, Office of Civil Rights, U.S. Department of Labor, September 30, 1981.

Hood, James P. Freedom of Information Office, Civil Rights Division, U.S. Department of Agriculture, December 30, 1981.

Malson, Robert A., Assistant Director, Domestic Policy Staff, White House, July 28, 1980.

Plummer, Wesley A., Director of Civil Rights, July 30, 1981.

SCHOLARLY PAPERS

Salamon, Lester M. *Rethinking Implementation*. Washington: DC: The Urban Institute, N.D..

Wasby, Stephen L. "The NAACP and the NAACP Legal Defense Fund: Preliminary Observations on Conflict Between Allies." National Conference of Black Political Scientists Meeting, April 1984, Washington, DC.

PRESS RELEASE

General Accounting Office. "Actions Taken by Federal Agencies to Implement Title VI of Civil Rights Act of 1964." April 5, 1980.

UNPUBLISHED THESIS

Hewitt, Gaye H. "An Evaluation of Civil Rights Legislation with Special Emphasis on the 1968 Civil Budget Act," (East Texas State College, M.A. Thesis, August 1968).

SPEECH AND DOCUMENT

Smith, Jr., J. Clay, "Keep Your Eyes on E.E.O.C." (Speech made before NAACP'S emergency Meeting on Friday, May 17, 1985 at Dupont Plaza Hotel in Washington, D.C.) in Author's files.

_____ . "Events During Acting Chairman Smith's Tenure March 3, 1981 to March 3, 1982," in Author's files.

INDEX

A "t" following a page reference denotes a table; an "f" denotes a figure.